'Never before have I seen a book covering this many techniques of social influence. The authors are the highest authorities currently researching in this area, so if they tell you a technique works, you can trust them. But just in case you are reluctant to take their word for it, each technique's summary includes an easy to understand description of the research that demonstrates the technique's effectiveness.'

Professor Christopher J. Carpenter, *Western Illinois University*

'Dariusz Dolinski and Tomasz Grzyb have produced an exceptionally readable and very entertaining survey of many – yes, 100! – social influence techniques. Each is described with an illustrative narrative, an account of one experiment that shows the technique can be effective, and a brief discussion of the underlying mechanism. Readers wanting an engaging introduction to the variety of available social influence techniques need not look further.'

Professor Daniel J. O'Keefe, *Northwestern University*

'Dolinski and Grzyb have done us all a great favor with this book. Not only have they described 100 effective influence practices, they have also reported on the psychological mechanisms that make the practices work. I can't imagine a more useful book for anyone looking to build persuasive success.'

Professor Robert Cialdini, *Arizona State University*

100 EFFECTIVE TECHNIQUES OF SOCIAL INFLUENCE

100 Effective Techniques of Social Influence provides a revolutionary look into the effectiveness of many techniques of social influence, providing an overview of the ways in which people use techniques to persuade others to meet various requests, suggestions, and commands.

For each technique, the authors explore the idea behind it, what empirical research says about it, and what the psychological mechanism behind its effectiveness is, aka, why it works. The techniques included span across multiple areas in people's everyday lives, ranging from business negotiations, managements, marketing, and close relationships, to people's behavior in public as well as in their private sphere. Covering research from the 1970s to the present day, the book describes techniques of social influence with the purpose of provoking certain behaviors, such as convincing an individual to donate to a charity or purchase a certain product. By exclusively focusing on techniques influencing human behaviors, rather than beliefs, biases, or emotions, the authors show how humans can be reliably convinced to behave in a certain way in a huge range of situations and contexts. Rather than being based on anecdotal evidence or legends of famous people, the authors have only included techniques that have been proven to be effective through scientific research.

With each technique described in an engaging manner, this is ideal reading for students and academics in fields such as social psychology, leadership, marketing, sociology, management, and communication. It will also appeal to professionals who need to influence others, and any readers who desire a better and more contemporary understanding of how people interact and influence others on a daily basis.

Dariusz Dolinski is a Professor at the University of Social Sciences and Humanities, Wroclaw Faculty in Poland, and editor of the *Polish Psychological Bulletin*. He was formerly the president of the Polish Association of Social Psychology and president of the Committee for Psychology of the Polish Academy of Sciences. He is the author of *Techniques of Social Influence* (Routledge, 2016) and (with T. Grzyb) *The Social Psychology of Obedience Towards Authority* (Routledge, 2020) and *The Field Study in Social Psychology* (Routledge 2022).

Tomasz Grzyb is a Professor at the University of Social Sciences and Humanities, Wroclaw Faculty in Poland and President of the Polish Social Psychological Society. His main area of interest is social influence and manipulation techniques. He is also a supporter of courses concerning the basics of social influence studies organized for military officers engaged in PSYOPS. He has published a number of articles about marketing, social psychology, advertising, and education.

100 EFFECTIVE TECHNIQUES OF SOCIAL INFLUENCE

When and Why People Comply

Dariusz Dolinski and Tomasz Grzyb

Routledge
Taylor & Francis Group

LONDON AND NEW YORK

Cover image: © Getty Images

First published 2023
by Routledge
4 Park Square, Milton Park, Abingdon, Oxon OX14 4RN

and by Routledge
605 Third Avenue, New York, NY 10158

Routledge is an imprint of the Taylor & Francis Group, an informa business

© 2023 Dariusz Dolinski and Tomasz Grzyb

British Library Cataloguing-in-Publication Data
A catalogue record for this book is available from the British Library

Library of Congress Cataloging-in-Publication Data
Names: Doliński, Dariusz, author. | Grzyb, Tomasz, author.
Title: 100 effective techniques of social influence : when and why people comply / Dariusz Dolinski and Tomasz Grzyb.
Other titles: One hundred effective techniques of social influence
Description: Abingdon, Oxon ; New York, NY : Routledge, 2022. | Includes bibliographical references and index. |
Identifiers: LCCN 2022001506 (print) | LCCN 2022001507 (ebook) | ISBN 9781032283920 (hardback) | ISBN 9781032283913 (paperback) | ISBN 9781003296638 (ebook)
Subjects: LCSH: Social influence.
Classification: LCC HM1176 .D649 2022 (print) | LCC HM1176 (ebook) | DDC 302/.13--dc23/eng/20220114
LC record available at https://lccn.loc.gov/2022001506
LC ebook record available at https://lccn.loc.gov/2022001507

ISBN: 978-1-032-28392-0 (hbk)
ISBN: 978-1-032-28391-3 (pbk)
ISBN: 978-1-003-29663-8 (ebk)

DOI: 10.4324/9781003296638

Typeset in Joanna
by MPS Limited, Dehradun

CONTENTS

INTRODUCTION

We, both of the authors of this book, participate from time to time in various social events. We chat with newly acquaintances about football, politics, or belles-lettres. The current weather is our least favorite subject to discuss but sometimes, when somebody directs the conversation to this topic, the problem of too low or too high temperatures, insufficient, or excessive rainfall becomes the subject of polite, but at the same time, incredibly trivial discussions. However, at some point, the "standard" topics run out and a moment of uncomfortable silence falls. It is at that moment when people who know very little about one another become interested in what is it that their interlocutors do for a living. "So what do you do?" we hear. The reply "I'm a psychologist" causes an instant re-action, which we refer to as "the Russian winter effect." Our new ac-quaintance takes two steps back and their face reveals astonishment and terror. Finally, after a while, which may be as long as a few dozen seconds, the person, fortunately, manages to cool down a little and replies with the following observation that sort of pretends to be a question: "I imagine

DOI: 10.4324/9781003296638-1

then, that you must have been watching and analyzing us all that time." Obviously, we hasten to explain that just like everybody else present at the party we are enjoying wine or vodka, chatting, telling jokes, or listening to jokes told by other people and that we could not be further from any attempts to analyze the personality of people around us. Nobody believes us though. It is a perfectly-known fact that psychologists, even when they are enjoying wine or vodka while chatting with other people, are constantly conducting complex observations to diagnose particular individuals around them based on indications, which are beyond the understanding of a layman. OK. With that out of the way, everything is clear now. Or is it? Not quite so! It turns out that the worst part is still to come, as our interlocutor, in his attempt to be polite, says the following: "I suppose you must have many patients in these difficult times." (It should be noted, just as a side note, that times are always difficult in similar conversations, it is only their cause that changes. Sometimes it is an economic recession, sometimes an economic boom and the intensified rivalry among companies that comes with it, as well as the resulting nervousness among employees; it may be a coronavirus pandemic, but in most cases, it is hard to tell precisely what it is. It reminds us of a satirical sketch featured in The New Yorker, where one man says to another: "I understand that we are in a crisis now. But why did nobody tell me when it was the prosperity period?") At this point, we need to explain that we are not clinical practitioners and that we do not offer psychotherapy. "You don't?" replies our surprised interlocutor, as it did not even cross his mind that a psychologist could do something else. "Well, what is it that you do then?" We kindly explain that we are social psychologists and that we have been focused on social influence techniques for quite a few years now. Except that it becomes immediately obvious that this explanation brings about our ultimate ruin. Our new acquaintance already knows that somewhere, in a laboratory located in the underground section of the university, we are up to devising a method that would allow us to manipulate people, change their personalities, brainwash them and make them do things they would never consider doing. We try to tell them about the so-called full-cycle social psychology but it appears that, at this point, nobody is listening to us anymore.

Nevertheless, we can explain, in a composed and methodical manner, the concept of full-cycle social psychology here. And this is exactly what we will do. In reality, a psychologist with a focus on social influence techniques rarely attempts to figure something out by himself rarely comes up with social influence techniques. What he does is observe the tricks used by individuals, who, due to their profession or social role, are effective in influencing others – measures applied by car dealerships that sell more cars than other dealerships, waitresses who get higher tips than others, politicians who can persuade their interlocutors into voting for them, or employees of charitable organizations who are true masters in procuring donations for noble causes. The basic question that a social influence psychologist asks himself after such observations pertains to the actual effectiveness of such a trick. Is it the trick in question that boosts the sales figures of the car dealership or, perhaps, its location, a wide range of offered vehicles, and the fact that customers can test drive offered cars without making an appointment plays a vital role? Is the trick the waitress always uses as she hands checks to her customers so extremely effective? Or perhaps the girl is exceptionally pretty and this (and only this) factor contributes to higher tips? Does the employee of the charitable organization actually play his ace at some stage of the negotiations, which makes his interlocutor ask for the foundation's bank account number, or perhaps he appears so trustworthy that people specifically choose to donate their money to him? How does one verify all this? Maybe one could ask the above-mentioned individuals how they know if the tricks they use actually work? Contrary to what one could expect, this is not a good idea. These people could be so certain of the effectiveness of their methods that it is quite possible they have never tried to see what would happen if they did not use them. (This approach would be rather reasonable: if doing something makes me effective, why would I stop doing it?) What is more, they may be unaware of the fact that using a particular trick makes them more confident about the effectiveness of their actions and that by the same token they behave in a somewhat different manner as compared to a situation where they would not use the same trick. There is one more important aspect. The fact that a given technique is effective when applied by one person does not automatically mean that it will also work when used by another individual. Due to all these factors, a conversation with social influence practitioners is only an initial step for preparing other methods to verify the actual effectiveness of a particular social influence technique.

What should we do, then? There is no better solution than to verify the actual effectiveness of a social influence technique in the course of carefully planned experiments.

Let us start with debunking a popular myth. Yes, we do conduct "studies on people." However, this does not mean that we become a demonic doctor Frankenstein, who tests the limits of human resistance to pain or attempts to hypnotize a person to make them follow instructions like a Golem from the Jewish legends of Prague. Our experiments are devised in such a way as to make sure subjects remain unaware of their contribution to science. In other words, our objective, in most cases, is to create a situation that resembles, as much as possible, a situation that we could encounter in our daily lives. Let us examine the process based on an example.

A feeling of puzzlement is always the starting point – in most cases, it refers to a specific situation one of us has experienced. It might be (and this is an actual story) a meeting with a door-to-door salesman offering water treatment devices. One day, such a salesman knocked on the door of one of our houses and asked if he could present his offer. It just so happens that drinking pure water fills us with nothing short of disgust. By that we do not mean that we prefer dirty water, it is just that we agree with the Bavarian saying, according to which drinking water is equivalent to wasting natural resources. This is because water is a great raw material for making beer and thus drinking pure water is, quite simply, a waste of resources. However, we always perceive a conversation with a social in-fluence practitioner as an opportunity to observe new techniques (or new versions of those we already know); therefore, a moment later, the salesman was sitting on the couch and presenting the device and its po-tential. Needless to say, it was an American product built using Japanese components, and it was, obviously, used on the international space station and featured structural elements made of gold ("after all, you can't go wrong with gold"). Until then, the arguments used by the salesman were neither new nor surprising. Yet, at some point he used a truly electrifying sentence – "I'm going to be honest with you. Ordinary folks don't buy it because they don't understand it. But I can tell that you play in a different league…"

Spoiler alert – none of us bought a magic water filtration device. However, several days later, we prepared an experiment designed to verify if emphasizing the "exceptionality" or "uniqueness" of the person we are addressing affects their willingness to grant a request. We prepared a challenging and time-consuming task (our intention was to deter the majority of subjects from agreeing to perform it). The task consisted in completing a survey featuring 248 questions. We assumed (rightly so), that the majority of the subjects asked to take part in such a study at a public transport stop would decline. Subsequently, we prepared two messages. One, intended for the so-called control group, was a standard message making no use of the technique applied by the door-to-door salesman. The message was as follows: "Good day, could I ask you for a favor? I'm a psychology student and I need to conduct a study to get a credit for one of my courses. This is a survey with 248 questions. Would you help me and answer these questions?"

The other was phrased in a very similar manner – it started identically but towards the end of it, the following phrase was added: "Today we are interested in obtaining answers from highly intelligent persons and you seem to be one of them."

When the messages were ready, we could start planning out the course of the experiment. First, we needed to determine the number of subjects to be tested. We would like to spare you the details of such concepts like the effect size, the power of the experiment, or statistical significance. It suffices to say that if researchers want their results to be considered applicable to the general population, they need to test a sufficient (but not excessive!) number of individuals. In our case, the target number was 1060.

We knew where we wanted to conduct our experiment (at public transport stops), how we wanted to test the subjects (with the prepared messages), and how many subjects we needed (1060). There was one more aspect to cover – who should the subjects be? It should be noted that when study results are discussed, the following question often arises: "perhaps the experimental group included extraordinary individuals?" This is a valid one – if this were actually the case, the whole experiment would be worthless. Therefore, in order to prevent such a situation from taking place, we use randomization – i.e., random selection of subjects (the so-called 1st-degree randomization) as well as random assignment to the experimental and the control groups (2nd-degree randomization). Using software based on random numbers, we prepared instructions for the researchers' assistants (i.e., the individuals who will actually be asking for help at public transport stops). The instructions specify who should be tested and to which group the given individual should be assigned – what is important here is this is absolutely random. This way, we make sure that both groups include very similar subjects.

Later on, we instruct our assistants to formulate the questions as consistently as possible and we "send them into town." If everything goes according to plan, we can soon examine our results. This is the most exciting part of the entire process. Our highly esteemed colleague, the prematurely late Professor Andrzej Szmajke, used to say that you are not a true researcher if you do not proceed with your calculations immediately after receiving an e-mail containing a database. Therefore, we proceeded with our calculations as soon as possible. What were the outcomes? In the control group, over 2/3 of respondents refused to complete the extensive survey – 32.3% agreed to do so. In the experimental group (in the case of which we "were searching for intelligent individuals"), more than 50% agreed to complete the survey! The exact figure was 51.8% of the subjects – the difference was also statistically significant and the effect was weak but clear (the so-called phi = 0.22). Consequently, we reached the point where we could conclude that the effect actually existed and was not of accidental nature.

So what happens next? In the event that experiments do confirm the effectiveness of the afore-mentioned tricks (as in the above-mentioned case), the next step is to explain the reasons for which the trick has a desired effect on peoples' reactions. Here we make use of our knowledge of psychology, various theories which explain the mechanisms behind human behavior. The accuracy of such explanations must also be verified empirically. It is again the time to use empiricism to either confirm or reject particular explanations. Additionally, to some extent unintentionally, thanks to the research conducted at this stage, we expand our knowledge of the conditions for the effectiveness of the technique in question – we learn in which situations and with what type of people the technique is particularly effective, in which conditions it becomes less effective, and in which conditions it may lose its value altogether. Only at that point does the technique become a fully-fledged element of psychological knowledge and, by the same token, a fully useful tool for practitioners.

So where does the term full-cycle social psychology come from? The term was coined by a true guru of social influence – Professor Robert

Cialdini (1980) of Arizona State University, the author of numerous, extremely ingenious studies related to social influence techniques and best-selling books on this subject. A social influence technique "comes into being" in real social life, it is applied by people in a particular situation – e.g., for the purpose of selling vehicles or offering life insurance policies. Psychologists observe people applying the technique and subsequently test its effectiveness in the course of experiments: they search for theoretical explanations for its underlying mechanism, test it in the course of follow-up experiments, and describe the outcomes of their experiments as well as theoretical investigations in scientific articles. Afterwards, this knowledge is disseminated. It becomes the subject for training and specialized courses, and it is also described in books read by practitioners. It is at that point where the full cycle (of social psychology) becomes complete. The technique emerged in a real-life environment; it became a subject of interest for academics and then, again, returned to practical application.

The book you are now holding in your hands also represents the closure of such a cycle. We want to take you on an intellectual journey into social influence techniques. Each time, we start by presenting a certain story, serving as an introduction to a particular technique, then we discuss a single empirical study (hand-picked by ourselves) documenting its effectiveness, and finally, we provide you with an explanation that tells you why this technique is effective. Hence the subtitle: "When and why people comply." It should be added that for each of the techniques described in this book, we provide the explanation that prevails in the literature on psychology or the one we consider the most accurate. Scholars will always dispute various things and hold never-ending debates on the reasons behind the effectiveness of various techniques are no different in this respect. For the purpose of this book, we decided to spare you a detailed account of these (otherwise interesting) disputes.

We have explained the rationale behind the subtitle of this book, i.e., "When and why people comply." Of course, there is also the title to address. The title reads: "One hundred effective techniques of social influence." The question that automatically emerges pertains to the number. We have to admit that there is no rational reason for which we decided to describe exactly one hundred techniques. To be perfectly honest, from a purely substantive perspective, eighty-eight or one hundred and four would be equally suitable numbers. We decided to go with the rounded number, i.e., one hundred because... it's just catchy. One hundred is a special number in mathematics. It is the sum of the first nine prime numbers $(2+3+5+7+11+13+17+19+23)$ and the square of the sum of the first four natural numbers $(1+2+3+4)^2$. According to the Bible, Abraham was 100 years old when his son, Isaac, was born and King David had to bring one hundred foreskins of the Philistines to Saul as the dowry. 100 degrees Celsius is the boiling temperature for water and the Kármán line – which sets the boundary between Earth's atmosphere and outer space – is 100 kilometers above the Earth. In many Slavic countries, on various occasions, we wish upon people that they live to be 100 years old. We suppose these are sufficient (although, to be honest, not the most rational) arguments in support of the magical nature of the number one hundred and in favor of the idea behind describing this many examples of social influence techniques in this book.

"And how many social influence techniques are there in total?" – one might reasonably ask. Frankly speaking, we do not know the answer to that question and there is really no way of answering it. Social influence practitioners regularly come up with new ideas to make people behave in a certain way. At the same time, social psychologists regularly test, through experiments, if (as well as when and why) these techniques actually work. Yet, we are inclined to believe that the one hundred examples we provide include (almost) all techniques that have been described so far in the literature on psychology and verified empirically. If we omitted any significant technique, it was not intentional and it should be treated as our mistake.

This book describes only the techniques, the effectiveness of which has been proven by psychologists in the course of experiments. Some of them were tested by us, because – as we have already mentioned – we have been working in this field systematically and consistently for a number of years now. Some were tested by our colleagues from all over the world, with whom we meet at various conferences and seminars, and others still by individuals we have never had the chance to meet in person. It should be added that even though the majority of the social influence techniques described in this book originated in the real-life environment, it also describes techniques invented by social psychologists. These have their source in various psychological theories and not in the observation of behavior of particularly effective social influence practitioners. We should also address one more aspect. In this book, we do not analyze techniques used to affect one's emotions, attitudes, or beliefs. We focus almost entirely on techniques designed to make people behave in a certain manner — agree to complete a survey, purchase an item, donate money to charity, or help a visibly pregnant woman carry a heavy bag to a bus.

To some extent, social influence techniques resemble dynamite. It can be used to quickly demolish old buildings or extract marble or granite in a quarry, but it can just as well be used to kill people in war. Social influence techniques can be used to persuade, more efficiently, people into engaging in charity, saving electricity, or voting for honest and intelligent politicians, but they can also be used to persuade pensioners into spending their money on a pea-filled pillow that will, allegedly, protect them against any and all cancers, or persuading drivers into purchasing insurance against collisions with UFOs. While writing this book, we hoped that it would be helpful for those people who want to honestly increase the sum of good on this planet by persuading others into taking actions that will contribute to this goal, and that it would help those who are subject to dishonest social influence to see it. Knowing that somebody is exposing us to a particular social influence technique does not automatically mean that we are being manipulated, but caution is always advised in such a case.

We put this book in your hands. As far as we are concerned, we might start taking this book with us to social events as a gift for those who are surprised to hear that we are psychologists who do not offer any therapeutic services. Perhaps this will make our attempts to explain that we do not work in an underground laboratory located underneath our University to come up with ways to manipulate people more credible.

1

SEQUENTIAL TECHNIQUES

As foreshadowed in both the title of this book as well as its Introduction section, this publication describes one hundred social influence techniques. We have arranged them according to a certain key to make reading this book easier. We will start with the techniques referred to by social psychologists as sequential. These techniques are based on the general premise that in order to increase the probability of someone complying with our request, we should first ask this person for another favor. Additionally, in the case of particular techniques, it is assumed that the initial request should be easier, more difficult, or be characterized by a similar level of difficulty as the key (actual) request. Historically speaking, the interest of social psychologists in social influence techniques started predominantly with studies of sequential techniques. What is more, these techniques have been the most common subject of psychological experiments. Therefore, we decided to start our book with their characterization.

DOI: 10.4324/9781003296638-2

Technique # 1 *Foot-in-the-door*

Idea

There are sayings in many languages of the world that illustrate the human tendency to escalate demands. The Americans and British say "give them an inch, they'll take a mile." Germans and Poles say "give someone a finger, they'll take your whole hand." Hungarians and Spaniards phrase it like this: "If you give someone your hand, they'll take the entire arm." In all cases, the idea is the same: If you give people something small, they will immediately ask for something bigger. These sayings describe the typical behavior of people with a sense of entitlement. From the perspective of social influence, however, what is more important is not so much the escalation of demands by people who are offered something, but rather the effectiveness of their actions. We are thus interested not in those who ask for something, but in those who are asked for it. Indeed, the question arises: does the fulfillment of an easy request make people subsequently more willing to fulfill another, clearly more difficult request? Returning to the metaphors cited above, if we assume that we are unlikely to want to give up an entire mile to someone, the question is whether we are significantly more likely to do so when someone employs the following strategy on us: first they ask us for an inch, and only after we give it to them do they ask for a mile. Social psychology calls this technique "foot-in-the-door." If you want to enter someone's house and you think it will be difficult, try to get them to open the door for you first.

Research

Imagine that you have a house in California, located along a busy road. Someone explains to you that a campaign is being organized to improve road safety. Billboards are being installed along the roadside urging people to drive carefully. Your lawn would be perfect for such a billboard, but they don't offer you any money for it; in addition, your property will suffer esthetically. Would you consent? Jonathan Freedman and Scott Fraser (1966) established that roughly 17% of people say "yes" in such a situation. We can thus characterize this request as difficult, and certainly quite exceptionally agreed to. Would the percentage of people agreeing to install a billboard increase if we first asked them to comply with a request that was clearly easier? Randomly selected individuals were visited by a man who formulated a simple request. Namely, they were asked to sign a petition to the governor of the state of California. In one case, it was a plea for boosting efforts to keep California clean; in another, it was for increased attention to road safety. Still, other respondents were asked to affix a small sticker to the corner of a car window or windshield. In one case it was an appeal to keep things clean, while in others to drive carefully. Of course, nearly everyone complied with the small request. When they were visited two weeks later by a man asking for permission to install a billboard, they agreed to the request significantly more often than did people who were asked to do so immediately. Keep in mind that when such a request was made straight away (that is, to use the language of the experimenters, in the control conditions), less than 17% of those approached agreed to the billboard. This time, nearly half of those who had previously signed some sort of petition or affixed a "Keep California clean" sticker agreed to the billboard. And in conditions where two weeks earlier people had put up a sticker appealing for careful driving, the proportion was as high as 76%! Thus, we see that the foot-in-the-door technique proved effective. Those who were first asked to comply with an easy request were then more likely to comply with another, clearly more difficult one, than those who were simply given the difficult request right away. There is still the question of why Freedman and Fraser tested in their experiment the consequences of people fulfilling as many as four different easy requests. Note that the difficult request, the one actually in question, concerned consenting to the presence of visual propaganda (billboard) about traffic safety. In two cases, the content of the first request was also about careful driving; in two others, it was about keeping California clean. Regardless, in two cases, the first request, like the second one, concerned visual propaganda ("put a sticker on it"), while in two others it was of a different character ("sign a petition"). The authors of the study wanted to see whether both requests had to be very similar (both in form and content) for the foot-in-the-door technique to be effective. This turned out to be unnecessary; it was enough that both subsequent requests "had something in common." In this case, it was engaging in a good cause to help others. At the same time, however, the technique proved to be by far the most effective in conditions of high similarity between the two requests.

Mechanism

Probably everyone knows that when women are unhappy, they sometimes start crying. Our beliefs, judgments about the world, views, mental states affect our behavior. But social psychologists say something else: sometimes, if women start crying, they then come to the conclusion that they are unhappy. Our behaviors can influence our beliefs and views. Why does someone who complies with the first request agree to fulfill a subsequent request? Freedman and Fraser hypothesized that humans reflect not only on what they should do but also on what they have already done. We also ask ourselves (not necessarily in a fully conscious way) why we agreed to fulfill a request. We first look for external causes. Did someone force us to do this, blackmail us? Not at all! Or maybe someone paid us a tidy sum of money? Nope! So, why did we agree? We ourselves come to the conclusion that we are "the kind of people who do such things." (In reference to the experiment described above: people who act to benefit the Californian community). If we begin to think of ourselves this way... we should then behave according to the belief we have just formed about ourselves. People who are committed to the well-being of residents of their state and think it is the right thing to do should agree to hosting a billboard that may reduce traffic accidents. Another interpretation of the effectiveness of the foot-in-the-door technique referenced by social influence researchers points out that our culture values consistency. If you said A, then say B; if you started something, finish in. So, if you've done something, and now someone's asking you to do something similar, then... do it, of course.

Technique # 2 *Two (or even more) feet in the door*

Idea

If fulfilling an easy request then leads people to fulfill another request, perhaps the effect would be even stronger if people were initially asked to fulfill not one small request, but several? After all, in that case, there would be both more reason to think of oneself in terms of "I am a person who fulfills requests of this kind" and to show consistency in one's own behavior. Would you lend a friend a dollar? Maybe you would, maybe not... It would probably be easier for you to reach for your wallet if the person asking you had already once borrowed a hundred dollars, then paid you back the next day. But perhaps you would agree to lend someone money even more easily if you had already lent that person money several times and always got it back the next day. While the technique we presented previously was called foot-in-the-door, this time we should talk about feet-in-the-door or even multiple feet-in-the-door.

Research

Nicolas Gueguen, Fabien Silone, and Mathieu David (2016) set out to see if the technique discussed here could be used to get people to stop smoking cigarettes. They focused on the conditions under which smokers would agree not to use tobacco for 24 hours. (A day without a cigarette is a trivial thing for non-smokers, but a real challenge for smokers.) In the control condition, participants were simply asked to refrain from smoking for 24 hours. The rationale for this was that the researchers were interested in learning about the impressions of smokers who quit for a while. The effectiveness of the now-familiar foot-in-the-door technique was tested in two different conditions. In the first, participants were asked to complete a short survey about their addiction. They responded to questions about their favorite brand of cigarettes, how long they had been smoking, whether their parents smoked, and whether they had ever tried to quit. They were then asked to abstain from smoking for 24 hours. In another condition, participants were first asked to refrain from smoking for two hours, and after a period of time, a request to refrain from smoking for 24 hours was made. In the two-feet-in-the-door condition, the participants were first asked to complete the aforementioned questionnaire, then to abstain from smoking for two hours, and only finally to abstain from smoking for a full 24 hours. In all the conditions of this experiment, the researchers first recorded whether the participants agreed to 24 hours of nicotine abstinence and then asked them if they managed to keep their word. The foot-in-the-door technique proved to be effective. While in the control condition, where participants were immediately asked to abstain from smoking for 24 hours, only about 27% of those questioned said they would do so and only about 12% said they actually managed to keep their word, both of these numbers were higher when participants first complied with the easy request. If they completed a short survey, 41.5% of the participants agreed to 24 hours of nicotine abstinence, and almost 21% declared post factum that they had not smoked for 24 hours. If the initial request was to abstain from smoking for two hours, both of these rates were even slightly higher (nearly 63% and nearly 28%, respectively). However, the effect was by far the best in the conditions in which participants first completed a survey, then abstained from smoking for two hours, and finally were asked to attempt 24-hour abstinence. In this situation, as many as 93% agreed to abstain from smoking for 24 hours, and 46.5% declared that they had not smoked a single cigarette for 24 hours!

Mechanism

The two-feet-in-the-door technique is an extension of the foot-in-the-door technique. We can also easily imagine even more complex forms of such interaction. The final request would then be preceded not by two clearly easier requests (as in the study described above), but three, four, or even more. Of course, it is assumed that the psychological mechanism underlying this technique is analogous to the technique in which only one easy request precedes the formulation of the final request. However, the more requests there are in the sequence, the factor inducing the participant to fulfill the final, difficult request should be stronger and act more strongly. The results presented above, as well as those of many other psychological studies, indicate that this is indeed the case.

Technique # 3 Four walls (Repeating yes)

Idea

Robert Cialdini and Brad Sagarin (2005) noted that people's inclination toward consistent behavior is often exploited by door-to-door sellers. Before such salespeople offer to sell "a great set of vitamins and trace elements," they have a short chat with the customer. They first ask their customer if health is important. Then, they ask whether it's worth taking care of one's health. Another question goes "Is it better to prevent diseases than to cure them?" All of these, after all, are rhetorical questions. The person being asked will answer "yes," "yes," "of course," "yes." And only now do they offer a sensational substance capable of preventing almost all diseases and ailments. How can people who have clearly and unambiguously declared that health is a very important consideration for them not buy this incredible product?

Research

A group of French psychologists – Nicolas Gueguen, Robert-Vincent Joule, Didier Courbet, Severine Halmi-Falkowicz, and Marie Marchand (2013) conducted a study that ostensibly was merely about the foot-in-the-door technique. It was a field study, and the participants were unsuspecting passersby. In the control conditions, they were asked if they would agree to fill out a rather long survey consisting of 45 questions. Of course, they could do it at home, and if they agreed, they would receive a stamped envelope into which they would put their responses after completing the questionnaire and send it back to the researchers. A total of 30% of the participants agreed to do so. In other conditions of this experiment, before participants were asked to take home a long questionnaire, they were asked a few questions. We know what this is, right? Foot-in-the door! Were those who first answered a few questions then more likely to agree to complete a long survey? Yes, this was indeed the case. But from the perspective of the technique, we are now presenting, the key point is how these initial questions were formulated. As it is, half of the time they were worded so that the obvious answer was almost always "yes" (e.g., "Have you ever assembled a storage unit?"), and the other half of the time so that respondents almost always answered in the negative (e.g., "Have you ever installed a solar water heater?"). It turned out that if the respondent answered in the negative several times within this short field survey, the percentage of people who agreed to take the long survey doubled, reaching 60%. But if the questions of the survey were formulated in such a way that the respondent said "yes" several times, the rate reached a skyrocketing 83%!

Mechanism

Four walls is a technique in which the interlocutor is induced to make statements that lead toward a consistency trap. Failure to accept the offer will constitute incorrect and inconsistent behavior. In fact, one could say that it would make the interlocutor a hypocrite. The French researchers have demonstrated that merely saying the word "yes" can cause an impact. When "yes" is repeated several times, the general tendency to agree and approve increases. This is because in many situations people function with little reflection and quite automatically. People who have in a fashion set themselves up to agree by saying "yes" to several statements are more likely to also agree to the next one than people who have set themselves up to disagree by responding "no" several times over. From this perspective, it is plausible to think that although salespeople might trick their interlocutors into a consistency trap by asking a series of questions that will be answered negatively (e.g., "Is it healthy to eat a huge amount of sweets instead of vitamins?"), more effective salespeople ask questions that evoke affirmative responses.

Technique # 4 *Service request*
Idea

In the case of the four walls technique we discussed earlier, the interviewee is initially asked a series of questions. The person's positive answers to these questions then make them more willing to comply with the request. The request is consistent with the content of the answers the person has just given. But what if, before asking us for something, someone uses a general and "smooth" statement like "Could you do me a favor?" or "Could you do me a service?". Unless we are tired, upset, or in a hurry, we are unlikely to say "no." Most probably we will either react normally, simply responding "yes," or we will answer a little more carefully, using the phrase "it depends." So if we answer "yes," we will not really be able to refuse the request that will appear in a moment (especially if it proves not too difficult to fulfill). If we answer "it depends," then probably... it depends. Depending on the nature of the request, we will accept or refuse it. As for the people who reject the question "Could you do me a favor/service?", they would probably also refuse a directly formulated request. So it would seem that preceding the request with the phrase we are talking about here may clearly increase the chances of its fulfillment. Is this really the case? Let us take a look at the results of a simple experiment.

Research

The study conducted by Sebastien Meineri, Michael Dupre, Boris Vallee, and Nicolas Gueguen (2015) was carried out in France, in a mid-sized city. It was conducted alternately by three young (20–21 years old), specially trained women. The experimenter approached a passerby walking alone and delivered one of two messages. Half the time she said: "Hello, sorry to bother you, I need to take the bus, but I haven't got enough money: could you give me 50 cents, please?" In the others, her statement sounded slightly different: "Hello, sorry to bother you, could you do me a service?", and the young woman waited for a response. If it was "yes" or "it depends," she continued: "I need to take the bus, but I haven't got enough money: could you give me 50 cents, please?". It turned out that if the woman simply asked people politely for 50 cents for the bus, this amount was given to her by 35.7% of those approached. However, if the request for half a euro was preceded by the phrase "could you do me a service, please?" the response was positive in as many as 54.9% of cases.

It is worth noting that a negative response to this initial request (or rather a polite formula) was rare. Only 8 out of 111 participants answered "no." Of the remaining 103, about half (49 to be exact) answered "yes," and the rest (54 people) said, "it depends." Interestingly, the responses to the main request were very similar in both cases. Among those who answered affirmatively to the question "could you do me a service, please?" 57.1% of people handed 50 cents over to the woman, while among those who answered more cautiously ("it depends") − 66.1%.

Mechanism

The most commonly cited explanation in the psychological literature for the technique presented here is the tendency of people to demonstrate consistency in their behavior. Someone who responds positively to a question (or rather, to a polite formula) such as "could you do me a service, please?" then fulfills the main request when it is made. Since they said A, after all, they should now say B. And this is what they do... One might think that someone who gives a different answer and says carefully "it depends" would not fall into such a trap of consequences. After all, it is worth noting that in the experiment presented Thus, consistent behavior in this case is more granting the request than not granting it. However, it is worth noting that, following the logic of the argument outlined here, it is possible to assume that the structure of the results of this experiment would be different if the final request were much more serious (e.g., a larger sum of money or sacrificing a few hours for some activity). In this case, an earlier "yes" should also increase the chances of the request being fulfilled, but an earlier "it depends" – not necessarily. However, we do not know of any empirical studies that show whether this would be the case for a difficult request.

Technique # 5 *Give to take (Reciprocity)*
Idea

Imagine that sooner or later you will need some kind of favor from a certain person. For example, you are planning to move, and you know that your friend has a big car that can carry many boxes of stuff in one go. What can you do to boost the chances that she will agree to your request for help? How about giving her a book that might interest her? Or buy her lunch out on the town? Most likely, you will do something that she will consider a favor, a nice gesture, giving something to her. You will also assume that when you ask her to lend her car to you, she will remember the gesture and take it into account when deciding whether or not to help. More or less consciously, you will use the "give to take" technique – you will give something to someone (it can be something material, like flowers or a bottle of alcohol, but also, for example, your time) in order to receive this gesture in the form of a favor.

Research

Hershey Friedman and Ahmed Rahman (2011) decided to test how the "give to take" rule works on strangers looking to buy something to eat at a small fast-food restaurant. Customers were randomly assigned to several groups. One was a control group (customers simply walked into the bar and ordered a meal). In the experimental group, customers entering the restaurant were approached by the manager, greeted warmly, and given a small gift – a little key ring. The amount of money that customers spent in the restaurant was then measured. While the control group averaged $7.11, the experimental group averaged $9.39 (32% more!). Of course, careful readers may say "now wait a moment – after all, we don't know if the higher amount spent in the restaurant was because of the customers receiving a gift or because the manager greeted them!". Indeed, this is a very important point – Friedman and Rahman also thought of this when they added another group that, although greeted by a manager, did not receive any gift. In this group, customers on average spent $8.39 in the restaurant – more than the control group, but still significantly less than the group in which customers received the key ring.

Mechanism

In many places around the world, especially in small communities, there is an interesting custom. When neighbors share something (for example, a piece of cake or a basket of fruit), they present it in a container – for example, a plate or a bowl. If, however, the recipients wish to give back the container, the social norm requires that it not be returned empty – something should be put in it (usually an item of similar value to the one previously received). The reason why this custom works is because of the rule of reciprocity, which says that every favor should be returned. This is a very powerful and, in evolutionary terms, quite old rule – sociologist Alvin Gouldner even calls it "the starting rule of societies." Gouldner (1960) argues that if we didn't have a deeply coded need to return favors, we could not have evolved as tribes, communities, groups. Only norms of returning reciprocal favors could make this possible.

Technique # 6 *Indirect reciprocity*
Idea

According to the reciprocity rule previously discussed, people are inclined to comply with the requests of those people who have previously complied with their requests, or have spontaneously (i.e., without being asked to do so) done something pleasant for them, for example by giving them an unexpected birthday present. So we are dealing here with a symmetrical interaction between two people. However, one can imagine a more complicated situation in which several people are involved. Suppose John gets help from Kate, who lends him her lecture notes. A few minutes later, Mary asks John to fill out a very long questionnaire on esthetic preferences. Mary has to survey dozens of people using this questionnaire in order to get course credit for her studies. John doesn't "owe" Mary anything, in the sense that she has never helped him with anything before. In fact, they don't even know each other. But doesn't the fact that John has just recently received help himself make it more likely that he will now decide to provide it himself? If it is the case that when someone receives help from someone else, that person is then more likely to help a completely different person, we could suggest a specific social influence technique. It would involve observing who has just received some selfless help and then making a request to that person to provide assistance.

Research

Redzo Mujcic and Andreas Leibbrandt (2017) conducted research at a shopping village car park area with more than 350 parking spaces. As concerns the implementation of the study, a particularly important aspect was that several side streets led to the main exit road from this parking lot. This meant that, especially in heavy traffic (which is when the experiment was conducted), many drivers were left to rely on the kindness of those on the main road. More specifically, these drivers had to brake before the intersection and let those on side streets join the traffic. It turned out that 15% of drivers behaved politely in such situations. Mujcic and Leibbrandt asked themselves how a driver would behave if, moments earlier, he himself had been allowed onto the main road and, while driving along it, sees another driver waiting outside the intersection for someone to allow her to merge with traffic. Note that this is a situation of indirect reciprocity. Someone has just done the driver a kindness, and now the driver may or may not do the same for another driver. The researchers found that in this type of situation, courteous driver behavior was more than twice as common as in the control condition, at 32%. For completeness, let's add one more piece of information about the structure of the results. The researchers conducted their experiment for a period of six months. Although the weather was mainly nice and sunny, there were also cloudy or rainy days. Did the weather affect the driving behavior they analyzed?

Under control conditions, yes. On sunny days, the politeness rate was 16%, but when it was raining or about to rain, it dropped to 9%. However, when drivers were tested under indirect reciprocity conditions, poor weather did not negatively impact politeness at all. This also means that when the weather was poor, the difference in driver politeness between the control and indirect reciprocity conditions was more than threefold (9% vs. 32%)!

Mechanism

It is widely accepted in the psychological literature that indirect reciprocity is the social foundation of altruism. People help others because they believe that when they themselves need help, someone will offer it to them. Of course, not all individuals share an equally strong belief that the social world is arranged in this way, and a given individual's understanding of this rule may be more or less probable in particular situations. It can be assumed, however, that if an individual receives disinterested help from someone, then it occurs to her that "people help each other." And if so, then shortly thereafter she herself should behave according to this rule. It is also worth noting that people in social interactions strive for balance (e.g., they like those who like them, support those who support them, etc.). When someone helps them, they are inclined to reciprocate. Then they feel good because the balance has been restored: they have helped those who previously helped them. They are not indebted. This is how the familiar classic rule of reciprocity works. But if, for some reason, they cannot return the favor to their benefactor, they achieve this balance by doing good for someone else. And this is what the power of indirect reciprocity is based on.

Technique # 7 *We've already given (Reciprocity-by-proxy)*
Idea

We know very well that the rule of reciprocity is one of the most effective forms of influencing other people's behavior – when others learn that we have done something for them, they are (in most cases) inclined to return the favor. This norm of reciprocal kindness is usually based on an exchange of mutual benefits – I did something for you, now you should do something for me. But what would happen if we included a third piece in this puzzle? For example, someone (a specific person or organization) whom we would help on behalf of the person whose behavior we want to influence? Imagine Mark and Andrew. Mark wants to influence Andrew's behavior, but he knows that Andrew might not appreciate a direct gift or favor. However, Mark knows that Andrew is an animal lover – so he decides to donate several bags of food to the local dog shelter and presents Andrew with confirmation of this gift as a birthday present. Will this lead Andrew to feel gratitude towards Mark? And will he feel obliged to do something Mark asks him for in the future? The matter is complicated because, after all, Andrew did not receive anything himself.

Research

Noah Goldstein, Vladas Giriskievicius, and Robert Cialdini (2011) planned an ingenious experiment in which they tested whether such a "transferred" reciprocity rule is an effective tool for influencing other people's behavior. In their study, they asked for help from students who came to the lab to perform simple research tasks for credits (at many universities, students are encouraged to participate in research with a system of extra credits that matter when calculating their final college grades). When the students had completed their work, they were asked an additional question – "we wanted to ask you whether you would be willing to volunteer to do an additional 20-minute survey assessing your thoughts about environmental practices taking place at UCLA and the greater Los Angeles area. If you are willing to do the survey, we will e-mail you a link later this week and ask you to complete the 20-minute survey." Up to that point, all students received the same message. Then – depending on the group they were randomly assigned to – it started to vary. In the control group, the message was simply about protecting the environment (since UCLA researchers believe in protecting the environment, we encourage you to engage in pro-environmental activities too: completing the survey is one of them). In the first experimental group, the students were informed that if they took the survey, UCLA would make a small financial donation to an environmental organization. In the second experimental group, the message was seemingly very similar – the students were informed that UCLA had already made a small financial donation on behalf of the participants in this study and that taking the survey and completing the survey would be a way to help defray that cost. There was a third experimental group, very similar to the second, which also reported that a donation had already been made on behalf of the respondents, but did not explicitly state that taking the survey would help defray the cost. Obviously, the researchers were interested in how many students would choose to take the additional survey in each group. The lowest number was in the first experimental group – 47.4%. There, the number of people volunteering to complete the additional survey was lower even than in the control group (52.9%)! Note that the first experimental group invoked a misunderstood reciprocity rule. It promised that UCLA would do something if the participants performed an action first – and this is one of the most serious mistakes you can make using this rule. Reciprocity is not a promise to do something when you do something. Rather, it's doing something first in order to create an obligation in you to "make your move"! And that is exactly what happened in the subsequent two groups. In the group in which it was directly indicated that the survey would serve as a means of covering the donation already made, the effectiveness exceeded 90%. In the one where there was no such direct reference (but there was information that the donation had already been made), 80% of the participants agreed to take part in the survey.

Mechanism

The studies by Goldstein and colleagues (because they actually tested this effect in a series of several experiments) showed that the mechanism of "transferred reciprocity" works very effectively. So, in reciprocity, an obligation does not have to arise only when the "recipient" has actually benefited – received a gift or real help. Reciprocity also works when others have benefited in some way, but that benefit has been transferred to them on our behalf. It seems that when someone has done something "for us" (even if they didn't ask us or coordinate with us in any way), it creates a kind of debt, or at least an imbalance in our relationship with that person. And because we generally don't like to owe people (and we believe in the norm that our debts should be repaid), we take action to zero out the balance as quickly as possible. And the easiest way to do that is to fulfill the request of a person who has done a favor on our behalf for someone else.

Technique # 8 *Door-in-the-face*
Idea

A group of social psychologists working on social influence techniques – Richard Miller, Clive Seligman, Nathan Clark, and Malcolm Bush (1976) – start one of their articles describing an adventure of characters from the popular comic strip "Blondie." The heroine comes home and shows what she bought while shopping to her husband Dagwood: shoes, a dress, and a hat, and asks him how she looks. A somewhat horrified Dagwood asks how much it all cost, and when he hears the number, he states that Blondie has to take it all back. Blondie starts crying, but after a moment asks if she could at least keep the hat. Dagwood agrees, congratulating himself in his head on his negotiating triumph: He has saved a lot of money because Blondie will return the expensive shoes and dress, while at the same time his wife appears pleased. Apparently, a new hat is enough to make her happy. If Blondie's goal really was to get a new hat, and she anticipated how things would develop, it means that she intentionally used the door-in-the-face technique. This is when, expecting your request to be refused, you make a request that is clearly more difficult. Of course, you will be turned down. But if you immediately follow up with an easier request (which is, in fact, the request you are most confirmed with), chances are good that it will be accepted. Dagwood said "no" when seeing the shoes, dress, and hat, only to say "yes" a moment later when just the hat was in question.

Research

Historically, the first psychological experiment devoted to the door-in-the-face technique was conducted by Robert Cialdini and a group of colleagues (1975) The person conducting the experiment introduced himself as an employee of an institution dealing with troubled youth (juvenile offenders) and asked people to engage in activities that would help these youth in finding their place in society. One of the primary problems is that these young people, left to their own devices out on the streets, become easy prey for drug dealers or various gangs. The idea is to keep them occupied in some way, to manage their free time. Would you, therefore, agree to go on a two-hour trip to the zoo in the afternoon as a caretaker of a group of such young people? Less than 17% of the respondents agreed to this request. Other participants are also presented with the problem of difficult youth but are told that probation officers are sought to be on call every week for two hours. In addition, since young people become used to the person in the role of probation officer, the idea is that they should not change too often. So would you agree to act as a superintendent for at least two years? Of course, the answer was almost always no. Upon hearing refusal, the experimenter did not insist, did not try to convince participants that they should take up the job, but asked whether, in that case, they would agree to go with some youngsters on a trip to the zoo – just once, for two hours in the afternoon. It turned out that every second participant agreed. Thus, we see that consent to comply with a request to chaperone during a trip to the zoo was much more frequent in conditions where the request was preceded by a clearly more difficult request that was refused.

Mechanism

An explanation that jumps to mind is the contrast between the difficulty of the first request and that of the final (main) request. We can compare it to being in a store where a shirt may seem quite cheap if the others are very expensive. Spending two hours on a trip to the zoo seems like an easier request when contrasted with the highly difficult request to serve as a probation officer for at least two years. The authors of the experiment described above considered this explanation. They also tested conditions in which the participant was presented with both options at once (would you agree to become a probation officer or go to the zoo?). Obviously, no one wanted to become a probation officer, while one in four people to whom the question was posed in this way agreed to go to the zoo. Thus, we see that the contrast plays a role here, but it cannot be considered the primary mechanism that accounts for the effectiveness of the door-in-the-face technique. The authors suggest that the effectiveness of this technique is best explained by the rule of reciprocity, which we are already familiar with. But this is a very specific kind of reciprocity. It is not about the mutual exchange of material goods or helping each other out in difficult situations. In this case, we are dealing with reciprocity of concessions. If someone who formulates a difficult request, which is then rejected, does not insist on its being fulfilled but makes a sort of concession by formulating a request which is clearly easier, then now the person being asked for help is in a way obliged to make a concession. If she said "no" before, she should now say "yes." There is another alternative explanation of the effectiveness of this technique, popular in the literature, which indicates an emotional mechanism (O'Keefe & Figge, 1997). Refusing a difficult request (especially when it involves engaging in a noble and desirable activity) can produce feelings of guilt or embarrassment. Accepting an easier request frees a person from these unpleasant emotions. For our part, we believe that the door-in-the-face technique is effective because of the combined effect of all three psychological mechanisms mentioned here – contrast, reciprocity, and the desire to rid oneself of unpleasant emotions.

Technique # 9 *Two-door-in-the-face*
Idea

If the effectiveness of the door-in-the-face technique described above is linked with a reduction of expectations that the person making the request formulates towards her interlocutor, the question thus arises of whether the effect would not be even greater if this reduction of expectations took place not once, but twice. In other words, while the door-in-the-face technique is based on the sequence: very difficult request – rejection – clearly easier (target) request, one can imagine a technique based on a slightly extended sequence: very difficult request – rejection – slightly easier request – rejection – clearly easier (target) request. If a sequence involving the formulation of one initial request that will be rejected is called door-in-the-face, then a technique based on the idea that two subsequent requests will be rejected should be called two-door-in-the-face. If we were to consider the effectiveness of such a technique, we should pose two questions: first, whether the use of a sequence of three successive requests, the first two of which are almost certain to be rejected, makes the final request (the third) more likely to be fulfilled compared to a situation in which this key request was posed immediately. Second, whether the effectiveness of such a technique would be higher than that of the door-in-the-face technique, which we are familiar with and which has been empirically tested by psychologists on numerous occasions.

Research

These were the questions asked by Morton Goldman and Christopher Creason (1981). They conducted their study at a time when cell phones were not yet in widespread use. (Although the first cell phones already existed – prototypes appeared as early as the 1950s). Instead, people in the United States used phones they had in their homes, and subscriber numbers were widely available in the phone book. Goldman and Creason used this for their experiment, randomly assigning said numbers to different test conditions. Between 12 and 4 p.m., the person conducting the experiment would dial a random number and say: "Hello, my name is Chris Walters. I am calling on behalf of KCST – a new radio station in the area." He went on to explain that the new radio station wanted to get an idea of listeners' preferences and was looking for volunteers who would agree to help survey Kansas City residents. In the control condition, the experimenter went straight to the point and asked if the caller would agree to call 25 people and ask them a few questions about programs they would like to hear on the radio. In the door-in-the-face condition, the caller was first asked to call 150 people, and then, after refusing, was asked to make 25 such calls. In the two-door-in-the-face conditions, the first request was also for 150 interviews; after the refusal, the expectation directed towards the participant was reduced to 100 interviews, and only after another refusal, it was pared down to 25. It turned out that in the control conditions almost no one agreed to comply with the request (to be more precise, around 3% did agree). The door-in-the-face technique proved to be effective. Under these conditions, exactly one in four respondents agreed to 25 interviews. However, what is particularly important from the perspective of the technique analyzed here, this rate was even higher under the conditions of using the two-door-in-the-face technique. Then it reached a level of 41%.

Mechanism

Of course, the psychological mechanism underlying the two-door-in-face technique is the same as that responsible for the effectiveness of the door-in-the-face technique. Note, however, that this mechanism is activated twice in this case, at very short time intervals. Presumably, this is what makes it not only effective but more effective than a technique based on reducing expectations once for the person being subjected to social influence.

Technique # 10 *Door-then-foot technique*

Idea

In the previous sections, we have described two classic social influence techniques: foot-in-the-door and door-in-the-face. In both cases, we use a sequence of requests. Foot-in-the-door is based on the principle that, according to which prior to formulating our request, the one we actually care about, we should first make a request that is significantly easier to agree to. We expect the latter to be complied with, which will increase the probability for also granting the following, more difficult, request. An opposite principle applies to the door-in-the-face technique. We start with a clearly difficult request, expecting it to be turned down. The refusal on the part of the subject will make them more inclined to accept the following, significantly easier, request. We also know that there are more elaborate forms of both the foot-in-the-door and the door-in-the-face methods. In the first case, the actual request is preceded by two requests, a simple one and a more difficult one, whereas in the second case the actual request is preceded by two consecutive difficult requests, in which the second one is slightly easier to fulfill than the first one. One can also imagine another sequence of requests that will pave the way for the actual one: first, there is a difficult request, which gets rejected, and it is then followed by a simple one, which is accepted, and only then is the actual request formulated – and this is clearly more difficult than the request that has just been accepted, but at the same time it is markedly easier to grant than the initial one, which was declined.

Research

Morton Goldman (2011) called randomly-selected individuals and introduced himself as a member of an organization supporting the local zoo. In the standard conditions, he asked the subject to manually address 75 letters with a request for financial support for the zoological garden. (It should be noted that back then, such a request was not extraordinary; the printers we use today for such tasks had not become common yet). Only 22% of the subjects expressed their willingness to participate in the project. The researcher investigated the effectiveness of various sequential techniques that, today, are well known and have become the standard. In the foot-in-the-door conditions, the request for addressing letters was preceded by a request to answer a few questions included in a survey, while in the door-in-the-face conditions, the first request was to conduct survey interviews with 150 individuals (which, obviously, was turned down). Both techniques turned out to be effective. In the first case, 42% of the subjects agreed to address the letters, while the result was 46% in the second case. However, we are particularly interested in the new door-then-foot technique. Here, the experimenter, having introduced himself, asked the subject to conduct 150 survey interviews regarding the zoological garden. After the refusal, the researcher asked the subject if, in this case, they would be willing to answer a few questions themselves. He asked the questions and then made a request for addressing letters to 75 potential donors. As it turned out, as many as 57% of the respondents agreed to fulfill the request in such conditions.

Mechanism

The door-then-foot method represents a combination of two classic sequential social influence techniques, namely door-in-the-face and foot-in-the-door. Its strength also results from a synergy of the underlying psychological mechanisms for the two techniques. It should be noted that the foot-in-the-door technique requires the subject to grant a relatively simple request. "Relatively" is the key word here. The request to be granted must not be trivial (e.g., replying to a question like, "what time is it?"), as this will not make the subject think of himself or herself in the "I'm someone who grants other peoples' requests" category. Due to the trivial nature of the request, everyone would be willing to fulfill it and thus the subject has no reason to believe he or she is special. However, if the initial request is not trivial, quite a few people will simply turn it down. If this is the case, they will be even more likely to refuse to grant another, even more difficult, request and thus the *foot-in-the-door* technique will not be effective. The *door-then-foot* method is designed to increase one's willingness to grant a simple, but not trivial, request. This is achieved by first presenting the subject with a markedly difficult request, which the subject refuses, but at the same time the refusal motivates the subject to accept the similar, yet clearly easier, request that follows. Let us emphasize: an easier, but not extremely easy, and not trivial request. Once this request has been granted, it will be very probable that the subject will be willing to accept another, more difficult, request. This is exactly the objective of an individual attempting to exert social influence.

Technique # 11 *Foot-in-the-face*

Idea

The foot-in-the-door and door-in-the-face techniques we wrote about in the preceding passages are among the most thoroughly studied social influence techniques. Both of them exhibit a sequential character, which means that before the actual request appears, a separate preliminary request is formulated. As we have already discussed, in the case of foot-in-the-door this initial request is easy, and one can expect that the person being asked will almost certainly fulfill it. In the case of door-in-the-face, exactly the opposite is true. The first initial request is difficult and you can be almost certain that it will be refused. But what if the first and the second request are at a similar level of difficulty? Will the probability of the participant complying with the second request increase after fulfilling the first one? Or vice versa: will it increase if the first one is refused? Or... will it increase regardless of whether the first request is fulfilled or refused?

Research

The experiment was carried out at a university (Dolinski, 2011). Students approached while in the hallway were informed that a campaign was being organized to provide comprehensive assistance to a student with a vision impairment. Thus, for obvious reasons, he has trouble both with preparing for exams and carrying out other tasks prescribed by the curriculum. All participants were presented with two requests in succession. In half of the cases, they were first told that the blind student was conducting a survey study. The survey is quite long and takes about half an hour to complete. Whether the participant agreed to do it or not, another request was made: would the participant agree to record a short chapter from a textbook (about five pages) on a tape recorder? Students with vision impairments study for exams by listening to such recordings. The other half of the participants were also asked to carry out these two requests, but the first request presented was to record a chapter from a textbook on a tape recorder, and only then were they asked to complete the survey. It turned out that whatever request (whether to record a chapter or to complete a survey) came first, less than half of the participants agreed to carry it out. However, for the request that came second (and was therefore preceded by the alternative request), there was an increase (to 58%) in compliance. In a follow-up study, one more factor was introduced into the experimental design. Regardless of whether the participant complied with the first request or not, the second request either immediately followed or came only after some time (two days to be exact). And it turned out that the foot-in-the-face technique is particularly effective when the second request appears immediately upon refusal to carry out the first one, but when the first request is fulfilled, the technique becomes effective only after some time. In this situation, almost 70% of the participants agreed to comply with the second request. The social influence practitioner should therefore take this into account and present the second request immediately after the first one is refused. However, if the first request is fulfilled, it is worth waiting a while before making another one.

Mechanism

The foot-in-the-face technique takes advantage of the fact that if the person being approached refuses the first request, upon observing that a second attempt is not made, one should not insist on its fulfillment but rather form an alternative request, as this will be perceived as a concession. First, the person being asked now has more freedom of choice, because there are two requests involved, rather than one, as there was just a moment ago. Second, this new request may subjectively seem easier than the original one. After all, the difficulty of both requests cannot be objectively estimated, and usually, after refusing the first request, salespersons and other similar request makers lower their expectations and formulate a more favorable proposal. Thus, most likely, the rule of reciprocity is activated here: a concession for a concession, which demands one who has just said "no" to fulfill the new request. And what if the participant carries out the first request? Well, both thinking of oneself in terms of "I am a person who fulfills such requests" and the human tendency for consistency should lead the participant to fulfill the next request as well. Especially since it is not clearly more difficult than the one already carried out. The magic of this technique is that no matter what the participant does upon hearing the first request, there is a high probability that the second one will be carried out as well.

Technique # 12 *Low ball*

Idea

This technique comes from observations of American used car dealers. They usually have dozens or even hundreds of cars on display in a large lot, and each of them has a price written in big letters on the windshield – usually quite attractive. The buyer walks around the lot, looks at the vehicles, and finally finds it – this is the car he was looking for! It looks nice, seems in good shape, has no visible problems, and even the color the spot. And the price isn't bad – so the buyer starts negotiations with the seller. After several minutes they come to an agreement, the seller has lowered the price a bit, and the customer has said he will pay immediately, in cash. They shake hands and go to the office to sign the contract. During the signing, however, it turns out that the car has summer tires, and the law forbids driving between November and March without winter tires. So we have to add this to the car's cost. The car is also without a valid technical inspection. You can take care of it at the dealer's, but it will cost extra. And let's not forget about sales tax, which must be added to the price. Will the buyer change his mind and walk away? In the vast majority of cases, no – he will stick to his earlier decision, and despite the fact that the deal is becoming less and less attractive, he'll still seek to finalize it.

Research

Research on the low ball technique was first conducted by Robert Cialdini, John Cacioppo, Rodney Bassett, and John Miller (1978). Their experiment involved psychology students who were contacted by phone and heard the following message: "I'm calling to schedule 100 students for an experiment on thinking processes. The experiment concerns the way people organize facts. We can give you one hour of credit for your participation in this experiment." At this point, the instructions differed for the group using the low ball technique and the control group. The control group was informed that the experiment would take place on Friday morning at 7:00 a.m. (for many students, this is the middle of the night). After this information, the students were asked if they wanted to sign up to participate in the experiment. In the low ball group, the students were first asked if they were interested; if they responded positively, they were enrolled, and only then were those students informed that the experiment would begin at 7:00 a.m. on Friday. The results confirmed the effectiveness of the technique in terms of verbal declarations that participants would attend the experiment – in the control group, 31% of them agreed. In the low ball group, it was 56%. But the most interesting thing happened later – the experimenters checked who actually showed up at the lab on Friday morning. In the control group, 24% of those asked to come actually did, while in the low ball group it was 53% (i.e., virtually everyone who said they would show up!). The results obtained by the researchers clearly confirmed that the declaration of consent to some proposal was maintained (both verbally and in terms of actual behavior) even when the conditions became decidedly unattractive for students.

Mechanism

The reason why people do not (usually) back out of their promises or declarations is the feeling of commitment – that is, the belief that if I have agreed to a deal, I should not back out of it. The feeling of commitment, in turn, is related to the rule of commitment and consistency – the strong belief that if I have already said A, I should also say B. People tend to behave consistently for reasons of self-perception as well – after all, none of us would like to see ourselves as people with unstable views, constantly changing our mind. On the other hand, the image of being steadfast in one's decisions and opinions is highly desirable. An additional reason is the foot-in-the-door self-perception technique we have also mentioned. After all, if I have already agreed to a request, I am a person who "does these kinds of things." We do them even when the going gets a lot tougher.

Technique # 13 *The lure*

Idea

The low-ball technique outlined above is undoubtedly unethical. Perhaps even more unethical, however, is the similar technique of the lure. While in low-ball, what is offered to the participant remains constant but the cost of achieving it increases (e.g., we have to pay more money, or spend more time, or get up early in the morning, as in the case of the research we described above), in the case of the lure technique, quite unexpectedly, it "turns out" that the promised thing is no longer available for some reason. The individual targeted may get something else (de facto less attractive, of course).

Research

In one experiment conducted in France, Robert Joule, Fabienne Gouilloux, and Florent Weber (1989) encouraged students to participate in a psycho-logical experiment. Under conditions that tested the effectiveness of the lure technique, they were invited to participate in an interesting study of emo-tions while being told that they would watch a movie 25 minutes or so in length and then answer a few questions about the scenes in the movie that moved them the most. They were promised 30 francs (equivalent to about $6) for participating in this experiment. When the students showed up at the lab, they were informed "with regret" that the experiment on emotions would unfortunately not be conducted. Jeśli student się jednak zgodzi, to może wziąć udział w innym badaniu, dotyczącym pamięci, za co jednak nie przewidziano żadnego wynagrodzenia. However, if the students agree, they can participate in another study dealing with memory, but for which no gratification was provided. In the control condition, students were simply offered the opportunity to take part in a memory study without any grati-fication for doing so. It turned out that using the lure technique roughly tripled the chance of recruiting participants for the laboratory memory study. While in the control condition only 15.4% of participants agreed to participate, in the lure condition this number jumped to 47.4%.

Mechanism

Not only is the lure technique very similar to the low ball technique described earlier, but it also relies on the same psychological mechanism; that is, a sense of obligation and motivation to continue with an action already commenced. In relation to the above experiment, participants who learn that the study they came for will not take place – but they can take part in another one without financial gratification – think "since I am already here, I'll join in some psychological study." Note also that by refusing to participate in an experiment for which there is no compensation, participants would have to admit that they came to the laboratory not because they're interested in psychology and psychological experiments, but just because they want the money. Some people are very reluctant to be perceived that way.

Technique # 14: *Two-in-one: Low-ball combined with foot-in-the-door*

Idea

We have already gotten to know the foot-in-the-door and the low-ball techniques. The basic difference between the two is that in case of the former, there is a sequence of two requests, where the second is more demanding than the first. In the case of the low-ball technique, the request essentially remains the same. The only thing that changes is the cost of granting the request. Initially, acting on the request seems easy but as the subject begins to initiate the action, it turns out that it will cost them more time, effort, or money. What would the combination of these two techniques be like? To put it simply, it would consist of asking someone to grant, in a short period of time, a reasonably challenging request. Once the person agrees to do so, we tell them that "since we are already on the subject," perhaps they would agree to act, right away, on a similar, very easy request that requires little involvement on their part. Obviously, the subject agrees to do so.

After a while, as stated earlier, we address the subject and we say that due to new circumstances that unexpectedly have come to light, we are asking them for somewhat greater involvement than we agreed on previously. Does it work? Let us examine some experimental studies on this subject.

Research

In the case of marketing research conducted over the phone, usually, the problem is that callees refuse to participate. Jacob Hornik, Tamar Zaig, Dori Shadmon, and Gabriel Barbash (1990) called residents of Tell Aviv on weekends between 4:00 p.m. and 9:00 p.m. and asked them to take part in an interview regarding health-related topics. The participants were informed that the interview would take 20 minutes and would take place in a few days' time. (If the respondent agreed to participate in such a long telephone conversation, they would be called three days later, but the interview would actually end after approx. six minutes). It turned out that 48.1% of the respondents agreed to participate in the interview. Hornik et al. wanted to see what percentage of individuals would agree if commonly known, classic social influence techniques were applied. As it turned out, the percentage of callees who were willing to spend 20 minutes of their time on a telephone conversation increases to 59% in the event the request to participate in a 20-minute long interview is preceded with a request to provide answers to three short questions. The low-ball technique proved to be even more effective. In this case, initially, the respondents were called and asked to participate, in the near future, in a ten-minute-long interview regarding health-related topics. If the respondent agreed, they would be called again after three days and told that the research team from the university decided to include a few additional questions in the interview, and thus it would last approx. 20 minutes. The result: 73.8% of the respondents agreed to participate in the extended version of the interview. But we already knew that the foot-in-the-door and the low-ball techniques were effective. What we are more interested in is how a combination of both of these techniques might work. In this case, a respondent was asked to participate, in the near future, in a ten-minute-long telephone interview. Once the respondent agreed, they would hear the following message: "While we are on the phone, could you please respond to three short questions concerning health matters?" This was, obviously, followed by said three questions. After three days, the respondent would be called again and told that due to the fact that the research team from the university decided to include a few additional questions in the scheduled interview, it would take not ten but 20 minutes. Was this technique effective? You bet it was! As it turned out, as many as 84.1% of the respondents agreed to be interviewed!

Mechanism

The power of the technique being a combination of two classic sequential methods, i.e., the low-ball and the foot-in-the-door techniques, results not only from the fact that it utilizes the basic elements of these two classic social influence techniques but also from the fact that it is based on somewhat different psychological mechanisms underlying the effectiveness of both of the above-mentioned methods. Let us remember: the low-ball technique is effective because the subject agrees to become involved in a certain activity and the sudden emergence of new, unfavorable circumstances does not negate the commitment they have previously taken on. However, the foot-in-the-door is commonly believed to be effective because of the self-perception mechanism (Bem, 1967). A subject who has agreed to grant the initial request is motivated to explain why they have acted in this way to themselves. If the subject sees no clear external motives for their reaction (no one forced them, no one paid them to act on the request), the subject begins to perceive themselves as someone who "does this type of thing" or someone who "grants requests of other people," and this new image turns out to be consistent with the new, more demanding request. The complex effect of maximizing the power of social influence, which we are discussing here, activates both of these mechanisms sequentially. Therefore, this technique can be described as a two-engine vehicle speeding towards a goal, i.e., towards making a subject act on a particular request.

Technique # 15 *Dump and chase*
Idea

When we make a request of someone, we may encounter acceptance or refusal. In the latter case, we can, in turn, either consider the conversation finished, or try to keep it going and continue to persuade our interlocutor to agree to our request. Sometimes the matter is quite simple. For example, our interlocutor tells us that she won't comply with our request because she is short on time. We can then reply that we will take less than a minute of her time because we want her to just answer three short questions. But what if she simply says "no" and cuts off the conversation? Imagine that we then politely ask her why she is refusing us. Perhaps… only then will she say that she has a little time. And could this new situation be treated as something that facilitates exerting social influence? Let see.

Research

Franklin Boster and his colleagues (2009) studied the reactions of passersby to a request from a woman standing next to a bicycle. She said that she has something to do in a nearby building, but she forgot to take her bicycle lock, and she's worried that it will get stolen. So she asks people to watch it, for about ten minutes. It turned out that 40% of the passers-by responded positively to this request. Those who refused sometimes gave a reason, which then provided an opportunity to present arguments that might induce them to change their mind decision. If they said, for example, "I'm in a bit of a hurry," the woman could reply: "ok, but it's only ten minutes, certainly no longer." But what if people gave no reason for their decision? Well, in this case, the woman politely asked about why they refused to help. After hearing their answer, she immediately tried to find holes in it that would allow her to convince them to agree to watch the bicycle. As a result, the percentage of people who agreed to give ten minutes of their time rose to 60%.

Mechanism

Refusal to comply with a request can take many forms. People may say "no" and end the conversation, but they can also say "no" and explain why they don't want to or cannot fulfill our request. In the first case, the refusal is a rebuff; in the second case, it is an obstacle. While a rebuff resolves the issue unfavorably for us, an obstacle opens the door to further talks and negotiations. For example, we may be able to present some additional circumstances or use additional arguments that will make our interlocutor agree to our request. But must a rebuff mean that the matter is definitively concluded? What if we simply ask our interlocutor politely about the reasons why he doesn't want to or cannot fulfill our expectations? If he is willing to answer us, the rebuff will turn into an obstacle. And now we have an opportunity to get him to change his mind.

2

EMOTIONS

Many people regard emotions as a redundant element hindering rational actions. If we refer to someone's behavior as emotional, it is a polite and euphemistic way to say that it was stupid. If we say that a decision was emotional, it essentially means that it was unwise and hasty. Meanwhile, emotions are necessary for our minds to be able to operate effectively. Imagine that you are deprived of all emotions and that you enter a shoe store to buy yourself a pair of shoes. You would have to consistently compare each pair in terms of at least several parameters: are they robust, is the sole going to provide good ground traction, will they be able to keep your feet dry if it rains, etc. As a result, you would spend the entire day choosing the right shoes. With emotions, though, you immediately know that a vast majority of the shoes displayed on the shelves invoke no positive feelings in you. You focus your attention on a few pairs and you will either buy one of them or you will go to another store. Emotions experienced by people can also facilitate or hinder a person from exerting social influence upon them. This section is going to be devoted to this very problem.

DOI: 10.4324/9781003296638-3

Technique # 16 *Take advantage of her (or his) good mood*

Idea

Common knowledge suggests that a good mood makes our attitude generally more positive; it makes us kinder and nicer. We see the world in bright colors and we think positively about the future. By the same token, we should also be more willing to act on various requests that are asked of us. It appears that this fact is already well known by children, who will wait for their parents to be in a good mood to ask (depending on their age) for a new toy, if they can go out to a disco, if they can stay out past midnight, or for a loan for their new car. We all know that this works. The good mood of the person we intend to approach increases the chances of having our request granted. Does it apply invariably or does it depend on the type of request? Psychological studies demonstrate that the problem is significantly more complex than it usually appears. Let us examine the results of one such study.

Research

Alice Isen and Stanley Simmonds (1978) took advantage of the fact that by the 1970s, cell phones had not been invented yet. As there were no cell phones, people had to use other communication devices when they were out. They used telephone booths, which we can still find in some places. They resemble the field exhibits at a telecommunications museum since today nobody uses them anymore (and our youth would probably not even know how to operate them). So with younger readers in mind, let us explain that a telephone booth featured a payphone that one could use after putting a suitable coin into the slot. The payphone featured a coin return compartment, into which the coin would drop if the call attempt was unsuccessful. Some payphones would give the change if the call was shorter than expected. Sometimes it would happen (it is uncertain why this would happen, probably due to an equipment defect) that the payphone would return the inserted coin even if the call attempt was successful. At that time, virtually everybody used telephone booths and almost everybody had a habit of checking if there was a coin in the coin return of the telephone after the call had ended.

The researchers assumed that if someone were to hang up and the payphone, unexpectedly, returned their dime, it would put this person in a good mood (it should be noted that in the 1970s, a dime had significantly greater purchasing power than today and that people generally enjoy pleasant surprises). The researchers' plan was to put a dime into the coin return compartment before an individual, unaware of the fact that they have just become a subject, entered the telephone booth. Once the caller has ended their call and found an unexpected gift (the dime), he would come out of the booth and be approached by an experimenter, who would introduce themselves and explain that they were conducting mood-related research. The experimenter would point to a book they were holding in the other hand and, depending on the experimental conditions, say that the statements included in the took were designed to put people in a good mood or that they were designed to put people in a bad mood. What the researchers needed was an empirical study that would confirm if the statements evoked the desired effect and if they were suitable for this purpose. The book did contain (positive in one part and negative in the other part) statements used by psychologists to evoke relevant affective states in people. The experimenter would approach subjects with an identical request in the control conditions. These were individuals who reached into the coin return of the telephone after their call but found nothing there. The researchers were interested in the following two aspects: the time the subject devoted to reading the statements and the number of statements read. The analysis of the results demonstrated that in the event the experimenter asked them to read the positive statements, those individuals who had just, unexpectedly, found a dime in the coin return compartment helped the experimenter for a longer time (on average by 50%) and read, from the book they were given, more statements (on average by 55%) than those individuals who simply had their call and walked out of the booth. As far as reading the statements designed to put the reader in a bad mood, the distribution of the results was the opposite. Those subjects who had been put in a good mood devoted less time to helping the experimenter (on average by as much as 70%!) and read less statements (on average by as much as 90%) than the subjects in the control conditions.

Mechanism

Our mood, unlike physiological arousal, which we addressed previously, is not related to observing changes in heart rate or respiratory rate. It could be said that it is a significantly milder (and in most cases also longer-lasting) affective state. Being in a good mood is very pleasant. It is so enjoyable that people are willing to go to great lengths to achieve this state and once they have, they are willing to do equally as much to maintain it. Granting other people's requests may put us in a good mood (it is pleasant to see someone else's joy and it is pleasant to believe that we are kind). At the same time, acting on other people's request may kill our good mood (we may, e.g., lose money when an employee of a charitable organization asks us for a donation, lose our time when someone asks us to fill out a survey, or get our hands dirty when someone asks us to carry a bag from a car's trunk to their door). A subject's good mood is conducive to said subject granting requests but only those requests that are not excessively detrimental to their good mood. But if you have a troublesome task that needs being taken care of, one that would significantly reduce the level of positive emotions experienced by the person you want to approach, you should not wait until this person is in a good mood (unless this person is so ecstatic that nothing will be capable of killing their good mood, although we should make the following reservation: social psychologists, as far as we know, have not examined such situations).

Technique # 17 *Take advantage of her (or his) bad mood*
Idea

The technique previously described was based on the premise that people want to sustain their good mood. While in a good mood, people gladly grant requests made by others but only those requests that will not kill their good mood. But what about being in a bad mood? You probably think that when they are in a bad mood, an individual does not feel liking doing anything and is only annoyed by other people's requests. Let us start by emphasizing that we are not referring here to emotions (e.g., experiencing anger or irritation directed towards a particular person) but to emotional states, which, on the one hand, are less intense and, on the other hand, are less specific, i.e., not directed towards particular social objects. Psychological experiments demonstrate that in certain cases a bad mood may also be conducive to an individual granting other people's requests. Let us take a closer look at one such experiment.

Research

Robert Cialdini and Douglas Kenrick (1976) invited teenagers (aged 15–18) to participate in their experiment. The experiment was individual in nature. The student designated to participate in the study would leave the classroom and would go to the improvised psychological laboratory on the school premises. At the laboratory, the student was told that he would participate in two consecutive tests: the first being a hearing task and the second being an imagination task. The subject was told that in return for his participation in the study, he would receive special coupons that he would be able to exchange for some (unspecified) rewards. During the hearing task, the subject was asked to listen to a series of sound pairs and identify the one they believed to be the louder of the two. Once the final answer had been given, the subject was told that his score was similar to the score of the majority of the tested students and was given ten coupons. The second test was to follow soon. The subject would receive another five coupons for participation at the start of the test. At this point, subjects were randomly assigned to one of two experimental conditions. In the control conditions, the subjects were shown a chair with a book on it; they were asked to close their eyes and imagine, individually, both of these items. Whereas in the alternative conditions, the subjects were asked to recall and imagine various negative events. As you can probably imagine, the objective was to keep some of the subjects in their current mood and to reduce the mood in the case of the remaining subjects. Regardless of the conditions, the subjects were assigned to, immediately after the imagination task they were told that not all students would have the opportunity to participate in the experiment and receive coupons and subsequently some gifts. "But if you wish," – the experimenter continued, – "you can donate your coupon or coupons to such persons. It is up to you and, obviously, you are not required to do so." As it turned out, the subjects who were kept in their current mood donated, on average, approx. 0.8 of their coupons to other students. (It should be noted that there were quite a few individuals who refused to give away any of their coupons). In the conditions where the mood of the subjects was reduced, they were more willing to follow the suggestion of the experimenter and donate their coupons to other students. In those conditions, the subjects gave away, on average, slightly above four coupons!

Mechanism

A negative mood is nothing pleasant, that is a truism and there is no need to convince anybody of that. It should be noted though that people use various strategies to get out of this negative state of mind. Some will go to the movies, some will get a beer with their friends, while others will put on their headphones to listen to their favorite music. According to Cialdini and Kenrick's negative state relief model, we can reduce our negative mood by helping other people. It makes us "feel better about ourselves" and such a belief, explicitly supported by the manifested behavior, elevates our mood instantly. Therefore, if the request is not difficult and does not require a great sacrifice from the person we are asking for a favor, this person may be very willing to grant our request. It should be emphasized here that we are referring to dealing with subjects with a slightly reduced mood, not suffering from severe depression, in which case people lack motivation to perform any tasks and their self-esteem is so low that acting on the request of another person would not restore it.

Technique # 18 *Physiological arousal*

Idea

Each one of you, dear Readers, has certainly noticed that sometimes your heart beats faster and your pulse, as well as your respiratory rate, increase. Sometimes you know exactly why this happens, while in other cases you are not exactly aware of the causes of your physiological response. Such changes in the reactions of our body, which we can observe ourselves (and others which can be precisely measured with specialist instruments), are symptoms of increased physiological arousal. Physiological arousal in humans can be caused by a variety of factors. It can result from the sheer physical presence of other people, by contact with a very attractive individual or with someone famous. It can also be caused by, e.g., a very strong odor (both pleasant and unpleasant) or by the sight of an individual standing on the edge of a roof of a building and threatening to commit suicide. In a car dealer's showroom, a customer's arousal may be caused by the sight of a magnificent sports car; whereas in a shoe store, a similar effect can be induced by the sight of super fashionable shoes available at a 50% discount, which appears to be screaming, "Buy me!" Increased arousal may also be induced by hearing a song by Pink Floyd, particularly if we have not heard this particular track for several years, or by a sex scene in an otherwise rather boring film. Honestly speaking, compiling an exhaustive list of events that may induce increased arousal is virtually impossible.

Research

Arnie Cann and Jill Blackwelder (1984) decided to verify if people experiencing elevated physiological arousal are more willing to grant requests they are asked to act on. The experiment was conducted in a university building. Some subjects (mostly undergraduates) were asked questions immediately after leaving the restroom and some away from it, in the middle of a hallway. The researchers assumed that a person approached by a stranger immediately after leaving a restroom will experience elevated arousal. A restroom is a place where we particularly need privacy, which, in the case of this experiment, was to some extent breached. The researcher conducting the experiment addressed all subjects with the same request. He told them that he was in a terrible hurry and that his friend was waiting for him at the entrance to the building to receive important notes. Would the subject agree to take the notes and deliver them to the person waiting outside? (It should be noted that the experiment was conducted in the pre-cell phone era, so the subject could not have said, "call your buddy and tell him to come over.") As it turned out, while 45% of the subjects agreed to grant the request when asked in the middle of the hallway, the percentage was almost twice as high (80%) in the case of those individuals who were asked to act on the same request by the door to the public restroom.

Mechanism

Numerous psychological studies have demonstrated consistently that negative physiological arousal hinders accurate assessment of a situation and making rational decisions. Some psychologists claim that this is caused by the fact that strong physiological arousal causes slightly less blood to be delivered to the brain. Due to the suboptimal amount of "fuel," we operate in a manner similar to a car with an almost empty gas tank – it is still moving forward but the engine is starting to choke. Meanwhile, when one becomes a subject of social influence, it becomes necessary, in most cases, to quickly think over the decision to be made: "How should I behave in this situation? Do I grant the request or not?" Provided that the request is formulated in a polite fashion, and it is not particularly weird or demanding, the subject experiencing strong arousal may be out of reasons for which they could refuse to act on the request.

Technique # 19 *Guilt*

Idea

Let us start with something obvious: the feeling of guilt is an emotion. An emotion is a state experienced also at the physiological level but it differs qualitatively from sheer physiological arousal, which we discussed in the previous section. This is because an emotion has its object and its contents; it is accompanied by certain thoughts that, in most cases, simply "come to our mind." We are angry at something or someone, we are saddened because of something. The feeling of guilt is a very peculiar emotion, as its object is the subject experiencing this feeling. It emerges when we realize that by behaving in a certain manner, we have violated the norm that we accept and consider important. People feel guilty, e.g., when they hurt an innocent person, when they are disloyal to their friends or when they fail to adhere to a diet and eat an entire bar of chocolate. The feeling of guilt is a strongly aversive state and, oftentimes, it is quite difficult to get rid of. It should be added that it is a so-called private emotion. This means that it does not matter if other people know that the subject has violated a norm or an ethical rule. What is important here is that the subject knows this.

Research

In their experiment, Paula Konoske, Sandra Staple, and Richard Graf (1979) created such conditions where some of their subjects, while performing a task, accidentally knocked over (or, to be more precise, they believed that it was accidental) a stack of computer punch cards. As a result, the punch cards got scattered all over the floor and thus it was impossible to recreate their stacking order. Therefore, the subject should experience the feeling of guilt related to the fact that their clumsiness ruined somebody else's work. Subsequently, the subjects were asked to call prospective subjects after the experiment had ended. Some of the subjects were told that the people they were supposed to call had not confirmed the date of their arrival at the laboratory yet and that the purpose of the call was to remind them about it. Other subjects were told that the purpose was to recruit subjects for an experiment designed to test people's reactions to fear-inducing stimuli. As it is difficult to recruit subjects for such experiments, the goal was to conceal the true nature of the experiment during the phone call and to say that the experiment would be pleasant. Identical requests (i.e., to remind the subjects about the time and place of the experiment or to lie to the prospective subjects about the true nature of the scheduled experiment) were also directed to the subjects from the control group, i.e., subjects who did not knock over the stack of punch cards and thus were not feeling guilty. Each time, the number of individuals that a given subject agreed to call was recorded. As it turned out, as far as simply reminding prospective subjects about the time and place of the experiment, the guilt-induced subjects clearly agreed to call a greater number of individuals (on average, 21.00) than the subjects from the control group (10.33). But when it came to lying, the guilt-induced subjects were willing to make calls to a slightly lower number of people (on average, 12.27) than the subjects from the control group (13.07).

Mechanism

Let us start by drawing your attention to the structure of the results of the above-described experiment. The feeling of guilt increased the subjects' willingness to grant the requests but only in those cases where acting on the request did not entail violating an ethical norm. When the subjects were asked to lie to other people, the guilt-induced subjects were even less willing to comply than the subjects from the control group. The feeling of guilt is not only about experiencing negative emotions, it also entails facing an influx of negative thoughts about ourselves, and in turn, thinking negatively about ourselves causes reduced self-assessment and self-esteem. Therefore, a fundamental psychological need in humans becomes endangered: the need for positive self-assessment. When in this state, an individual is strongly motivated to do something, which will help them restore the lost self-esteem. For this reason, this state is accompanied by an increased tendency to grant such requests, which will help the subject feel better about themselves but the subject's readiness to act on just any request is not increased.

Technique # 20 *Shame*

Idea

The emotion of shame often occurs together with the feeling of guilt. This is the case when other people witness the violation of a norm or a rule on the part of the subject. At the same time, these other people do not have to be physical and literal witnesses. Shame can also be present when the subject, who has violated a norm, begins to wonder how other people would react to it, what they would think of him, how they would judge him. By the same token, unlike the feeling of guilt, shame is a public emotion. Other emotions that often occur together with experiencing shame are regret and repentance. The public nature of shame consists of the subject communicating all these feelings to other people. What is more, the subject does it, in some measure, independently of their intentions. There is a typical blush on the subject's face (as well as on the neck and the upper chest, in women). This blush is a non-verbal message: "I regret what I have done, I am aware of the fact that I violated a norm or a rule, I am ashamed of my behavior, and I promise it will not happen again." Obviously, shame, similar to guilt, is a strongly aversive state. Naturally, the following question arises: will a person experiencing shame be more willing to comply with other people's requests similarly to someone experiencing the feeling of guilt?

Research

John Wallace and Edward Sadalla (1966) conducted an ingenious experiment designed to examine the relation between the feeling of shame and one's compliance with other people's requests. It was, historically speaking, one of the first psychological experiments pertaining to social influence techniques. Each time, there were two subjects sitting in the laboratory and filling out questionnaires. At the same time, the experimenter, in a rather demonstrative manner, checked the correct operation of various pieces of equipment set on a table. Then the experimenter left on the pretense of a need to prepare additional questionnaires and scales for the subjects. While the experimenter was gone, the subjects either sat neutrally and waited for his return, or one of the subjects (actually a confederate) would attempt to persuade the other subject to fiddle with one of the devices set on the table. This fiddling resulted in damaging the device. Various lights started blinking and there was smoke coming out of the device. There was a noticeable smell of burning wires. Immediately after the experimenter had returned to the room, the confederate either admitted that, together with the other subject, they wanted to see how the device worked and, unfortunately, they damaged it or said that they noticed something strange happening with the device as they were filling out their tests. The experimenter checked the device and (accordingly) either confirmed that the subjects had damaged it or concluded that the device became defective in a completely spontaneous fashion. In the control conditions (i.e., where nobody attempted to persuade the subject to fiddle with the device), the experimenter verified the operation of the device and concluded that it was defective. In all three conditions, this caused the experimenter to cancel the remaining part of the experiment due to the same reason: equipment malfunction. Therefore, the experimenter would declare the experiment to be complete but, at the same time, he would ask the subjects to participate in another experiment devoted to physiological determinants of stress reactions. In this experiment, the subjects would be, from time to time, shocked with electric current. As it turned out, only approx. 15% of the subjects from the control conditions agreed to take part in such an experiment. The percentage was markedly higher in those conditions where the subjects believed that they had damaged the device but also thought that the experimenter was unaware of it (approx. 38% of the subjects). However, in those cases where the subjects believed that the experimenter knew they had damaged the equipment, a clear majority (as many as 69%) of them agreed to participate in the unpleasant experiment.

Mechanism

Experiencing shame is a very aversive emotion. Doing something positive, such as acting on the request of another person, may help us get rid of this unpleasant feeling. If the individual asking for a favor is the same person who was wronged by the subject (and this is how the situation arranged in the above-described experiment could be described), granting the request may be perceived as an attempt at redemption: "True, I have damaged the equipment but I will help the experimenter out by participating in another experiment." It should be noted that those conditions that created the feeling of shame ("the experimenter knows that I, even though I was not instructed to do so, fiddled with and consequently damaged the device") were particularly conducive to granting the experimenter's request. However, it should also be noted that other research into the role of the feeling of shame in inducing compliance demonstrates that individuals experiencing this emotion are also more willing to grant requests in those conditions where the request is made by a person who did not witness the subject's reprehensible behavior. By the same token, this indicates that doing something positive (helping someone who is asking for help) is, for the subject, primarily a chance to get rid of the negative emotion of shame or to at least reduce its intensity.

Technique # 21 *Embarrassment*
Idea

Embarrassment is an emotion we experience quite rarely but, undoubtedly, almost every adult person has experienced it at least once in their life. We feel embarrassed, e.g., when we do not know how to behave in a given situation. Should we extend our hand to greet someone we are being introduced to or should we wait for this person to extend theirs? We feel embarrassed when we receive a gift and have nothing to give in return, and thus we violate the reciprocity rule discussed in the previous sections of this book. We also feel embarrassed when we are not certain whether we should speak or remain silent, or when we do something that is considered unseemly for respectable and cultured people. Embarrassment is a negative emotion, although it is not as aversive as experiencing shame or the feeling of guilt we discussed above. It is relatively rarely the case that psychologists who deal with emotions address states of embarrassment. Empirical studies of whether embarrassment may increase one's compliance with social influence are also quite rare. A description of one such study can be found in the following section.

Research

The study by Robert Apsler (1975) involved pairs of individuals: one was an actual subject and the other only pretended to be one. In reality, the other person was a confederate working with the experimenter. The experimenter flipped a coin to allegedly randomly assign different roles to both individuals. As a result of this "random" assignment of roles, the actual subject was asked to perform certain tasks while the other person (the confederate working with the experimenter) was to observe them from an adjacent room through a one-way mirror. The subject was to perform, consecutively, four different tasks. Depending on the experimental conditions, the tasks were either neutral and standard (such as turning on a cassette player and listening to a piece of music, reading a passage from a book out loud, counting from one to fifty out loud, or walking around the room) or potentially embarrassing – if they were to be performed publicly (such as turning on a cassette player and dancing alone, laughing for 30 seconds with no apparent reason, singing a song or imitating the hysterical reactions of a child who refuses to go to kindergarten). Once the subject has completed the last of the four tasks, the subject was rejoined by the "other subject," who asked for help with a private matter. The other subject explained that he was given an assignment at his university, which required him to examine a group of people with a questionnaire. It would be ideal if people filled it out regularly over the next 20 days but even if the questionnaire were to be filled out only once, it would provide important data. Would the subject agree to fill out the questionnaire? And how many days would the subject devote to this task? It turned out that the answers to these questions depend largely on what the subject was doing shortly beforehand. The individuals who performed four standard activities agreed to fill out the questionnaire over an average period of 8.7 days. Among the individuals who most likely experienced embarrassment as a result of performing the other tasks, the percentage was significantly higher and amounted to 14.9 days.

Mechanism

The psychological mechanism underlying the effectiveness of the technique consisting of taking advantage of the state of embarrassment experienced by a person who we want to ask for a favor is not exactly clear. One might assume that it is related to the desire, on the part of the embarrassed person, to save face. Acting on a request articulated by another person is equivalent to sending the following message: "I am not as odd as it would appear based on my behavior as you have just observed. I am eager to help other people. I am a reasonable person of worth." However, experimental studies where an embarrassed person was asked for a favor by someone other than the person who had observed them indicate that in such conditions the state of embarrassment was also conducive to compliance. This does not preclude the above-mentioned motivation on the part of the embarrassed person to restore his image in the eyes of other people, but it does show that it does not necessarily have to involve an improved assessment on the part of the person who witnessed the embarrassing behavior. Yet, it is more probable that the mechanism that makes embarrassed individuals more susceptible to the influence of other people is intrapsychic in nature. By acting on the request of another person, we can feel better about ourselves – we can get rid of negative emotions and elevate our self-assessment.

Technique # 22 *Fear and anxiety*

Idea

To say that anxiety or fear can make people follow orders is stating the obvious. For this reason, psychologists hardly ever conduct empirical studies devoted to this problem. This does not mean that such studies have not been conducted. For obvious reasons, the few studies available did not pertain to such extreme situations as putting a gun to somebody's head or threatening to reveal something that could potentially ruin somebody's life. Strong, extreme fear for one's life occurs in absolutely extraordinary situations. On the other hand, people often experience various types of anxiety or concern: their health, fire breaking out in their apartment, their children advancing to the next grade, etc. Such negative emotional states can motivate them to have their health examined, have their apartment insured, or hire a tutor for their child. It would seem that the stronger the anxiety, the more likely it is for this state to cause the above-mentioned actions. In other words, one could expect a direct relationship between the strength of the anxiety experienced by a subject and his susceptibility to some form of persuasion designed to make him perform a certain action. The more frightened we are, the more willing we are to do what is being suggested to us. However, psychological experiments demonstrate the opposite.

Research

Clive Skilbeck, James Tulip, and Phillip Ley (1977) invited visibly over-weight women aged 20–60 to participate in their research. The women were randomly divided into three groups. A 20-minute long lecture on the health risks related to obesity was presented to each group. A low level of fear was induced in the subjects from the first group. The message of the lecture was that overweight individuals, particularly past a certain age limit, experience increasing problems with mobility and are more exposed to various conditions. In the case of the second group, the researchers' intention was to induce a medium level of fear in the subjects. This time, the lecture was devoted to the connection between obesity and rather minor cardiological problems, as well as arthritis-related problems. In the third group, where the intention was to induce a high level of fear, the problems related to one's heart condition and arthritis were presented as very serious. Subsequently, the subjects were asked to fill out a special questionnaire, which was designed to measure their level of anxiety. As it turned out, contrary to the intentions of the researchers, inducing a low level of fear in the first group, a medium level of fear in the second and a high level of fear in the third group was not exactly successful. This was because some might be most concerned with potential heart problems, while others might be most concerned with potential problems with mobility. Therefore, the researchers divided the subjects into three groups (slightly concerned, moderately concerned, and very frightened), not based on the contents of the delivered lecture but based on the level of the fear induced by the lecture in the subjects. At that point, subjects from all three groups were presented with detailed dietary instructions that they should follow in order to lose weight. Needless to say, it would be difficult for the researchers to verify the degree to which the women followed the instructions but it was relatively easy for them to obtain even more in-teresting data. They could simply weigh the participants. Weighing took place on four occasions: after two weeks from the date on which the women listened to the lecture, after four weeks from this date, after eight weeks, and after sixteen weeks. For each of the measurements, the distribution of results was identical: the smallest weight-loss was recorded among those women who experienced the strongest fear, while the biggest weight-loss was recorded among those who experienced medium-level fear. For example, according to the final measurement (conducted after 16 weeks from the date of the lecture on the connection between obesity and health problems), the women who experienced low levels of fear managed to reduce their body weight on average by 14.9 pounds, the women who experienced medium levels of fear by 20.3 pounds, and those who were very frightened by only 13.9 pounds.

Mechanism

The distribution of the results of the above-described experiment may at least seem odd to some people. However, it is not surprising in the light of the psychological pattern, which assumes a curvilinear relationship between the fear induced by a message designed to make a person do certain things and the degree to which this person follows the instructions. Low-level fear is not enough to stimulate the interest of the subject, let alone to make the subject behave in an expected manner. (Particularly to behave in a manner that is problematic or burdensome for the subject). Very high-level fear, on the other hand, causes psychological defense reactions. The subject considers incoming information unreliable or instantly reinterprets it, assuming that perhaps the threat applies to the majority of people but, for certain reasons, not to them. In other words, in such a situation, the subject focuses on reducing the feeling of threat and not on reducing the actual source of the threat. It is different in the case of medium-level fear: the concern is strong enough to motivate the subject to start thinking seriously about their position but, at the same time, mild enough not to trigger psychological defense mechanisms against thinking clearly about the threatening situation.

Technique # 23 Anticipatory regret

Idea

People regret different things. Some regret getting married, others regret getting divorced, while some will regret both. Regret is an unpleasant emotion and relates to past events. If only we could travel back in time, we would have made another decision, put more effort into something, or made a different choice. By definition, regret pertains to the past. Sometimes a very distant past, e.g., when mature individuals reflect on their youth, and sometimes not-so-distant past, e.g., when people regret something they have just done. Nevertheless, it is always about the past. And yet, one can imagine the state of anticipatory regret. One could think: "If I don't do it, I might regret it in the future," or "If I make this choice now, I might regret it in the future." Psychologists are not unanimous as to whether such anticipated regret is or is not an emotion, but from our perspective, settling this dilemma is not the most important thing. What is more important to us is this: can inducing anticipatory regret be an effective social influence technique? From the description included in the Bible, it follows that Eve plucked the forbidden fruit only because the serpent told her: "You will regret it if you don't do it." Isn't that what it said?! Well, OK, perhaps these were not the serpent's exact words but it was something along those lines... To speak more broadly and less biblically: can you make someone do something by using the argument of anticipatory regret?

Research

Ronan O'Carroll, Jennifer Dryden, Tiffany Hamilton-Barclay, and Eamonn Ferguson (2011) conducted an experiment that may seem like a simple survey. In reality, they made the questions that particular subjects were asked to answer a little different, and they did so in order to make some of the subjects consider the possibility of experiencing regret in the future. In order to be eligible to participate in the online survey, candidates had to be at least 16 years old, they had to be UK residents, and they could not be registered as potential organ donors in the event of their sudden death. In total, 286 individuals were deemed eligible. In the control conditions, the questionnaire filled out by the subjects consisted of standard demographic questions regarding one's age or sex and four questions regarding medical procedures or pertaining to donating one's organs after one's death. The subjects who were randomly assigned to the alternative conditions were asked to fill out a questionnaire in which, apart from the standard questions regarding their demographic status, they were asked about the degree to which they agreed with the following statements: "If I do not register as an organ donor in the next few weeks, I will feel regret," and "If I do not register as an organ donor in the next few weeks, I will later wish I had." One month later, the researchers verified if the subjects did register as potential organ donors in the case of their death. As it turned out, while the figure was 12.9% of the subjects in the control conditions, the percentage was much higher, i.e., 20.7%, in those conditions where the subjects were asked to assess their potential future regret as a consequence of failing to register as organ donors.

Mechanism

The emotion of regret is experienced when there are states of affairs that the acting subject assesses negatively. The simplest and the most effective way to prevent this emotion from occurring is, obviously, to prevent such a situation from taking place. As it turns out, people may also be willing to undertake measures aiming at preventing merely hypothetical regret, that which might occur in the future. As demonstrated in the above-described experiment, it was not even necessary to directly motivate people to imagine their future regret. It sufficed to subtly make them consider the possibility of their future regret. The above-described experiment pertained to experiencing, in a more distant future, the feeling of regret resulting from a failure on the part of the subject to perform a certain action (here: to register as a potential organ donor in the event of a sudden death) in a more immediate future. Obviously, in many other cases, potential future regret could pertain to the consequences of our actions: actions that might lead to undesired ramifications. Clearly, persuading an individual to start thinking that in the future they will regret their action should prevent them from undertaking it.

Technique # 24 *You will regret not thinking this over*

Idea

People regret both the things they have and have not done. More often than not, they regret their inaction. "If I had gone to college when I was young, my life would have turned out better"; "if I had taken the opportunity offered to me by my friend 20 years ago to become a partner in the company, I would be rich now"; "If I had accepted John's proposal, I would be happier than I currently am with my alcohol-abusing husband," etc. Needless to say, sometimes people also regret things they have done. The anticipatory regret technique addressed previously is based on making people imagine a situation where they will either regret that they did something or that they failed to do something in the event there are negative consequences that could have been avoided. The technique we are referring in this section also pertains to the possibility of future regret, but it does not specify whether the subject is going to regret their action or inaction. In the case of this technique, the subject, who is about to make a decision, is warned to act in such a manner as to make sure they will not regret not thinking this decision over thoroughly enough.

Research

John Hetts, David Boninger, David Armor, Faith Gleicher, and Ariel Nathanson (2000) invited university students to participate in a computer game. Each student was given USD 10 and told that the point of the game was to get from the starting line to the finish line. On their way to the finish line, there were various pitfalls, and falling into one of them represented a financial loss. The participants in the game were randomly assigned to one of two routes leading from the starting line to the finish line. One of them was easy – there were few pitfalls and it was possible for the participants to reach the finish line without losing any money or with only small losses. The other route was beset with pitfalls. In these conditions, participants could lose everything and save only a small amount – in the best-case scenario. The probability of being assigned to either of the two routes was identical, 1:1. The subject could (but did not have to) purchase insurance that would allow him to recover some of the lost money. The cheap insurance cost USD 1.50. If the subject decided to purchase this insurance, they would be left with USD 8.50 and would be reimbursed 25% of all incurred financial losses. The more expensive insurance cost USD 3. In the event the subject decided to choose this option, they would be left with only USD 7 but would be reimbursed 50% of all incurred losses. Four different conditions were created under the experiment and participants were randomly assigned. In the control conditions, subjects were reminded that they had equal chances of getting assigned to either the easy or the difficult route; they were also asked to take this into account when making their decision regarding the potential purchase of insurance. In the pro-insurance regret conditions, the subjects were told that if they decided not to purchase the insurance and they lost their money, they would regret not having bought the insurance, whereas, in the anti-insurance regret conditions, the subjects were told that if they decided to purchase the insurance unnecessarily, they would regret having spent money on it. In the last condition (thought regret), the subjects were told that if they failed to thoroughly think over their decision, they would regret not having devoted enough time to considering what they should have done once they had finished the game. Obviously, the researchers were interested in the decisions made by the subjects regarding the purchase of insurance in each of the four above-mentioned experimental conditions. As one might expect, the average amount spent on insurance was higher in the pro-insurance regret conditions (USD 1.39) than in the anti-insurance regret conditions (USD 1.02). The average amount spent on insurance in the control conditions fell between the above-mentioned figures and amounted to USD 1.26. Therefore, the results can be interpreted as confirmation of the effectiveness of the anticipatory regret technique discussed above. However, the most interesting aspect here is that the most money was spent on insurance (on average, USD 1.67) by those subjects who were told that they might regret, in the future, not having thought their decision over thoroughly enough.

Mechanism

The above-described experiment clearly demonstrated that if we make somebody think that in the future they will regret not having devoted enough time to make a rational decision, this person, as a result of that, will choose a safe option and will avoid the risk. Why is that so? In those conditions where a person is induced to imagine their regret resulting from both potential negative situations (i.e., purchasing the insurance unnecessarily or failing to purchase the insurance that would cover some of the losses), this person does not feel persuaded to undertake any action. Therefore, the subject is fully convinced that the decision is his own and it is autonomous. As shown by results of numerous psychological studies, even though, mathematically speaking, the gains and the losses may be equal, the losses, from the psychological perspective, outweigh the gains (Kahneman & Tversky, 1979). Imagine that you get a raise of USD or EUR 25 per month. You probably think: that is laughable, what kind of a raise is that? And you are not particularly thrilled with it. But what would happen if your salary were to be reduced by the exact same amount? A real tragedy! That would be horrible! (Never mind the amount, but the reduction of salary!) In those conditions where subjects are led to believe that in the future they might regret not having thought their decision over thoroughly enough, they experience stronger conceivable regret in the hypothetical conditions where they failed to prevent a loss than in the conditions where they failed to use the opportunity to maximize their gains. Therefore, it should come as no surprise that in the above-mentioned experiment, in such conditions, subjects are willing to purchase the insurance, and in real-life situations, to make risk-mitigating decisions. So, if we want someone to play it safe, we can increase the chances for this by saying, "if you do not think the entire situation over thoroughly, you may regret it bitterly in the future."

Technique # 25 *Positive cognitive state*

Idea

Have you ever been highly intrigued by something? For example, by the demonstration of a card trick or a demonstration of one of those manual puzzles, where you need to untie some sort of a knot or separate two metal rings that are joined together? The ingenuity behind those puzzles is often combined with the sophisticated sadism of their creators — for example, when you need to untie an almost Gordian knot just to be able to open a bottle of wine. Your fingers are simply itching to use the corkscrew but no, first you need to pull a wooden ball over a steel band in order to be able to lace a string through an opening in a piece of wood... Yes, people can be cruel. Yet sometimes such puzzles can be interesting, or even intriguing. They can cause a pleasant tingling and a slight urge to challenge oneself — will I be able to solve this? But what if I can't and somebody has to show me how to do it? How will I feel then? And could this state be treated as something that facilitates exerting social influence?

Research

In 1997, Bruce Rind (1977) conducted a study designed to examine this effect. For this purpose, he decided to use a puzzle (quite popular in English-speaking countries). The task was to count the letter "F" in the following text:

FINISHED FILES ARE THE RE-
SULT OF YEARS OF SCIENTIF-
IC STUDY COMBINED WITH THE
EXPERIENCE OF MANY YEARS.

If we perform this task, the outcome will largely depend on our command of the English language – if we are proficient in this language, our answer is most likely going to be that there are 3 "Fs" in the above text. If this is your answer, you will surely be surprised to learn that this is incorrect. The above text contains six "Fs" – in most cases, we omit the Fs in the word "of" and hence the mistake. A mistake – let us add – that causes surprise and puzzlement. How have I made a mistake while performing such a simple task?

Rind conducted his experiment by dividing his subjects into two groups. The subjects assigned to the first group were asked to perform the above-mentioned task (and, by the same token, most of them made a mistake and provided an incorrect answer). The subjects from the second group were asked to count the letter "R" in the same text (there are 5 and almost everyone counts them correctly). Once the subjects had performed their task and received feedback (regarding mistakes in the "F" letter group and correct answers in the "R" letter group), the undergraduate conducting the experiment added that he was a student in the sociology department and that he was conducting research as part of his final assignment for the semester. The research consisted of filling out a questionnaire containing 80 questions but it was not a requirement to provide answers to all of them. So how many questions would someone agree to answer? For Rind, the differences between the two groups in terms of the number of questions the subjects were willing to answer was a measure of the effectiveness of the intriguing puzzle as a social influence technique.

Apparently, Rind was right. When people made a mistake counting the letters (and they always did when they were asked to count the letter "F"), they declared that they would answer, on average, 46.25 questions. When they were asked to count the letter "R," the result was significantly lower – only 25.75 questions. Hence, one may assume that a situation where someone shows us an interesting puzzle, particularly one which we are unable to solve, creates a natural opportunity to exert social influence.

Mechanism

When Bruce Rind explained the reasons for which people are more willing to act on requests after an interesting puzzle has been demonstrated to them, he used the term "positive cognitive state." He assumed that directly after being taken in by a smart trick, we are in a peculiar state of mind, which could be described as curiosity, puzzlement, surprise, perhaps even combined with a mild feeling of guilt ("after all, they pulled a fast one on me and I was taken in by a simple trick"). Of course, the puzzle does not have to be about counting letters. In our studies, which were conducted in Poland and designed to replicate the effects achieved by Rind, we, for obvious reasons, did not use the same "letter" puzzle. Instead, we used the above-mentioned manual puzzles (separate two rings, take the ball out of the box, etc.). We also asked about various optical illusions. Each time, the results were similar: those subjects who were asked to solve an intriguing puzzle agreed to do more (answer more questions, donate more money) than the subjects asked to solve a not-very-interesting puzzle.

Was Rind correct in justifying the reasons behind the differences between the experimental and the control groups with the existence of a "positive cognitive state"? This is not exactly clear. It is also possible that people made assumptions regarding the nature of the questions to be included in the questionnaire based on the nature of the puzzle ("the puzzle was boring – count the letter "R" – so the questionnaire will probably be uninteresting too, so I will not declare my readiness to answer too many questions"). It is possible that they felt guilty ("I was unable to solve the puzzle, but perhaps I can at least help this person who is seeking assistance"). There are at least several tracks leading to the solution for this puzzle. However, all of them explicitly indicate that intriguing someone, asking them to solve an interesting puzzle, jigsaw, or another charade, maybe the key to obtaining their consent to grant a request in the future.

Technique # 26 *Hide your anger, show your disappointment*

Idea

Imagine that you are going to a post office to buy a stamp. You want to send a postcard with Christmas wishes to your grandmother, who has no e-mail account. Only one counter is open at the post office. This seems normal – after all, people send real letters less and less often these days. The queue is short. Except for the person being served at the counter, there is only one overweight, sweaty guy in front of you. However, you notice that he has put a pile of letters on the counter, which he intends to send by registered mail; this task will take a long time for the post office clerk to perform. You ask the man politely, "How long do you think it will take you to send these letters?" And the surly man replies, "fifteen minutes or so." "Oh, dear! I only want to buy a stamp, it will take me about 20 seconds. Would you let me buy my stamp first?" You say this and hope for a positive reply. But it does not come. The man says nothing. Will you increase your chances of the disobliging man letting you buy your stamp first if you express anger at that point? Or perhaps it would be better to show disappointment in the absence of his positive reply? It is also possible that the best option would be to remain silent and show no emotion at all, hoping that the man, once the post office clerk asks him to approach the counter, will tell you to "go first but make it quick." It should be noted that the question of whether it would be better to show anger, disappointment, or not to express any emotion at all is a question pertaining to the role of affective states in exerting social influence. At the same time, it is formulated in a completely different context than in the case of the techniques we discussed earlier. In those cases, we focused on the emotions experienced by the person we want to exert influence over (for example, is this person experiencing sadness, guilt, or shame at this point in time). It is a very different story this time around: we are asking whether an expression of emotion on the part of the person wanting to exert influence increases their chances for success.

Research

Evert van Doorn, Gerben van Kleef and Joop van der Pligt (2015) invited university students to join a game in which they could either lose or earn money. A subject received ten dimes and was told that their partner was being given the same amount. When told to do so by the experimenter, the participants, having no contact with each other, were to decide how many of their coins they wanted to give to their partner. The experimenter would double the amount donated by each player. It would be most profitable for both players to give all their 10-cent coins to their partners. In such a case, the experimenter would give ten coins to each player, and thus each would have a total of two euro. But if the partner fails to do so and decides not to give any coins, the player will be left with nothing and their partner will double their initial amount. Even if the partner decides to give away four of their coins, the player who decides to give away all their coins will gain a total of eight coins, which is less than the initial capital. It should be also noted that the number of coins gained throughout the game determines one's chances to win a special bonus of 50 euro. In such a case, perhaps it is reasonable to give all the coins to your partner? Maybe you should give away less? Or perhaps it would be most reasonable not to give any of the coins? It is a difficult choice. Before commencing with the actual game, in order to make sure the rules of the game were clear, the player was to make a "trial" contribution while believing that their decision would not be revealed to their partner. Once the player had made this decision, the experimenter showed him a chart illustrating the behavior of the previous participants in the experiment. The chart demonstrated that, on average, they contributed 2.19 of their coins to their partners. The subject does not know that, in actuality, their partner in the game is not a real subject but an associate of the experimenter. The real game is about to start in a moment, and the alleged partner says: "Could you give me as many of your coins as possible?" In some conditions, he adds a comment to the above request. In some cases, it has the following wording: "I am angry about your contribution in the trial round," while in other cases, the comment is: "I am disappointed about your contribution in the trial round." How many coins do you think the player will give to their partner? As it turned out, in the control conditions (i.e., when the partner did not disclose their emotions), the player gave away, on average, 3.24 coins. When the partner expressed anger, the number of contributed coins was slightly lower (on average 3.01). But when the partner showed disappointment, the players gave him, on average, as many as 5.24 coins.

Mechanism

Why might showing disappointment be an effective social influence technique? Let us start with the emotion itself. Disappointment, similar to sadness, belongs to emotional states characterized by relatively low physiological arousal. Experiencing disappointment is also connected with the feeling of helplessness and our conviction that we have no control over the course of events. The expression of disappointment is a social signal of a request for help but, unlike anger, it does not indicate our readiness to become aggressive. What is more, a disappointed person is not, directly, blaming anyone for the existing state of affairs. In the above-described experiment, the information on disappointment was of verbal nature. Yet, in their other studies, Van Doorn, van Kleef, and van der Pligt demonstrated that similar effects could be produced with an image of the face of a disappointed person. A person receiving a signal of disappointment may become motivated to improve the emotional state of the person experiencing the disappointment and, by the same token, feel better themselves. The route to both of these goals is simple: it will suffice to act on this person's request! Their disappointment will change into satisfaction and the person granting the request will feel like they can easily make another person happy.

Technique # 27 *Fear-then-relief*

Idea

Fans of action films know exactly how the typical good cop/bad cop interrogation scene looks. The bad cop starts by threatening the suspect, and sometimes he even tortures him or shouts at him while putting the barrel of his gun to the suspect's mouth. Yet, the interrogated person does not break. Not only does he not confess but he also refuses to testify. Unexpectedly, the bad cop is replaced by his colleague, who behaves in a very different manner. He brings a cup of hot coffee, gives the suspect a cigarette (for some reason, the characters interrogated by the police almost always drink coffee and smoke). More importantly, he does not threaten, blackmail, or shout at the suspect. With a calm and warm tone of voice, he tells the suspect that he wants to help him; he does not want him to be sentenced to many years of imprisonment and waste his life. He only needs him to start talking. And behold, something remarkable happens. The man who just a few moments earlier was determined to refuse to testify, even though the police officer put a gun to his head, now starts, when nobody is threatening him, to give evidence which incriminates both him and his associates. The above-described interrogation scene is connected with the emotions experienced by the suspect: first, it is fear (when the suspect is interrogated by the bad cop) and then, suddenly and unexpectedly, relief (when the bad cop is replaced by the good one). Needless to say, a similar emotional see-saw can be experienced in other circumstances, not just during an interrogation at a police station. We could easily imagine a university student who is doing rather poorly during an exam and is thus frightened to see the examiner reaching for a pen to enter, as the student suspects, his grade on the exam. However, the student will experience a sudden and unexpected relief when it turns out that he has actually passed the exam. Another example would be an employee who has been told to report to his superior during a period when people are being laid off at the plant. Once he steps into the director's office though, he learns that the boss only wanted to ask a trivial question. First comes fear. Then comes the relief. The interrogated individual starts to testify (and, by the same token, meet the expectations of the police officer) in a state of unexpected relief, which followed fear. Do other situations in which people experience a similar emotional see-saw also make them compliant?

Research

This is precisely the question that one of the authors of this book asked himself and, together with Richard Nawrat, they decided to investigate the reactions of people who experience unexpected relief preceded by fear (Dolinski & Nawrat, 1998). Before we move on to describing one such experiment, it should be explained that it was conducted in Poland during the communist regime era. Any contact with a police officer called up very negative associations. Subjects were individuals who were crossing a street outside of the designated spot, i.e., not at a pedestrian crossing. When such an individual was, more or less, in the middle of the street they were crossing, the experimenter, who was standing on the pavement, blew his whistle. The scared subject looked around but did not see any police officers (as there were none). Surely enough, the subject must have felt relieved since the police officer was nowhere to be found. Therefore, he continued crossing the street and once he had reached the pavement he was approached by another experimenter who asked the subject to fill out a questionnaire. The problem was that the questionnaire needed to be filled out right away, while the subject was standing on the pavement, and the autumn weather was not particularly favorable. As it turned out, 59% of the subjects agreed to fill out the questionnaire. A similar request was made of individuals who were crossing the street in the same (improper) spot but who were not alarmed by the sound of a whistle, as well as individuals who were simply walking along the pavement. In both cases, a lower percentage of subjects agreed to fill out the questionnaire (46% and 41%, respectively) compared to those in the conditions in which the subjects experienced the fear-then-fear sequence.

Mechanism

The emotions we experience are a product of evolution. Each emotion instantly triggers an action program typical of this particular emotion. Even though nowadays it may not always be the case, emotions used to make it easier for us to survive and thus facilitated the survival of our species. In the case of fear, the above-mentioned action program consisted of changes taking place in our body that are meant to make us ready to either escape or defend ourselves. In both cases, our body would be required to make a huge effort. Therefore, when we experience fear, our heart starts beating faster to pump more blood, some of which is moved from our intestines to muscles in order to supply them with extra oxygen and nutrients; blood coagulability also increases. Other changes of physiological nature also prepare our body for the requirements resulting from the current circumstances. Such a response is appropriate in the case of a serious threat. Yet when the threat disappears suddenly and unexpectedly, the above-mentioned action program becomes completely inappropriate for the new circumstances. The problem is that a new program (not necessarily based on emotions), appropriate for the completely different circumstances, has not been initiated yet. In such a situation, our body remains, for a short period of time, in a state of inertia. And if we, while being in such a state, have to perform a task (because we are asked to do so or we are expected to make a decision), we act in an automatic and mindless manner. If the request is polite and the situation seems safe, we are caught off" guard and we say "yes." We say "yes" when we are asked to fill out a questionnaire while standing on the pavement and when we are being persuaded to testify in an interrogation room at the police station. The mechanism is identical.

Technique # 28 *Humor*

Idea

Hello! Is this the radio station? Great, I'm calling from a bus station. I've just found a black, leather wallet. There is a driving license and a credit card inside the wallet issued to John Smith. There is also a substantial amount in cash: 800 euros and 460 American dollars. Oh, and there is also a ticket for tomorrow's Metallica concert! So I was thinking that perhaps Mr. Smith is listening to your station at this moment and since the show is live... Perhaps you could play some nice piece from me to Mr. Smith!

The thing with jokes is that some find them funnier than others. Surely enough, John Smith would not find the above message funny. Presumably, some readers will consider it less, and some – like us – more entertaining. Yet the point here is not to discuss differences in terms of our sense of humor. In the context of this book, we would like to ask the following question: can a joke help us exert social influence? Will a verbal message, delivered by a person who wants to persuade another individual into doing something, become more effective if it contains humorous elements?

Research

Karen O'Quin and Joel Aronoff (1981) invited 250 university students to participate in their experiment. Each of the subjects met, in the laboratory, another individual who pretended that they had also been invited to participate in the study but they were really associates of O'Quinn and Aronoff and behaved in line with the previously designed scenario. The person who headed the experiment explained that it consisted of testing various negotiation situations and that the task of the subjects was to succeed in the negotiation. The subject of the negotiation was a valuable painting with one subject acting as the seller and the other acting as the buyer. There actually was an oil painting of a landscape on the wall in the laboratory. Needless to say, the measure of success was to achieve the most favorable outcome (i.e., to sell at the highest price possible, for the seller, and to buy at the lowest price possible, for the buyer). Obviously, in order for any side to succeed in the negotiation, both parties must first reach an agreement as to the price of the work of art. As a result of a (fixed) random assignment of roles, the actual subject became the buyer and the experimenter's assistant became the seller. In line with the received instructions, the seller's asking price was USD 70,000, whereas the buyer was offering USD 25,000. In the course of the negotiation process, the seller lowered their expectations and the buyer offered an increasingly high price. At some point, where the discrepancy between the seller's price and the buyer's offer was still considerable, the experimenter would say that there was little time left for negotiations. It was then that the seller would say, "Well, my final offer is…" and state the amount, or would say, 'Well, my final offer is […] and I will throw in my pet frog." Of course, the key issue was the extent to which the joke on the part of the seller made the buyer give in. The measure of concession adopted by O'Quin and Aronoff was the quotient of the following two values: the dollar amount of the subject's concession and the total dollar amount of concession possible (e.g., the subject proposed, at that point, an amount that was USD 1000 higher than before, and for an agreement, the subject would have to offer an amount that was USD 5000 higher. The index value, in this case, would be 0.20).

It turned out that in the case of the standard text uttered by the seller, the index value was 0.45, and when the seller offered to throw in their pet frog, the index value increased to 0.53. Hence, the joke made the subject more prone to concession.

Mechanism

It was approximately one hundred years ago when the then-guru of advertisement, Claude C. Hopkins, made his famous statement, namely that "people don't buy from clowns," which was the expression of his deep belief that using humor in an advertisement is detrimental to its effectiveness. Today, advertisers have no doubt that either Hopkins was wrong or that, for some reason, his thesis has lost validity. Psychologists who study the effectiveness of modern advertising point to the fact that humor catches the attention of the target audience to such a degree that they lose the ability to critically analyze the underlying content of the message. To put it simply: humor throws us off guard and impairs our critical thinking ability. The same psychological mechanism may be active not only in advertisements but also in other instances of social influence. If someone asks us for something in a humorous manner, chances are we will not analyze the costs of granting the request (e.g., the time we will have to devote or the physical effort involved in acting on the request). As far as the above-described experiment is concerned, there could have also been another aspect at play: humor, which evokes positive emotions, might have made the subjects more willing to compromise, and at the same time this might have caused them to see less of an opponent or a rival in the person they were negotiating the price of the painting with.

Technique # 29 *Foot-in-the-mouth (How are you feeling?)*
Idea

Several years prior to the outbreak of WWII, Winifred Johnson (1937) conducted a simple and yet very original study. He asked his students to indicate their moods throughout several consecutive days. Each time, they were to use an 11-point scale, where the extreme left side (-5) denoted the worst possible frame of mind and the extreme right side ($+5$) denoted the best frame of mind ever. The midway zero point denoted a standard, typical mood. Obviously, on some days we feel better and, on some, we feel worse, but most of the time, we feel neither better nor worse than usual. Therefore, one would expect that the majority of the subjects should produce an average outcome of their measurements close to zero. Yet, the majority of the subjects recorded an outcome significantly above that value. (The average for all the subjects was $+1.2$). In other words, even though it should be mathematically impossible, the majority of the individuals tested by Johnson usually felt better than usual! It would therefore appear that in the USA, and in fact the majority of other countries too, it simply is not right for people to complain about their poor frame of mind. We are expected to say that we are good even when we are not. Can this tendency to say that we are good when asked about our mood be used to persuade us into granting requests we are asked to act on? Let us examine an experiment designed to explore this problem.

Research

Daniel Howard (1990) wanted to check to what degree asking people about how they feel can affect their willingness to get involved in charity. In the course of his experiment, he called randomly selected Dallas residents. The experiment was conducted immediately prior to Thanksgiving. In the control conditions, the researcher introduced himself and stated the name of the charity he represented; then, he explained that an employee of this charity could deliver cookies to the house of the interlocutor at the price of 25 cents and that profits from each such transaction would be used to support starving residents of Dallas. Only 10% of the respondents agreed to purchase the cookies. In experimental conditions, the course of the telephone conversation was somewhat different. Once he had introduced himself and revealed the name of the charity he represented, the researcher asked the callee how they were. In the vast majority of cases, the reply was positive; the respondents said that they felt great, good, or at least not bad. At that point, the researcher said he was happy to hear that. (In rare cases, where the reply from the callee suggested that they were doing poorly, the researcher said that he was sorry to hear that). Only at that point did Howard talk about the opportunity to purchase the cookies and about using the profits generated from their sale to support the hungry. As it turned out, significantly more (25%) of the subjects agreed to buy the cookies in this variant. According to Howard's conclusions, this might be due to a specific social influence technique, which he referred to as the foot-in-the-mouth technique.

Mechanism

The foot-in-the-mouth technique is based on the premise that people are more willing to help those less fortunate (e.g., homeless, suffering from hunger or incurable diseases) when they are persuaded to compare their own situation with that of the aforementioned less fortunate individuals. A positive reply to a question regarding one's frame of mind stands in clear contrast with the situation of such people. It should be noted that once a subject replies that they "are great" or "OK," they are offered the opportunity to support people in a significantly worse situation – people who have no reason to feel great and whose lives have not turned out as they had expected. Clearly, the technique is very effective and, at the same time, very subtle. After all, the individual exerting the influence is not saying: "You are much better off than homeless people, so you should help them." It is somewhat the other way around: it is the subject who arrives at a similar conclusion only because they have just described their mood as great (or at least good).

Technique # 30 *Foot-in-the-mouth-then-door-in-the-face*

Idea

It should be noted that the foot-in-the-mouth technique described in the previous section is, in a way, natural. We frequently start our con-versations with other people by asking them how they are. We even believe that some of our readers have, unconsciously, used this tech-nique on other people. After all, it is only right to get the conversation going before we ask our interlocutor for something. We also ask other people how they are even if we do not intend to ask them for anything or offer them anything. The above-mentioned naturalness of the foot-in-the-mouth technique makes it easy to combine it with another method to be applied after our subject has answered the question about their mood. In the following section, we have described an experiment de-signed to verify the effectiveness of the door-in-the-face technique, which we have already addressed in this book, which was either applied in the standard manner, i.e., subjects were first asked to act on a difficult request followed by an easier one, or it was combined with the foot-in-the-mouth technique. In the latter case, the aforementioned procedure, consisting of formulating a difficult request followed by an easier one, was used on individuals who had first been asked about their frame of mind.

Research

Valerie Fointiat (2000) examined housewives by asking them to donate food to the poor. In the control conditions, the experimenter simply formulated the request. As a result, 26.6% of the housewives agreed to comply. In other conditions, Fointiat tested the aforementioned foot-in-the-mouth technique as proposed by Daniel Howard. Prior to asking the housewives to donate food, they were asked how they were. Obviously, the vast majority of the ladies answered in a way that suggested that their mood was great (or at least good). The outcome turned out to be yet further proof confirming the effectiveness of said technique (let us emphasize that in this case, the technique was applied face to face and not over a telephone as in the original experiments). As it turned out, 40% of the subjects decided to prepare a food package for the poor in the experimental conditions. However, Fointiat was mainly interested in the effectiveness of the above-mentioned technique when it is combined with the door-in-the-face method we are already familiar with. This time around the housewives were first asked about their mood and once they had replied, they were asked to participate in a charity campaign consisting of providing food for the poor. A food package for the poor would have to be prepared every week throughout the upcoming period of three months. After a refusal, the housewives were asked to prepare a single food package for the poor. It turned out that in such conditions, as many as 60% of the subjects agreed to prepare a single food package.

Mechanism

The foot-in-the-mouth and door-in-the-face techniques are based on different psychological mechanisms. The former is effective, as it makes the subject, who is asked to act on a request, aware of the big contrast between their mental state and the situation of other, less fortunate, people. As far as the mechanism behind the latter technique is concerned, we already know that psychologists either argue in favor of the interpretation of its effectiveness referring to the reciprocity rule or claim that the feeling of guilt or shame experienced by the subject is of key importance. From our perspective though, it does not matter which mechanism we are actually dealing with. In any case, the subject who refuses to act on the initial, i.e., difficult, request will be more willing to grant the second, i.e., easier, request, as their attention has been already redirected to a person, i.e., the beneficiary of the request, who is poor, hungry or sick. Therefore, there are two different psychological forces at play when it comes to the technique discussed in this section that could push the subject, in a concordant manner, towards agreeing to the request they have just heard. It should be also noted that the sequence of both elements of this complex technique, as used in the experiment, seems very natural. First, we ask someone how they are and only then do we ask for a favor.

Technique # 31 *Negative emotional see-saw*
Idea

We have already learned that when a source of fear is suddenly removed and replaced with a state of relief, a person experiencing such emotional see-saw is willing to act on requests as well as follow instructions or suggestions. Yet, when we discuss emotional see-saw, it does not necessarily mean that this phenomenon must consist in the disappearance of fear or another negative emotion. It may also happen that a positive emotion occurs and lasts over a given period of time but suddenly becomes invalid and thus the subject has no reason to experience it any longer. For example, let us imagine a person who regularly plays the lottery and bets, each week, on the same numbers. This week he has also played the lottery, only he asked his mother-in-law to place his bets. During a Sunday dinner, the whole family gathers around the table. Everyone has had their veal chop, dessert is about to be served, and the radio is announcing the outcome of the lottery drawings. It cannot be!! Our protagonist has just won a fortune. Yet, he sees a look of horror on his mother-in-law's face... No, this cannot be true! And yet it is. "Listen," she says quietly to her son-in-law: "I forgot to buy your lottery ticket." Obviously, the nature of the emotional see-saw does not have to be as extreme as it is in the above-mentioned example. Therefore, the state of emotional see-saw will be also experienced by a pedestrian who finds a banknote on the pavement only to learn, upon closer inspection, that it is actually a flyer for a night club, or by a university student who has just taken an exam and feels that he did well only to learn, one hour later, that his initial euphoria was unfounded as he actually had failed the exam. Needless to say, what is important from our perspective is whether inducing the state of such emotional see-saw in people can be used as an effective social influence technique.

Research

Magdalena Kaczmarek and Melanie Steffens (2017) conducted their experiment by recruiting subjects from among university students, who came to the university library. For their participation in the experiment, the students were offered only 1 euro but they were also told that 2.5 euro would be paid to everyone who does well on the quiz. In half of the experimental conditions, the quiz consisted of easy questions, and in the other half, they were more difficult questions. Some subjects were told, truthfully, that they did either well or poorly on the quiz. Others received completely surprising feedback. Some of the students who tackled very difficult questions learned that they did exceptionally well, while some of the students who tackled easy questions learned, unexpectedly, that they did poorly. Regardless of the experimental conditions, a given subject was assigned to, they were asked to walk along a corridor to another room, where the following part of the experiment was to take place. In the corridor, the subject was approached by another student (in fact an associate of M. Kaczmarek and M. Steffens) and asked to sign a petition. The petition made no sense whatsoever – in the petition, the student community demanded, from the university authorities, to be allowed to get to the university via a means of public transport of their choice. As it turned out, the situation where students initially experienced negative emotions, as they believed they did poorly on the quiz, only to learn later on that they did exceptionally well, made them significantly more willing (67%) to sign the nonsensical petition than those who experienced positive emotions in a stable manner – i.e., who expected good results on the quiz and who received feedback confirming their expectations (35%). The above outcome provides yet another confirmation for the effectiveness of the fear-then-relief technique we are already familiar with. As far as our perspective is concerned, though, we are more interested in the behavior of those students who experienced a negative emotional state. From among those subjects who expected a negative result and received feedback that confirmed their expectations, approximately half (53% to be exact) agreed to sign the nonsensical petition. Yet, if subjects experienced a negative emotional see-saw (i.e., they initially believed they did well on the quiz only to learn later on that, in fact, they did poorly), as many as 74% agreed to sign the petition. Evidently, the state of negative emotional see-saw also makes people more willing to comply with requests.

Mechanism

Kaczmarek and Steffens thoroughly analyzed the interaction between the person collecting signatures under the nonsensical petition and the subjects in various experimental conditions. It turned out that in the states of emotional see-saw, people are less prone to ask questions, express surprise, or pay attention to the nonsensical nature of the petition than they are when in the state of experiencing one emotion in a constant manner. It also turned out (this aspect was also examined by the experimenters) that they do not remember the course of said interaction that well. All this clearly demonstrates that the state of emotional see-saw impedes the effectiveness of one's cognitive functions. It is quite probable that due to a sudden change in the situation (i.e., the fact that the situation plays out completely not as expected), the subject analyzes what has just happened and tries to comprehend it. By the same token, the subject fails to focus on the "here and now" and, as a result, responds in a rather automatic and mindless fashion to the request being formulated. It should be noted that Kaczmarek and Steffens checked if the students would agree to sign a petition. It was thus a rather standard situation (university students are often asked to sign petitions) and the request was formulated in a polite manner. It is unclear whether the negative emotional see-saw technique would also be effective if the request were challenging, unusual, or formulated in an impolite manner. It should be also noted that the emotions induced in the above-mentioned experiment were not excessively strong. We do not know if a terribly embittered or even emotionally devastated person would be willing to act on requests formulated by a stranger. At this point, we feel obligated to emphasize these doubts, as there are still very few empirical studies on the determinants of the effectiveness of the negative emotional see-saw technique. Therefore, we still do not know, precisely, the limitations to its effectiveness.

Technique # 32 Hold flowers in your hand

Idea

Millions of (especially young) people around the world try to get from point A to point B by taking advantage of a free form of travel: hitchhiking. Even more car owners stop to pick them up, or just pass by them on the way. The latter is much more common. The reasons why a driver does not pick up a hitchhiker vary and are not always due to selfishness. It is usually the case that women in particular rarely stop to invite a man inside. This is mainly due to their fear of becoming victims of rape, aggression, or theft. A few decades ago, this was not a big problem because the vast majority of drivers were men. Today it is different, and as a result, for the male hitchhiker, the fact that he cannot actually count on help from female motorists is a serious problem. What could a man do to increase his chances that a female driver would stop and invite him inside her car? Studies show that not only women but also men stop on the side of the road extremely willingly when a request for a ride is made by a man in a fire fighter's outfit. However, it is difficult to see this as a very useful and convenient social influence technique. French researchers decided to see how drivers would behave if a male hitchhiker were to hold a bouquet of flowers in his hand.

Research

The study was carried out at the entrance to a peninsula in the south of France, in a place where hitchhikers usually try to stop cars (Gueguen, Meineri & Stefan, 2012). The experimenter-hitchhiker (male or female) stood by the side of the road, looking at oncoming cars with his or her hand extended and thumb stretched upward. Depending on the experimental conditions, the experimenter held a bouquet of flowers in the other (left) hand, or the hand was empty. His colleagues, positioned discreetly on the other side of the road, counted passing cars and identified the gender of the drivers. (There was a lot of counting because the behavior of 2000 drivers passing by was taken into account.) This procedure made it possible to determine the percentages of both women and men who stopped at the sight of an unambiguous gesture of a hitchhiker. Of course, since this was an experiment, if the car stopped in front of the experimenter, the experimenter did not get in, but explained that a psychological study was being conducted, thanked the driver for their willingness to help, and apologized for the "confusion." It turned out that in the case of female drivers, flowers in the hands of a man were almost magical. While only 1.3% of ladies stopped in conditions where the hitchhiker's hand was empty, the percentage was as high as 10.5% when there was a bouquet of flowers in their hands. Interestingly, flowers in the hands of a man also had a positive effect in conditions where the drivers were men (up from 6.8% to 13.6%). And what were the results in the conditions where it was the woman who was trying to stop cars? It turned out that whether or not she had flowers in her hands did not matter in the least.

Mechanism

A man with a bouquet of flowers in his hands is more associated with someone who is about to meet his beloved girlfriend than with someone who is about to rob or rape someone. Flowers in his hands therefore greatly reduce the fear of aggression on his part. This effect is especially true for drivers who are women, but after all, men also don't want to take a hitchhiker into their car who might intend to do them harm. However, a female hitchhiker does not increase her chances that a car will stop in front of her. Women are unlikely to give flowers to their beloved men, so the same mechanism does not work in their case. A man with flowers also evokes sympathy in other situations. Studies show, for example, that people are more willing to spontaneously help a man holding a bouquet of flowers in his hand. If a passer-by drops an object that lands on the sidewalk (of course, he is only pretending to lose it in order to conduct an experiment), a witness to this event is more likely to inform him of this fact if the unfortunate soul is holding flowers in his hands. Drivers are also more likely to let a pedestrian cross the road if he has a bouquet in his grasp. So, it is good to carry a bouquet in your hand sometimes, particularly if you are a man.

Technique # 33 The word "love" in your surroundings

Idea

There is probably no other place on Earth that is more pink and red than a florist's on Valentine's Day. In every corner of the shop, there are red hearts and chubby cupids stringing their bows, ready to send their arrows and consequently produce another happy couple. Every flower (and definitely each rose) is decorated with a red ribbon so that you have no doubts as to what day of the year is being celebrated. Even helium-filled balloons are in the shape of a heart and for all enthusiasts of tradition, there are big, red, kitschy lollipops in the shape of — yes, you guessed it — a heart. But apart from all this, there is also the word, "love." It is all over the place — on mugs, candleholders, pictures, gypsum figurines, key rings, earrings, refrigerator magnets, pillows, and plush teddy bears... This word (most often left untranslated, i.e., in English), can be found literally everywhere — even on a metal pendant in the shape of a human skull, which, let us be honest, is a little disturbing. Naturally, with such large exposure to words related to love near Valentine's Day at least some of us are sick of it (perhaps some of us even fail to notice them thanks to the blessed consequences of perceptual defense). Yet, the very word "love" brings about positive associations — we simply associate it with warmth, attachment, and the presence of someone close to us. Therefore, it should come as no surprise that social influence researchers decided to verify whether it can be used as a social influence tool.

Research

Studies designed to verify the effect that the exposure to the words "Loving" or "Helping" can have on the behavior of people seeing these words were conducted by Virginie Charles-Sire and her associates (2016). The study was very simple in its design but, as usually happens in similar situations, it was very time-consuming as far as conducting it is concerned. It was conducted in a parking lot, where the experimenter's assistant was pushing a shopping cart with a large cardboard box. When the assistant was given the prearranged signal from the observer (who was to monitor the course of the experiment and record the results), the assistant approached a car, opened the trunk, and attempted to put the cardboard box inside. They acted in a manner that suggested that the box was very heavy and that putting it into the car's trunk was too difficult a task for them alone. What the researchers were interested in was the number of people who decided to help the assistant (i.e., who would approach the experimenter's assistant and at least ask if they needed any help with the apparently difficult task).

Naturally, the researchers wanted to know if there would be differences in the subject's behavior depending on the words they might notice in their surroundings. This was resolved with the t-shirt worn by the experimenter's assistant – in the first group, the t-shirt had a large "Helping" inscription on the back, in the second group, the inscription read "Loving," while in the third, the control group, there was no inscription on the t-shirt.

As it turned out, the expectations of the designers of the experiment were very accurate. In the conditions with no inscription on the t-shirt, people were the least eager to help (12.7% of the subjects helped). When the t-shirt read "Helping," the figure increased, even though not markedly (to 16%). However, when the t-shirt worn by the experimenter's assistant had the "Loving" inscription on the back, the percentage of subjects willing to help increased significantly (to 28%).

Obviously, one more aspect should be taken into account: the sex of the subjects as well as the sex of the experimenter's assistant. To be more precise, certain prevailing stereotypes seem to be the most important, for example, stereotypes about women being physically weaker and those according to which men should help women by carrying heavy items. Regardless of their questionable validity, one has to be aware that these stereotypes exist and may affect the behavior of subjects participating in experiments. For this reason, in the course of her experiment, Charles-Sire tested the behavior of subjects in various conditions – when it was a woman or a man struggling with the cardboard box (and when it was a woman or a man watching this). As expected, in all conditions, it was the male subjects who were most eager to help a woman struggling with a heavy box, but even here the results varied depending on the inscription on the t-shirt (40% of the male subjects were willing to help when the inscription read "Loving"; 26.1% when it read "Helping"; and only 21.4% in the control group).

Mechanism

We are scientists and as such we will most likely not be presented with this opportunity anywhere else; therefore, let us, dear Reader, make our dream come true and quote someone we would never be able to reference in a strictly scientific text and whose words are simply a perfect match for this occasion. The godfather of all guidance, the spring of wisdom, and a titan of self-awareness, Paulo Coelho once wrote that "it is not time that changes man nor knowledge the only thing that can change someone's mind is love." Well isn't that just lovely? Especially since it resonates with the results obtained by Charles-Sire, in that the exposure to the word "Loving" alone can change someone's mind (well, all right, at least someone's willingness to help and that is something in itself). Why is that so?

So far, we have no clear answer to this question. Undoubtedly, we associate love with helping other people. We know this from other studies, for example, those conducted by Lubomir Lamy and his co-workers (2012), who labeled the moneyboxes used in the course of fundraisers for charity with the "Loving – Helping" slogan and, by doing so, managed to collect more money than in the control groups which used moneyboxes without such inscriptions. It is, therefore, possible that the sheer exposure to the word "Loving" triggers the desire to help people. We still do not know exactly why.

Perhaps we should look for an answer in social norms. As we have pointed out numerous times throughout this book, these norms have a profound effect on our lives even if we deny this on the declarative level. Therefore, it cannot be ruled out that the presence of the word "Loving" activates a certain norm pertaining to our behavior. Just as you do not break up with your partner on Valentine's Day, you do not refuse to help in the presence of the word "Loving." Or at least the vast majority of people do not.

Would, by the same logic, a request for a raise submitted with a red heart, wrapped with a red band with the word "Loving" across it, increase our chances of success? Well, that might be a little over the top but, as demonstrated by Charles-Sire and her associates, asking for a raise while wearing a t-shirt that reads "Loving" might slightly improve our position.

Technique # 34 *Birthday effect*

Idea

One's birthday constitutes a kind of caesura in a person's life. Subjectively, we become more adult (when we are children), older (when we are adults), or "more old" (when our adulthood is already advanced). A birthday is so important that - as statistics show - people more often die just after their birthday than just before it. As if they didn't want to spoil the birthday mood in their family home with their death, or as if they cared about the fact that on the tombstone and in the obituaries their life would appear that one year longer... Of course, in this book we are particularly interested in the relationship between a person's birthday and the effectiveness of social influence exerted on them. So imagine that you want to ask someone for something. It is not very urgent. You can do it today, but you can do it tomorrow, or even in a few days. You know that today is the birthday of the person you want to ask. You will probably think that it is not appropriate to bother them right now. After all, the matter can wait. But from the perspective of the effectiveness of social influence, what is more interesting is whether addressing a request to someone who just happens to have a birthday can decrease or increase the probability that the request will be fulfilled.

Research

Nicolas Gueguen and Celine Jacob (2013) took advantage of the fact that a certain store selling musical instruments provided them with a mailing list of its customers. They, therefore, had at their disposal both the birthdays of people who had shopped there and their phone numbers. These customers, willingly or unwillingly, became the participants in a study by Gueguen and Jacob. The researchers randomly divided them into three groups. People in the first group were called the day before their birthday, those in the second group on their birthday, and those in the third group the day after their birthday. The call was always made between 6:30 and 8:30 p.m. If the music store customer did not answer, the call was made again. If this again proved unsuccessful, another attempt was made. In each case, the experimenters introduced themselves and made the following request: "Sorry to disturb you Madam/Sir. It's the Music House in Vannes where you have previously bought some products. We are currently conducting a customers' survey in order to improve our service quality. Would you accept to respond, by phone, to a nine-item questionnaire that will take two minutes of your time?". If the respondent refused, the experimenter politely bid farewell. If they consented, a brief survey was actually conducted with them whose results could help improve the store's operations. A total of 264 customers were called, with 30 not picking up the phone despite three attempts to contact them. Of those called on the day before their birthday, 51.5% agreed to participate in the survey. In conditions where the call was made on the client's birthday, the rate was significantly higher, at 75.6%. If, on the other hand, participants were called the day after their birthday, 48.7% agreed to participate.

Mechanism

In trying to explain the obtained effect, one may invoke two mechanisms. First, note that the study was conducted in the late afternoon and evening. Thus, it is quite likely that those celebrating their birthday had already experienced some cheer from other people on that day. Someone has wished them warm wishes, someone else has given them a gift. The mechanism of indirect reciprocity, which we have already written about in this book, thus makes them feel a kind of obligation to fulfill the request of some other person. An alternative mechanism that can explain the structure of the results obtained in the study discussed above is mood. A good mood is conducive to kindness towards people who ask for some small favors, and this was the nature ("answer 9 questions") of the request used in this experiment. It should be noted, however, that numerous psychological studies show that people who are in a good mood may be particularly reluctant to fulfill such requests that could lower their positive mood. Thus, if it is precisely the good mood that would be the reason why people are more likely on their birthdays to fulfill the requests of others, it should be assumed that this is true only with regard to small and unproblematic requests. Asking the birthday boy or girl for serious and troublesome requests, however, would not be a good idea. However, we are not aware of empirical research that answers the question of whether this is really the case.

3

FRAMING

Several dozen years ago, when Ronald Reagan, already an elderly man at that time, was the current president of the United States of America, and the Soviet Union's leader was Leonid Brezhnev, who was five years older than Reagan, there was a popular joke about the two leaders intending to race each other in a dash. On the following day, the American press published articles informing the public that Reagan had won the race in great style and crushed his opponent. The Soviet press announced that Brezhnev came in second in an international dash competition, which was a very respectable result, and that Ronald Reagan, representing the United States of America, came in second-to-last. This shows that the same fact can be presented from very different angles and that the way it is described bears serious ramifications. As the cliché says: some see the glass half full and some half empty. Both sides are right but the former are satisfied, while the latter are not. Similarly, you will probably be more interested in a product described as expensive but good than in a product that someone describes as good but expensive. You will also be

DOI: 10.4324/9781003296638-4

more willing to buy beef with bone and 85% meat content than meat with 15% bone content. Any verbal message can be framed in a specific manner and this triggers a specific way of thinking about a given topic. This chapter is devoted to the presentation of social influence techniques that use message framing.

Technique # 35 *Validation-persuasion*

Idea

When someone urges you to do something you don't particularly want to do, you naturally resist. In all likelihood, you will not do it, and you will perceive the person who is trying to change your attitudes and behavior as an opponent (or even an enemy) rather than a partner. Forcing you to do things you don't want to do is simply limiting your freedom. You are certainly not unique in this regard. So, if you make a request of someone else, they too may perceive it as a threat to their personal freedom. How to deal with this? Clinical psychologists have come up with an interesting way, as they often want to induce their clients to behave in ways that they are not particularly keen on. A victim of tobacco addiction should give up cigarettes, an alcoholic should not reach for alcohol, an obese person should avoid sweets and start running. The validation-persuasion technique used by clinical psychologists is based on the premise that in addition to simply presenting arguments to show the client the necessity of changing some behavior, one must also acknowledge that the client's resistance to change is perfectly under-standable. An obese person might be told, "I know sweets are delicious and it's hard to resist the temptation of a scrumptious donut, but because of the serious risk of diabetes, giving up sweets is essential in your case." A smoker might be told: "It is a fact that it is very difficult to get rid of addictions and habits, and nicotine abstinence is very extremely un-pleasant and burdensome for the smoker, but in your case giving up smoking is a condition of recovery." Clinical psychologists have some very interesting ideas, but they rarely take care to verify their accuracy in replicable experiments. However, social psychologists are doing this without necessarily focusing on changing the behavior of clients in therapy rooms. So let's take a closer look at one such experiment.

Research

The struggle for a clean environment is the challenge of our time. Undoubtedly, it is Homo Sapiens and not any other species on Earth that litter the planet the most. The idea of recycling waste, one of the most important measures for reducing the pollution of the Earth, has been known for a long time. Already in the 10th century, the Japanese collected wastepaper and recycled it. The pioneers of waste segregation were, in turn, the 19th-century *chiffoniers*, the poorest residents of French metropolises, for whom shoveling heaps of waste was a basic source of income. Today, the idea of waste segregation and recycling is universally approved in the declaratory sense, but it would be far from the truth to claim that this verbal approval directly translates into human behavior. Carol Werner, Sara Byerli, Paul White, and Matthew Kieffer (2004) asked whether the validation-persuasion technique discussed here could be used to increase people's willingness to put paper in specially placed bins. They placed such bins in university buildings, whose signage clearly stated that they were for throwing paper that was no longer needed into them. In these buildings, students were able to take the university newspaper, the *Utah Chronicles*, free of charge. The question is, what will they do with it after reading it? In the different conditions of this experiment, the container only stated what it was for, or there was additional content. When the validation-persuasion technique was used, the caption read: "It may be inconvenient, but it is important"; in other cases, the container contained only argumentation ("It is important"), and in still others, only validation ("It may be inconvenient"). This last case may seem strange, but methodological rigor demanded that the experimenters introduce such conditions into the scheme of the study. It turned out that while in the control conditions (i.e., when the container only had a label on it saying what it was for) the students threw 46.6% of the collected newspapers into it, and when the validation-persuasion technique was used this rate reached as high as 66.3%! The use of validation alone or persuasion alone did not prove to be particularly effective. The respective percentages were 49.9 and 52.5. Let us add to this another important and interesting result concerning the students to whom the validation-persuasion technique was applied. When the slogan "It may be inconvenient, but it is important" disappeared from the paper bins, and only the marking that it is used to collect waste paper remained, their willingness to throw read newspapers there only slightly decreased, stabilizing at 59.8%.

Mechanism

When people receive a message composed of two elements: validation and persuasion, it is easier for them to agree with the content of this message. After all, from the very beginning, they agree completely with half of the information that reaches them, i.e., with the content of the validation. In the experiment described above, the phrase "It may be inconvenient" was used because the authors' previous research had shown that this was the main reason people gave for not separating waste. Of course, the student reading this information approves completely! In real social situations where you are influencing one particular person, you do not need to do any preliminary research. You can use exactly the same argument that the person uses in conversation to explain their resistance to a certain behavior. This will have the added benefit that the person will feel that they are being listened to carefully and that their arguments are indeed relevant. The key point is that the validation-persuasion technique builds a collaborative relationship, thus minimizing the degree to which the influencer is perceived as an adversary. Moreover, the influencer admits that there are reasons not to do what they insist on. Only now these reasons become less important. Or in any case, less important than the ones that indicate that one should do it.

Technique # 36 *Default settings*
Idea

One of us has a rather poor Internet connection at home. While it's not that you can't use email or browse what the newspapers are saying in the morning, things aren't always at their best even when chatting on Skype. Also, watching movies involves the image suddenly freezing, and you have to wait a while until you can return to watching again. The question that naturally arises is, "Why don't you change your Internet provider then?" The honest answer is, "Because you'd have to do something: terminate the contract, take the leased router to the current provider's office, and then carefully select a new provider and enter into a contract with them." Sure, if the Internet stopped working at all, or was completely hopeless, having to do these things wouldn't be a deterrent. But it's not that bad after all, and there are even days when everything works perfectly. So while on the one hand, people have freedom of choice in many situations (and value having it), very often they do not exercise it. You could say that they prefer inaction over action and constancy over change. Even when students come into a lecture hall and can take any seat they want, they tend to sit where they have sat before. Moreover, it does not seem to be some deliberate strategy of site selection. Rather, it is an aversion to change, or (looking at it from another angle) a preference for constancy. Can this type of human tendency to "do nothing" be used to exert social influence?

Research

This time, instead of researchers, the experiment was carried out by real life, or to be more precise, by governments, and rather parliaments of countries that make laws in them. Medical advances in recent decades have meant that more and more often human lives are saved through transplants of organs such as the heart, kidneys, or liver. But of course, for someone to receive such an organ, someone must (usually after their clinical death) donate it. Most often these are drivers who lose their lives in road accidents. Some countries in the world require the so-called explicit consent of people for the possible use of their organs for transplantation. So if residents of such a country want to give their consent, they must do certain things: go to an office and fill out an appropriate form, or at least do it online. In other countries, a diametrically different solution is adopted – the so-called presumed consent. In this case, if someone would like a person in need to use their organs after their death, they do not have to do anything. However, if they object, they must fill out the appropriate paperwork. Germany and Austria are countries where people speak the same language, are very similar culturally, and have many centuries of shared history. According to Eric Johnson and Daniel Goldstein (2004), in explicit-consent Germany, 12% of citizens consent to organ donation. So what about Austria, which uses presumed consent? Here, it applies to almost everyone (99.98%)!

Mechanism

Every change poses some risk. If things are good so far, or even great, is it worth taking the risk? After all, it is possible that it will turn out to be worse after the change. Change also requires activity. Why make an effort if you can avoid it? All this causes that in most situations people accept the status quo and are not willing to engage in any actions aimed at change. This is why people may decide not to change their electricity supplier, even though it could save them a lot of money, or – like one of the authors of this book – not to change their Internet provider, even though it could make their work and entertainment more convenient. In many cases, another, additional mechanism comes into play. Contracts with customers for various services (Internet, water, electricity, home or car insurance) are often constructed in such a way that the customer must terminate them within a certain period of time (e.g., two weeks before a given date) in order not to incur additional costs. However, if the customer misses the deadline (which often happens), even pure economic calculation tells them that, faced with the need to pay contractual penalties, making such changes ceases to be worth the effort.

Technique # 37 *Script of mindless action*

Idea

Fewer and fewer people watch on their wrist; more and more just use the clock in their cell phones. Still, there are enough such people who use wristwatches for you, the reader, to perform a simple experiment. Imagine that you see someone, say a 40-year-old man wearing a shirt and jacket, who is just raising his left hand towards his eyes, while pulling up his sleeve a little and revealing his watch. He has just checked what time it is. If you walk up to him now and say: "Excuse me, what time is it?" – he should answer you right away. After all, he knows the answer; after all, he just checked a moment ago. But most likely this will not happen. Most likely, this man will make the same movements as before: bringing his left hand closer to his eyes, with his right hand he will pull up the cuffs of the shirt and jacket of his left hand, look at the watch face and tell you, "6:54 p.m." Apparently, your question triggered just such an automatic response from him. Can such automatic reaction patterns, which appear as a response to certain verbal messages, be used for the effective application of social influence? One of the most famous experiments in social psychology proves it.

Research

Today, when students are expected to read a book or article for class, they usually sit somewhere with laptops on their laps and read pdfs of the assigned material. Once upon a time, in the pre-Internet era, when words like "book" or "article" meant that something was printed on paper, one of students' most common activities was to go to a copy shop and make prints of the material needed for class. Of course, before an exam session, this was particularly popular, and queues formed in front of copy shops. Ellen Langer, Arthur Blank, and Benzoin Chanowitz (1978) decided to take advantage of this fact for their experiment. The researchers sought to explore the structure of the various requests that each of us very often both formulates and receives. They determined that a typical message of this type consists of two elements: a request and an explanation for why the requester is making it. One person says to a friend: "can you lend me twenty dollars, because I forgot my purse?" while a student asks a classmate "can you share your notes from the last lecture with me because I missed it?" Importantly, in the vast majority of cases, these types of requests are met with approval and fulfilled. Thus, Langer and her colleagues conclude that if we formulate a request to be let through without queuing at a photocopy shop, we increase the chances of it being fulfilled if the request is of such a "binary" nature. And indeed: when the researchers in question said to a person standing in line: "Excuse me, I have 5 pages. May I use the xerox machine, because I'm in a rush?" 94% of people agreed to this. If, on the other hand, they simply said: "Excuse me, I have 5 pages, may I use the xerox machine?" significantly fewer (60%) people let them pass without queuing. Langer, Blank, and Chanowitz argue that because people have repeatedly responded positively to "two-factor" requests in their past lives, now, too, when encountering a message of this kind, they automatically and unreflectively say, "Why of course." How do we know that they do it without thinking? Well, in the scheme of the experiment in question there were also conditions in which the justification for the request... did not explain anything. This time the message was: "Excuse me,

I have 5 pages. May I use the xerox machine, because I have to make copies?". It turned out that a positive reaction was presented just as often (in 93% of cases, to be exact) as when the requester explains that he is in a hurry! So people do not analyze in detail the content of the message they hear. They react to its very structure. If a message with such a "two-factor" structure in the past caused them to comply with a request, now they comply as well.

Mechanism

Human beings are generally lazy. It is not only about "behavioral" laziness, about the fact that we do not want to vacuum our apartment, or clean up the desk. Human beings are also cognitively lazy: we often don't want to think deeply, consider in detail all possible issues and focus our attention on individual elements. If in our past, a situation repeated many times and we developed a generally adequate reaction to these situations, then now the appearance of such an event or a sequence of events automatically triggers that very reaction. Therefore, a man asked for, say, the hundredth time in his life, "Excuse me, what time is it?" does not answer immediately, but aims his watch at his eyes, because he has always done this when hearing such a question. Similarly, participants in the experiment described above respond positively to a request accompanied by a justification for making it. And it does not matter whether the justification is sensible or not. However, it should be very clearly emphasized here that Ellen Langer and her colleagues do not claim that humans are mindless, but only that humans can sometimes be mindless. More specifically, they assume that humans function either in a state of mindlessness (as was the case in the experiment presented above) or in a state of mindfulness. If the situation becomes serious, if the subject can lose a lot by relying on automatic responses, they begin to analyze the situation more carefully.

The experiment described above also included conditions in which a person standing in line at a photocopier was addressed with a message beginning "Excuse me, I have 20 copies...". Clearly, people in general would be less likely to let such a person pass, because in doing so they would lose more time. But what exactly are the results under three different conditions? This time, when the request was not accompanied by any justification, 24% of people complied; when the requester explained "because I'm in a rush" – 42%. What if he said: "because I have to make copies?". It turned out that the percentage agreeing to comply with this request was exactly the same as in the condition with no justification (24%). Apparently, only the vision of having to wait patiently for a stranger to make 20 copies caused people to analyze the content of what was being said to them. Only then did they begin to think, "after all, you don't buy doughnuts or take your jeans to the copy shop for washing, so why would you explain that you want to make copies!" So remember, that when you ask someone for something, you should give a justification. But if it's a serious request, think hard about how that justification should sound.

Technique # 38 *Do not state the reason (unless you want to lie)*

Idea

In the case of the previously discussed technique, i.e., the script of mindless action, we said that throughout our lifetime we are, on numerous occasions, faced with various requests that might include an explanation for making them in the first place ("Would you borrow me your lawnmower? Mine has just broken down."). In the case of trivial requests, it is enough to provide literally any explanation ("Would you let me use the copier first because I would like to make a copy?") for the subject to initiate the widely-used behavior pattern and grant the request. Yet, as you may remember, this mechanism does not work with serious, not trivial, requests. This is because a person receiving a serious request switches from mindlessness mode to mindfulness mode, stops initiating ready-made, automated behavior patterns, and analyzes the message more thoroughly. In such a situation, the request must be followed by an actual explanation that justifies making it in the first place. In the experiment we described when presenting the script of mindless action technique, the request was justified by the fact that the person who wanted to use the copy machine without waiting in line was in a hurry and pressed for time. It should be noted, though, that reasonable justifications (those which actually provide a valid explanation) may vary considerably in terms of their importance. A student may ask an examiner to postpone an exam. Both of these explanations, "because I have a surgical procedure scheduled at the same time" and "because I have plans to go on a trip out of town at the same time," justify, logically, the desire on the part of the student to postpone the exam. Yet, there is no doubt as to the fact that the former explanation is of significantly greater importance than the latter. What is more, providing the second explanation might anger the examiner.

Imagine that you want to make someone grant your request, which might be, in some way, problematic for this person. As you already know, providing just any justification is not going to be helpful. How about a reasonable justification? You've got one, but it is rather "poor." You do not expect it to be of much help to you. It even might make things worse for you! (Students, when asking to postpone an exam, tend to avoid justifying your request with a desire to take a trip out of town on the exam date). Obviously, there are solid and serious reasons that may come to your mind but they would not be true and you do not want to lie. What are the options then? Let us examine a certain experiment.

Research

Stanley Milgram and John Sabini (1978) examined the behavior of passengers traveling on an NYC subway car as they were asked to give up their seats. The experimenters were young individuals – both men and women – and they addressed both male and female passengers of various ages. The experiment was really simple. It was conducted when all the seats were occupied. The experimenter, holding a book in his/her hand, would approach a sitting passenger and address this person in the following manner: "Excuse me. May I have your seat? I can't read my book standing up." In those conditions, 37.2% of the passengers gave up their seats, while an additional 4.7% slid over to make room for the experimenter on their seat. And what happened when the experimenter simply said: "Excuse me. May I have your seat?" In those conditions, 56% of the passengers gave up their seat and an additional 12.3% slid over so that the asker could also sit down. As evidenced by the results, the chances of the passenger to give up their seat were significantly higher when no explanation was provided to support the request.

Mechanism

Would you give up your seat on a subway car (or a bus, a tram, or a train) if you were asked to do so by a person telling you that they would like to be able to read their book and for this specific reason they would like your seat? Surely not. Why on earth would you agree to significantly reduce the comfort of your travel only to make it more comfortable for somebody else? The fact that reading a book standing up is uncomfortable is, evidently, a very poor justification in this particular case. It would be a very different story if someone told you that they did not feel well, or that they felt pain in their chest or had difficulty breathing. But nobody used such a justification in the above-described experiment. Truly, it is very probable that upon hearing "May I have your seat?", the passengers concluded that the request for giving up their seat was made due to the asker's poor condition. This is because we all know that one's poor condition legitimizes a request for somebody's seat. A person who is not feeling well has the right to a seat! The asker does not articulate these reasons directly but it is, to some degree, obvious. If the asker were fine, he probably would not ask for the seat. Obviously, we are not making reference here to the experiment conducted by Milgram and Sabini in order to provide instructions on how to wheedle a seat in means of public transport, but to illustrate a rule that tells us that sometimes it is better to have the subjects themselves come up with (obviously serious) reasons for which they are asked for something.

Technique # 39 *The pique technique*
Idea

Imagine that you are not particularly punctual. If someone makes an appointment with you for 5 p.m., you assume that coming ten minutes earlier or later doesn't really change anything. If you're driving a car and you see a 40 mph speed limit, you'll probably slow down, but slowing down to 43 or even 45 mph is probably OK… What if someone has an appointment with you at 4:55 p.m., or the speed limit is 42 mph? First of all, you will pay close attention to what is happening. The situation is highly unusual. After all, no one makes such precise appointments, and you've never seen a speed limit posted on a road sign in such detail! It is very likely that you will come to the meeting precisely on time, and your foot will press the brake just hard enough for your car to stay under the speed limit. Similarly, imagine that you are involved in a negotiation and a representative of the opposing party says that the minimum amount for which they can do something for your company is 800,000 (in whatever currency). Will you take this as accurate and definitive information? Will you believe that this is really a price that cannot be altered in negotiations? Now imagine you hear that the minimum amount is 801,027... How much more serious this sounds! Surely they have calculated everything carefully and there is no point in even trying to negotiate this issue.

Research

Michael Santos, Craig Leve, and Anthony Pratkanis (1994) are the researchers who first described and empirically examined the technique known as the pique. They did so inspired by their observation of the very low effectiveness of American beggars asking for alms. In doing so, they usually ask for "any spare change" or "a quarter" (more like a dollar these days, thanks to inflation). However, people have learned not to pay attention, "not to hear" these requests, and walk by the beggars. They had automated just such a response. However, if the beggar asked for alms in an atypical manner, he could engage the attention of passers-by and make them interested in his hard-luck story. If, for example, he asks not for 25 cents (a typical request) but for 17 cents or 37 cents, he may arouse in the person being approached an interest in why they need exactly such an amount. As a result, the person being asked may want to give it to him. Santos, Leve, and Pratkanis carried out a study on this issue and demonstrated the effectiveness of the technique in question. However, we will present here the results of another, very similar experiment conducted on a larger number of participants. Jerry Burger, Joy Hornisher, Valerie Martin, Gary Newman, and Summer Pringle (2007) implemented an empirical study related to a money begging situation. In the control condition, a young person said to a lone walking adult: "Excuse me, can you spare any change?" In the conditions involving application of the pique technique, he said: "Excuse me, can you spare 37 cents?" In the control condition, the person being questioned did not ask what the requester needed the money for. In the pique condition, such a question was asked relatively often – 29.9% of the participants did so. In half of the cases, the experimenter answered: "Because I need to buy a stamp," and in the other half "Because I need to buy some things." (Note that this last answer does not explain anything. Thus, it reminds us of the pseudo-explanation "because I want to make a copy" from the technique presented previously). It turned out that in the control condition 18.8% of the subjects handed over some money, while in the pique condition 41.7% did. Let us add here that in the pique conditions, those who asked why the asker needed 37 cents were especially willing to give money. Among those who received a specific answer (Because I need to buy a stamp) as many as 87.1% gave money. A response that did not explain anything, however, did not discourage most participants from ignoring the request for change. It was given by 70% of the participants. Let us add that also the average amounts of money handed out were clearly (almost three times) higher in conditions where the pique technique was used.

Mechanism

While the script of mindless action technique discussed earlier takes advantage of the fact that people respond automatically and without thinking, the pique technique is based on the exact opposite mechanism: if you anticipate that the automatic response will be to refuse your request, you must behave in an unusual way. In other words, you cannot allow the chain to be set in motion: a defined situation – a typical message to the recipient – a refusal of the request. While you may have little or no influence on the situation itself (e.g., you are a person in need of help at the moment who needs to approach another individual who is approaching), you can influence both the form and content of your message in such a way as to minimize the likelihood that your request will be denied. For this to happen, your message should be strange, or at least unusual. We note that the pique technique is not reserved strictly for asking for money. Other studies have shown, for example, that people are much more likely to agree to take a short survey when, instead of being assured that it will last a very short time, they are told that it will last 37 seconds. So if you want to approach your boss for a raise, and you know that he always answers "no" in such situations, you should try to do something weird immediately before doing so – like stumble at the threshold of his office and fall to the floor, then crush his hand in a shake. (We don't guarantee this will work, but since the alternative is an obvious no, it's worth a try…)

Technique # 40 *Disrupt-then-reframe*
Idea

A key element of the pique technique that we introduced a moment ago is the emergence of something new, something surprising. This "something" causes things to veer from a set course. In doing so, we reduce the likelihood of rejection where it would be routine in a standard situation. What if we are faced with a situation that is first standard and routine, and suddenly a strange element appears, but only for a moment because the situation returns to normal again? You, dear reader, will probably agree that if circumstances have changed twice in a short time, a person may feel strange or confused. It's a bit like when your mother-in-law, who is fussy as usual, suddenly becomes cordial and then fussy again. And what if your mother-in-law suddenly asks you for something just then? Perhaps you will be so "confused" that, against your own interests, you will agree to fulfill her wish. Is that possible? Maybe the example with the mother-in-law is not the best, but it's what came to mind. In any case, let us move on to presenting a study on a very interesting, original, and also effective social influence technique.

Research

Barbara Davis and Eric Knowles (1999) conducted their experiment just before Christmas. The experimenter played the role of a door-to-door salesman who visited people in their homes, offering them a set of Christmas cards. The situation is rather typical. Peddlers offer just such items in the first half of December. The cards are quite nice. But does it really make sense to buy them? After all, when we send wishes to our relatives and friends for Christmas, we use the Internet more and more often and send traditional cards much less frequently. On the other hand, the cards are nice… The seller is saying they cost $3 and claims that's a bargain. It turned out that 35% of people decide to buy under such conditions. But what if the peddler presenting the cards says "The price of these Christmas cards is 300 pennies," and after two or three seconds he explains: "That's three dollars" to end his statement with "It's a bargain?" It turned out then that almost twice as many people (65% to be exact) decided to make the purchase. Further research has shown that in order to achieve this effect, it is necessary that the following sequence of events occurs during the interaction: the interaction seems to have a normal, routine course – something strange happens – an explanation is provided, which makes the interaction seem to resume its normal course – an argument emerges. Everything has to happen in a very short time. If any of these elements are missing or appear in a different order (e.g., the salesperson says: "It's a bargain, the price is three dollars, that's 300 pennies"), people are not made more likely to buy.

Mechanism

Most people who want a wooden bookcase in their home buy it from a furniture store or order it from a carpenter. However, there are those who, using pine boards, a few tools, and wood glue, construct such a bookcase themselves. Imagine that you visit such a person absorbed in this work and ask them what they are doing. You may hear very different answers – for example: "I'm decorating my daughter's room," "I'm making a bookcase," or "I'm trying to join these two boards together," "I'm gluing these two pieces together because I can't screw in the fixing screw." In their action identification theory, Robin Vallacher and Daniel Wegner (1985) point out that people who perform different actions may think about them in different ways. If things are going well, they identify their action at a high level (with reference to the example above they think and say they are decorating their daughter's room or making a bookcase). However, if something strange or unexpected happens that disrupts the subject's action in some way, they begin to focus on the details in order to regain control of the situation. So if our do-it-yourselfer has just come across a knot in the wood and is having a problem because of it, they will rather respond: "I'm trying to join these two boards together," or "I'm gluing two pieces of wood together," rather than "I'm making a bookcase," or "I'm decorating my daughter's room." In the case of the experiment discussed above, we have the subject changing the level at which they identify their action twice in very short intervals. First, the interaction with the peddler proceeds normally (so the subject expresses it at a high level of identification), but suddenly the peddler quotes the price in a strange way (300 cents) that causes the subject to drop to a lower level of identification. In a moment, however, everything becomes clear: 300 cents is, after all, simply 3 dollars. So the subject goes back to a high level of identification because the situation has become normal. However, their mind is in a strange and unusual state of disorientation. And in this peculiar state of disorientation comes the argument used by the peddler: "It's a bargain." In this specific state of mind, the argument turns out to have extraordinary power.

Technique # 41 DTR: Beyond selling and buying

Idea

The disrupt-then-reframe technique, which we have already described, was tested almost exclusively in the course of empirical studies devoted to selling and buying various products. By quoting, initially, the price in cents instead of dollars or euros, and in the case of our studies conducted in Poland in grosz instead of Polish zloty and, subsequently, by presenting the price in the conventional fashion (i.e., in dollars, euros or Polish zloty) and, lastly, by adding an argument supporting the purchase decision, researchers were able to significantly increase people's willingness to buy, e.g., Christmas cards, notebooks, candles, lottery tickets or condensed canned soups. It is worth noting that from the perspective of the underlying psychological mechanism behind the effectiveness of the DTR technique, its use cases should go well beyond the mere sale of products. After all, we can try to persuade someone into rewriting, by hand, three pages of text by specifying the number of letters only to explain, later on, that these make three pages, or to ask someone to carry a bag to the second floor by saying, earlier, that there are 42 steps to climb. Lastly, we can ask someone to spare their time. In such a case, instead of days, we can first use hours, instead of hours, we can use minutes, and instead of specifying the amount of time in minutes, we can initially express it in seconds. This is precisely the version of the disrupt-then-reframe technique that we tested in one of the studies designed to examine various possibilities of persuading people into participating in a telephone marketing survey.

Research

The problem often faced by people conducting telephone marketing surveys is that many of their callees refuse to participate in such surveys. The
fact that you first need to call a few individuals before any of them agrees
to talk about, e.g., pasta or gas prices is not a major problem in itself. It
only makes conducting the survey more time-consuming and a little more
expensive. The real issue is that the tested sample is not representative.
Who is willing to talk to a stranger over a telephone? Unemployed,
pensioners, retirees, and people who are stuck in bed because they have a
cold and are bored. All of them have a lot of time on their hands and are
often bored. Who would say no? Hard-working people who are always in
a hurry. We want to know the opinion on pasta or gas prices held by
residents of a given area and instead, we will learn the opinion, on these
topics, of people living in this area who are unemployed, pensioners and
retirees, or who have a cold. In the course of a study devoted to the use of
the DTR technique, Iza Kubala (2002) called randomly selected people and
said, in the standard conditions, that she was conducting a survey regarding consumer goods that would take approx. seven minutes and asked
the callees if they would agree to take part in it. As it turned out, less than
10% of the subjects agreed to talk to the researcher. In the conditions
where the disrupt-then-reframe technique was used, the researchers informed her callees that the interview would take approx. 420 seconds,
after 2–3 seconds she would explain, "it means approx. seven minutes."
She ended with: "it'll just take a moment." In such conditions, a significantly greater number of people (approx. 24%) agreed to take part in
the survey.

Mechanism

The underlying mechanism behind the effectiveness of the technique
based on presenting a time frame in an unusual manner only to present it
in the conventional fashion and to add an argument is, obviously, exactly
the same as in the case of using the DTR technique to boost sales. In both
cases, cognitive reframing plays a crucial role. The subject is first surprised by the way important details are presented. Before they fully
understand it, these details are presented in a conventional manner and

the entire message is concluded with a simple argument, which, as it would appear, requires no in-depth analyses. It should be emphasized that it is necessary for the above-mentioned three elements (details provided in a weird format – the explanation – the argument) to occur in this particular order. This is because studies clearly demonstrate that should their order be different, the technique is no longer effective, which, after all, is perfectly understandable, given its underlying psychological mechanism. It should be noted that even though in the study described above the DTR technique was used in a telephone conversation, there is empirical evidence that such a specific presentation of the time (i.e., in seconds instead of minutes) the activity the subject is asked to perform requires significantly increases the chances for granting a request also formulated by direct (face-to-face) contact.

Technique # 42 *Emotional disrupt-then-reframe*
Idea

An attentive reader of this book might have noticed a similarity between the above-described *disrupt-then-reframe* technique and the *fear-then-relief* technique, which we earlier described in a section "Emotion." In both cases, circumstances change suddenly and the subject is completely confused. As far as the *disrupt-then-reframe* method is concerned, the change stems from the fact that something odd has just happened, which makes the subject lose full cognitive control over the situation. A salesclerk does not present the price of an item in the typical fashion (e.g., three dollars) but in an odd way (300 cents) or someone asking for a short interview specifies its duration not in minutes (e.g., five minutes) but in seconds (300 seconds). In the case of the *fear-then-relief* technique, the situation also changes completely and unexpectedly, which makes the experienced fear inappropriate. What clearly separates these two techniques though is the fact that there is a need for one additional element in the case of *disrupt-then-reframe*. This element is an argument that should make the subject act on a request or accept a proposition. This element is not required when it comes to the *fear-then-relief* technique. Or perhaps this technique would be even more effective if the subject were faced with an argument intended to make him act in a certain manner at the moment of experiencing an unexpected relief? This is the question one of the authors of this book and Katarzyna Szczucka asked themselves.

Research

The subjects in this experiment (Dolinski & Szczucka, 2013) were drivers who parked their cars in a restricted place. The researchers decided to use this fact in order to induce the emotional seesaw: initially, they triggered fear and subsequently, relief. They left a sheet of paper behind the windshield wipers of illegally-parked vehicles that resembled, both in terms of dimensions and color, a parking ticket. It is reasonable to assume that a driver, when approaching his car, believed that he had been caught parking illegally by the police. The driver would remove the sheet from underneath the windshield wiper only to learn that it was not a parking ticket but a flyer for Arcoon hair shampoo (the brand does not actually exist). Needless to say, the driver experienced unexpected relief at that moment. In the control conditions, the Arcoon shampoo flyer was attached with a piece of adhesive tape to the door of the car next to the door handle. Obviously, this is not where parking tickets are usually left, so in these conditions, the driver did not feel fear or relief. Regardless of where the sheet of paper was left, when the owner of the vehicle was taking a look at it, he was approached by a young male (age 22) who offered him a chance to purchase a certain product. He said: "Hi, I am selling a summer windshield wash with insect formula. Would you like to buy a liter container from me? The price is six zlotys." In half of the cases, he added an argument in favor of making the purchase: "It's a bargain." As it turned out, only 7% of the subjects purchased the offered product in the control conditions. The *fear-then-relief* technique, which we had already been familiar with, again proved effective. This time, 26.25% of the drivers decided to make the purchase. From the perspective of the technique analyzed in this chapter, the key aspect is the number of drivers who bought the summer windshield wash when the seller used the argument designed to urge potential customers to make the purchase. As it turned out, in those conditions where the emotional seesaw was not applied, the phrase "It's a bargain" did not increase the drivers' willingness to purchase the windshield wash. However, if the argument was used at the time the driver experienced the unexpected relief, the role of this argument became very significant. In such conditions, as many as 41.25% of the subjects bought the windshield wash.

Mechanism

In the studies devoted to the investigation of the disrupt-then-reframe technique, a simple argument such as the phrases, "It's a bargain," "It's a great deal," or "It's really inexpensive," had little impact in the standard situation but at the same time proved to be very significant in those conditions where the subject, at some point, felt confused. In the case of the fear-then-relief technique, subjects also experience confusion. And even though the nature of this confusion is different and is caused by a sudden change in the experienced emotions, in this case, the above-mentioned argument also proves to be remarkably effective. In our considerations, we should return to the reality of the interrogation. It appears that once the suspect has been introduced to a state of emotional seesaw, the good cop also uses certain arguments intended to make the suspect testify. For example, he says, "You will be able to walk out of this room in a few moments," or, "You will receive a suspended sentence." Apparently, a state of short-term confusion, typical when experiencing unexpected relief, not only disables our ability to think in a fully rational manner but also makes us susceptible to simple (not always necessarily true) arguments.

Technique # 43 *That's not all*

Idea

People love a bargain. If you can buy jeans for half price then you should definitely do it. If you pay for one shirt and get another one free, it would be a sin not to take advantage of such an opportunity. In the vast majority of cases, these bargains are static in the sense that the customer sees that the jeans used to cost a certain amount, but the price is crossed out and the current price is twice as low. As for the shirt, you actually have to figure out that the current offer is better than the one in effect before. Previously they probably weren't giving a second one at no charge. But what if the offer dynamically becomes more favorable, so to speak, before the very eyes of the subject... We are considering buying jeans, and only then does it turn out that they are clearly cheaper; we are considering buying a shirt, and only then do we find out that if we buy it, we will get another one as a gift. This situation resembles one often used in teleshopping. A nice gentleman demonstrates the operation of a sensational, latest generation vacuum cleaner and gives its price, saying that it is especially reduced for viewers, and then states: "That's not all," explaining that those who buy it today will get an additional 10% off. The show goes on, however. Because... that's not all, and the vacuum comes with four nozzles for free, enabling you to clean up dust from just about anywhere. That's not all!

Research

Jerry Burger (1986) was selling cookies at a booth set up specifically for this purpose. However, there was no price information attached to them. People who approached the booth and asked how much the cookies cost were randomly assigned to one of two conditions. Half of the people were told that the cookies were sold in a bundle of two packages, and such a set cost 75 cents. The others heard the short answer when asked about the price: 75 cents. It must seem obvious in such a situation that this is the price of a single package. However, after a moment the salesperson explained that this is not the price for a single package, because the cookies are sold in a set consisting of two packages. As we can see, the offer is the same in both cases, but that half of the respondents initially thought it was less favorable. It turned out that while in the control conditions 40% of those who asked about the price decided to buy, in the conditions in which the "that's not all" technique was used this number was as high as 70%. In other experiments, Burger demonstrated a similar effect when participants asked for the price of a product, were given the price, and were told a few seconds later that the price was lower. This effect occurred regardless of how the reason for the reduction was explained (e.g., sometimes it was because all the products had been sold before the store closed, and sometimes it was because the sales-person made a mistake in initially giving the wrong, inflated price).

Mechanism

In most decision-making situations, we weigh the arguments on a scale: on one side are those that tell us "do it," on the other side are those that tell us "don't do it." Very often the decision is extremely difficult because it is impossible to know objectively how much each of the arguments we consider weighs. The two scales are therefore in relative balance, and we are completely at a loss as to what we should do. Would it be different if one of the many arguments were removed? Probably not. The situation would also be uncertain and unclear. The that's not all technique is based on exactly that. If you want to get someone to do something, you have to assume that there are arguments against doing it. You may not even know them all, but the person you are making the suggestion to knows them. And it will probably be difficult for this person to make a decision regardless of whether you put all your arguments on the table right away or whether you put almost all of them on the table, but keep one argument up your sleeve for later. For now, you wait until someone you want to influence starts to hesitate. The aforementioned scale remains in balance. And now (right now!) you are adding weight to one side.

Technique # 44 *Endowment rule*

Idea

One of the authors of this book sometimes buys antiques at a flea market. Needless to say, the flavor of such places is related to, inter alia, the bargaining ritual, which takes place even if the potential buyer does not consider the asking price to be excessive. You are simply expected to bargain with the seller. In such cases, it may happen that after purchasing, e.g., an Art Nouveau lamp for PLN 200, instead of PLN 300, which was the initial asking price, the buyer may feel that he bought it at a discount. How much is the lamp worth? PLN 300? After all, this was the amount the buyer was willing to pay for this item in the event the seller refused to negotiate the price. Well not exactly, according to one of the authors of this book, the lamp is worth much more. He would not sell it even for PLN 600. It is very probable that you feel the same way about various items that you own (not necessarily purchased at a flea market). Particularly those items that are unique in some way and cannot be easily purchased in a regular store. This may be a ring made 20 years ago by a jeweler-artisan or a rug bought during an exotic vacation. Can this mechanism be utilized as a social influence technique? It most definitely can and the results are simply remarkable.

Research

In his extremely interesting book titled *Mindware. Tools for smart thinking*, Richard Nisbett (2015) describes marketing activities implemented by a branch of his university responsible for organizing concerts. Obviously, the marketing personnel's task is to attract the largest audience possible and almost everyone likes using discounts. Therefore, music lovers received letters including a promotional code that enabled them to purchase their tickets at a discount of USD 20. The campaign turned out to be a moderate success. Apparently, for many people, the idea of a discount worth USD 20 was not tempting enough. As a result, the marketing strategy was somewhat modified and instead of the above-mentioned letters, there were coupons for USD 20 inside the envelopes, which the addressees could use when purchasing their tickets. Needless to say, if the addressees did not buy their tickets, the coupons would go to waste. In other words, they would lose USD 20. What was the outcome? With the modified marketing campaign, the organizers were able to sell up to 70% more tickets as compared to the traditional, previously implemented promotional action!

Mechanism

People tend to avoid giving up what they have, even in the event the cost-benefit analysis seems to suggest that it would be reasonable to give up what they have in exchange for something better. This phenomenon, known as the endowment effect, is based on loss aversion. The disutility of giving up an object is greater than the utility associated with acquiring it. It was the economist Richard Thaler who first came up with the idea of the endowment effect. Thaler had a friend who was a great wine aficionado. He would purchase good vintage wines made of high-quality grapevine varieties but he was not careless with his money. Actually, he never bought a bottle of wine for more than thirty dollars. Yet, when he was to sell one of the wines kept in his cellar, the price of USD 100 seemed to be too low for him (Kahneman et al., 1991). A similar mechanism was at play in the case of the above-described promotional campaign. Even though, mathematically speaking, in both cases the customers would be purchasing their tickets at a USD 20 discount, they were more willing to do so when they felt they were avoiding a loss than in a situation when they felt they could gain something. Both the loss and the gain, mathematically speaking, were identical. And yet, psychologically, the loss is considered to be (sometimes significantly) greater than the gain.

Technique # 43 *Valence framing*

Idea

An argument intended to affect a subject's decision may, sometimes, be presented in the category of gain or loss. Even though both the gain and the loss may be identical mathematically, in most cases they are not considered identical in the psychological sense. Imagine that you get a raise in your monthly salary. You will be paid 20 euro or 20 dollars more. Are you happy about it? Well, I guess, but it is not like you are thrilled. What kind of a raise is that? Hardly anything really. The joy is not that great. And now, imagine that your salary was reduced by the same amount. How would you respond? Surely, you would be very angry! They reduced your salary! In this case, the very fact that your salary was reduced (never mind the amount of the reduction) is enough of a reason to be upset. Following the same logic, people are usually less excited about getting an attractive job than they are worried about losing it, or they are less excited about finding something (e.g., a banknote on the pavement) than they are worried about losing the same thing. The conclusion should therefore be that if we want to persuade someone into doing something, we should emphasize what this person could lose if they do not do what is being suggested rather than what they could gain if they do. Research into valence framing is very frequently conducted by psychologists who study people's economic decisions and actions. Here, however, we will discuss studies designed to advocate health-promoting behavior as we rarely made reference in our book to this crucial area of exerting influence on people, and this is a perfect opportunity to do so.

Research

Beth Meyerowitz and Shelly Chaiken (1987) decided to check if the "it is better to say what someone can lose rather than what they can gain" rule applies to advocating health-promoting behavior. To be more precise, they

wanted to check which type of message will be the most effective in pro-
moting the performance of breast self-examination among women. College
female students were asked to show up at the laboratory and fill out several
questionnaires. In one of the questionnaires, the female students were asked
how often they performed breast self-examination throughout the previous
year. The questionnaire also verified their knowledge on how such self-
examination should be carried out and included questions regarding their
subjective feelings related to this activity. Subsequently, the female students
were assigned to one of four experimental conditions. In three of those
conditions, the female students were asked to read a leaflet entitled, "Some
Basic Facts," which stated that breast cancer was a frequent condition (affecting 1 in every 11 women in the USA) and that physicians recommend
performing breast self-examination. Additionally, the leaflet included instructions on how to perform self-examination. This was the final piece of
information included in the leaflet presented to the first group of women.
The women from the second group received additional information on the
benefits of breast self-examination. One of the paragraphs read as follows:
"Research shows that women who do BSE (Breast Self-Examination) have an
increased chance of finding a tumor in the early, more treatable stage of the
disease." In the third group, the aforementioned additional information was
virtually identical but it was formulated differently. The above-mentioned
exemplary paragraph had the following wording: "Research shows that
women who don't do BSE (Breast Self-Examination) have a decreased chance
of finding a tumor in the early, more treatable stage of the disease." The
fourth group did not receive any information of this nature. Four months
later, the experimenters called these women and conducted a 15-minute long
interview, during which the women were asked, inter alia, how many breast
self-examinations they did during the past four months. Needless to say, the
point was to check if (and to what degree) the female subjects became more
willing to perform this activity. Meyerowitz and Chaiken designed a special
indicator that allowed them to estimate this value for each subject. According
to the results, the frequency of breast self-examination increased in all groups
included in the experiment. In the three groups, however, the increase was
minor (the researchers determined its value to be in the range of 0.74 to
0.75), while in one group it was significantly higher (on the same scale:
1.42). This marked increase was recorded in the group where the women
read about the risks related to not performing self-examination.

Mechanism

In 2002, the psychologist Daniel Kahneman was awarded the Nobel Prize in economics. He got the prize for the research (most of which he conducted in cooperation with Amos Tversky, who died in 1996), which consistently demonstrated that the decisions we make in conditions of uncertainty are not completely rational. One of the most significant discoveries made by Kahneman and Tversky (1979) was demonstrating that people perceive potential gains and possible losses in a different manner. In most decision-making situations, people behave as if avoiding a loss was, subjectively, more important than achieving a gain. The valence framing technique refers to this observation and takes advantage of the fact that the same situation can often be described in terms of losses as well as in terms of gains. When referring to our health, one can say that cutting down on sweets will help us retain good health or that having too many sweets can lead to illnesses. When discussing insurance policies, one can say that by purchasing comprehensive coverage, we are guaranteed to be paid in the event our car gets stolen or we will lose our money if we fail to insure the vehicle and someone steals it. It appears (from the logical perspective) that both messages are identical but the consequences for the decisions made by people, as demonstrated by the experiment discussed above, are different. Torry Higgins (2005), while admitting that in most cases people, in their actions, are driven by their desire "not to lose," notices that there are areas where people are focused predominantly on improving their situation. One of such areas is the situation when a person is considering buying a new car. For the potential buyer, the arguments regarding the new car's acceleration or comfortable seats are more important than those related to the fact that their old car might break down at any moment.

4

AGENCY AND FREEDOM

In the early 20th century, psychology, in most cases, treated a human being as either a creature controlled by external circumstances (behaviorism) or as someone controlled by instincts and drives they were not consciously aware of (psychoanalysis). Modern psychology, or at least its prevailing trend, perceives a human being in a completely different manner: as an individual who is an agent of their actions and who appreciates being able to influence their life. Agency and freedom represent values that people not only highly appreciate verbally but also try to implement in both their everyday life as well as the process of achieving their long-term goals. This section demonstrates how these human aspirations can be used in social influence processes. Consequently, we are dealing with a certain paradox in the case of the techniques discussed in this chapter: by exerting influence on people, we emphasize, in various ways, the fact that they are the agents behind their own actions and we demonstrate how important it is for them, but at the same time, we increase the probability of them doing something we want them to do.

DOI: 10.4324/9781003296638-5

Technique # 46 *Evoking freedom*

Idea

Do you like being forced to do something? Of course not! Each of us wants to feel like the agent of our own actions and choices. That's probably why most kids don't like school and don't like to learn. Many adults don't like their jobs either. Not because school knowledge is boring and work is tiring, but because both young and slightly older people feel forced into these activities. In other words: because it is not their own choice. The same is true in situations where someone urges us to do something, such as suggesting that we buy a product, sign an appeal, or watch our bike or dog for someone who wants to go into the store. That is why we sometimes refuse in such situations. We feel that someone is putting pressure on us, limiting our personal freedom. We rebel and, as if in defense of our own subjectivity, we say "no." Imagine, however, that someone addresses you with a request and at the same time insists that the choice is yours, or insists that although they are asking you to do something, you will do what you think is right anyway. Can this kind of message influence your decision? And if so, how?

Research

Nicolas Gueguen and Alexandre Pascual (2005) conducted an experiment in which passersby were approached and asked to answer several survey questions. They added that it would take them about 5 to 8 minutes. It was explained that this survey was about evaluating local merchants and craftsmen in their town. Apparently, the subject matter of the survey must have seemed interesting to the people interviewed because as many as 75.6% of them agreed to answer the series of questions. Is it conceivable that the percentage of those agreeing could be even higher? The researchers tested conditions in which passersby were addressed as follows: "Excuse me Sir/Madame, I would like to ask you for something but you are free to accept or refuse," and only then was the survey mentioned. It turned out that in these conditions as many as 90.1% of people agreed to spend a few minutes responding! Let us add here that this emphasis on freedom of choice does not have to be done using the exact phrase from the experiment described above. In other experiments, the effectiveness of social influence was increased with equal success when the request was supplemented with phrases such as: "do not feel obliged" or "do as you wish."

Mechanism

The need for freedom and subjectivity is one of the most important human psychological needs. It is obvious that if someone asks us to fulfill a request, the choice is ours. After all, no one is able to force us to do anything of the sort. And yet emphasizing this obvious fact by the person making the request probably makes us feel better, more subjective. However, let us note a paradox here. Readers of this book have already been introduced to quite a few social influence techniques. We probably all agree that in the control conditions of individual experiments presented here people did what they wanted; after all, nobody forced them neither to comply with the request nor to refuse to comply with it. Also, in the case of the experiment testing the *evoking freedom* technique in control conditions, people experienced no external pressure. In the experimental conditions, however, they complied more frequently with the request addressed to them. Not because they were objectively freer (of course they weren't!), but because under those conditions it was easier for them to feel that they were fulfilling that request of their own free will (because they themselves wanted to) and not because they were being pressured to do so by someone else.

Technique # 47 *Get it while you still can (unavailability)*
Idea

Imagine that it is a hot afternoon. You are walking along a beach, you can feel your skin getting hot from the sunshine and you are simply dying to cool off. Unfortunately, there is nowhere to buy a cold beverage. You keep walking and suddenly you see an ice cream cart on the horizon. You run to the young ice cream vendor. After a while, you reach the ice cream cart and you say: "It is sure hot today... thank God at least you are selling something cold. What ice cream flavors do you offer?" The ice cream vendor looks into his cart and says: "I've got something for everybody, I've got chocolate, strawberry, sweet cream, pistachio, mango, and yogurt flavor. No wait, I'm out of the yogurt-flavored ones." And most likely, precisely at this moment, you feel like having yogurt-flavored ice cream.

What has just happened there? The answer is unavailability: a mechanism through which items that are unavailable (or at least difficult to obtain) immediately seem to be the most attractive ones. Do you remember when your parents told you as a child not to do something? Not to eat a cookie right before dinner or not to get on a swing at the playground if the swing is in poor condition. Did the cookie or the swing not seem to be most attractive and desirable at that exact moment? It is a similar story with the most famous pair of lovers in international literature: Romeo and Juliet. Would they actually be so attracted to each other if the Montagues and the Capulets were not so hostile to each other and their relationship were not forbidden?

Yet there is still a question as to whether this technique could be used in everyday life. After all, we cannot forbid everything and hope that the forbidden items will become attractive to those individuals over whom we want to exert influence. However, we can, e.g., present one option as the most attractive by describing it as limited.

Research

Michal Maimaran and Yuval Salant (2019) decided to investigate how presenting an option as limited, in some manner, affects the behavior of pre-school children. Fifty-one children, with an average age of five years, participated in their study. The children were asked to go into a room with building bricks scattered on the floor. In the control conditions, the experimenter said: "Go ahead and play with the bricks. When you are finished, simply walk to my desk." In the experimental conditions, the experimenter added: "Unfortunately, you can only play with the bricks for ten minutes." Subsequently, in order to minimize the impact of the observation, the experimenter sat at his desk and pretended not to pay attention to what the child was doing. When the child approached the experimenter to tell him that they had finished playing with the bricks (or, in the experimental conditions, when ten minutes had passed and the child was interrupted – even though it was not always necessary, as in many cases even the children in the experimental group finished playing before the set time was up) the second part of the experiment followed. The experimenter asked the child to approach his desk and said that there was a snack waiting for them – a plate of baby carrots (exactly 42 grams of carrots). The child was told to eat as many carrots as they wanted. In the conditions designed to induce the unavailability effect, the experimenter added "... and I'm sorry but these are all the carrots we have."

According to the results obtained by Maimaran and Salant, even five-year-olds are very sensitive to having their choices (or the availability of some goods, e.g., building bricks or carrots) limited. The children who were told that they could play with the building bricks for just ten minutes played with the bricks longer than the children in the control group – almost 8.5 minutes and 6.5 minutes, respectively. Similar effects, which might be particularly important for parents of picky eaters, were observed in the case of eating baby carrots. When the children were not told that these were all the carrots available, they ate 21.84 grams of carrots. Yet when the children were told that there would be no more carrots, they ate 33.76 grams. Interestingly enough, the researchers also asked the children if they enjoyed their snacks. On a scale of 1 to 5, the group with the "unavailability effect" rated the carrots at 4.92 points, whereas the control group gave the carrots a rating of 4.25 points.

Mechanism

The psychological mechanism most often referred to in order to explain the effectiveness of the rule of unavailability is the theory of reactance described by Jack Brehm (1966). Reactance consists, inter alia, of a desire to regain one's freedom of choice should someone take this freedom away or restricts it. Brehm conducted his studies, inter alia, on two-year-old toddlers, who were allowed to enter a room where there were two identical teddy bears. However, one teddy bear was positioned behind a Plexiglas board, which made it difficult for the child to reach the toy. As it turned out, the higher the board was and the more difficult it was for the toddlers to cross, the more they wanted to play with the teddy bear they were separated from. Their reasoning was simple: it is more difficult to reach this teddy bear, so it must be more attractive.

Obviously, Brehm had only given a name to something that had been known for years. In "The Adventures of Tom Sawyer," first published in

1876 Mark Twain describes the painting of a fence. Aunt Polly tells Tom to paint the fence, which the boy does not want to do since to him this task seems like a punishment and drudgery. Yet, with his natural cunning, talent for acting and reactance (although it is unlikely for Tom Sawyer to know this term), he manages to convince his friends that painting the fence is an exceptionally responsible and remarkably attractive task available only to the chosen ones. After a while, he graciously allows the chosen friends to be granted the honor of painting the fence. Obviously, not for free, because in exchange Tom receives two marbles, a broken harmonica, a piece of blue glass from a bottle to look through, a spool of sewing thread, a key that did not open any lock, a piece of chalk, a glass decanter stopper, a lead soldier, two tadpoles, six percussion caps, a one-eyed cat, a brass door-knocker, a dog collar, a knife handle, four orange peels, and an old, broken window frame. All this is only because we strongly dislike situations where someone tells us that we cannot do something.

Technique # 48 *You will probably refuse, but...*
Idea

Perhaps you remember, dear reader, some incident from your childhood when someone dared you to do something and then told you that you probably wouldn't manage. For example, that you won't be able to climb to the top of a tree, walk on all fours to the nearest raspberry bush and back, or that you won't be able to come home after 10:00 p.m. for fear of your parents' wrath. Very likely, you immediately wanted to prove not only to your interlocutor but also to yourself that you would do just that. Now imagine that today, at a time when you are already an adult, someone asks you to do something, but at the same time says that they think you won't do it. Will it be like it was when you were a kid? Would you want to show that you are about to do it? If that were the case, then to get you to sign a petition, for example, one would have to say "I don't think you'll sign that," and to increase the likelihood that you'll agree to answer a few survey questions, one would have to say "I don't think you'll agree to spend five minutes answering that." But then again, you're not a child anymore, and I suppose such a thing wouldn't work on adults....

Research

The experiment was conducted by Nicolas Gueguen (2016) in two small towns in southern France just before Christmas. The experimenter (a 20-year-old male) was dressed in a red t-shirt with the logo of the Thousand and One Smiles organization and had an official badge pinned to his chest. He questioned passersby who, in his estimation, seemed to be between 30 and 55 years old. He first introduced himself as a volunteer of the said organization and then asked if he could speak with them for a moment. Where the passerby agreed to this, he would say: "Our organization helps children who have serious health problems and their families. We help them overcome some of the difficulties in their live." In the control condition, he immediately followed this up by asking for a donation for this purpose. He said: "I wonder if you could help us by making a donation." In the experimental conditions, on the other hand, the request was phrased slightly different: "You will probably refuse, but I wonder if you could help us by making a donation." It turned out that while in the control conditions exactly one in four participants donated, in the experimental conditions the percentage of those who did so was significantly higher, at 39.1%. Let us add that the average amounts of donations among those who gave money to the volunteer were similar in both conditions.

Mechanism

The "evoking freedom" technique we discussed previously is based on the participant being explicitly told that the choice of behavior is up to them, that they are the author of their decision, and that their freedom is in no way threatened. The "you will probably refuse, but" technique is more sophisticated. It suggests to the interlocutor that they will probably refuse to do something. The reactance theory mentioned earlier assumes (and a great deal of research concurs) that what is forbidden or made difficult immediately seems more attractive. (After all, that's why the biblical Eve in the Garden of Eden had a special craving for fruit from the forbidden tree, even though a whole bunch of other trees were growing around it, full of probably no less tasty fruit). Telling someone that they are unlikely to agree to a request can cause a similar reaction. It is then that its fulfillment becomes subjectively particularly attractive and desirable. (After all, that's why the biblical Eve in the Garden of Eden had a special craving for fruit from the forbidden tree, even though a whole bunch of other trees full of, presumably, no less tasty fruit grew next to it.) Telling someone that they are unlikely to agree to a request can cause a similar reaction. It is then that its fulfillment becomes subjectively particularly attractive and desirable for the subject. People's need for freedom is so strong that it sometimes leads to a restriction of freedom – people then do what others expect them to do.

Technique # 49 *The power of limited choice*
Idea

In the case of some of the social influence techniques described above in this section, the key factor was that the request was formulated in such a way as to emphasize the freedom of choice of the person being addressed. This freedom was either mentioned directly (this is the basis of the evoking freedom technique), or indirectly (this is the basis of the you will probably refuse, but… technique). There is no doubt that people usually want to have freedom and want to feel free. In psychology, it is commonly assumed that freedom consists of three aspects: the subject can do what is consistent with their preferences; the subject is not subject to external pressures; the subject has a choice between different options. Let us stop at this last point. The greater the choice, the greater the freedom. This is, after all, rather obvious. Let us note that from the perspective of social influence, it happens that we do not care that someone engages in a strictly and precisely defined behavior, but that they simply manifest some activity toward a certain goal. For example, we don't necessarily want someone to agree to participate in a psychological study on Friday, March 13 at 5:15 p.m., but to agree to participate in such a study at all. Similarly, it may be important to us that a bookstore customer buy any book, not that they necessarily reach for a particular title. We might think that in this type of case, the more choice someone has, the more likely they are to exhibit the behavior we expect: to participate in psychological research, to buy a book in a bookstore, etc., etc. Are we sure? It is precisely to answer such seemingly obvious questions that social psychologists do experimental research.

Research

Sheena Iyengar and Mark Lepper (2000) conducted their study at an upscale grocery store located in Menlo Park, California. The Draeger's Supermarket chosen for the study was characterized by an unusually wide range of different products (for example, there were 250 types of mustard and 75 types of olive oil to choose from). Customers frequently had the chance to participate in various promotional campaigns – they received free samples of various products, or they sampled them on the spot. Thus, the marketing action in this store (actually an experiment) conducted by the researchers could not arouse any surprise among customers. It was part and parcel of everyday business. The researchers set up a special Wilkin & Sons stand in the store, where they offered jams with exotic flavors. Customers could both sample these jams and buy them at a bargain price. Customers who approached the stand received a promotional coupon worth $1, which they could use to buy a jar of jam. All customers were also allowed to sample the different flavors of jam that were offered before a possible purchase. The researchers created two different experimental conditions. In the first, six different jams were offered to the shoppers. In the second, 18 more types of jam were added to the aforementioned 6 different types. Now the customer had an impressive 24 different Wilkin & Sons products to choose from. The study tested whether the difference in experimental conditions would be reflected in consumer behavior. It turned out, as expected, that when the choice was very rich more customers (60%) stopped at the jam stand than when it was limited to only six different flavors (40%). But did those who had a richer selection try more jams? No! The difference was so small that it could be considered random. In the high choice condition, an average of 1.5 different flavors were tried, and when the choice was limited, the ratio was 1.38. Most important from a social influence perspective, however, is the result on the number of jars of jam bought. It turned out that under conditions of limited choice (six different flavors of jam), 30% of customers made a purchase. You are probably curious, reader, how much this rate increased when there were four times as many different jams. Well, it was… ten times lower! This time, only 3% of the customers decided to buy!

Mechanism

The result showing that the abundance of different jams on the shelf made almost no one decide to buy any of them is very puzzling. After all, quadrupling the offer should result in higher sales, yet exactly the opposite turned out to be the case. Let us recall that the need for freedom (and thus the need to choose between available options) is one of the fundamental human needs. However, it turns out that if there are too many decision options, people may feel lost. Probably they try to make comparisons between the parameters of different options, and since one thing is better than another in some respects but worse in others, especially with a large number of options they feel lost. Of course, there are situations in which individuals feel they have to make a choice one way or the other (e.g., they're at a restaurant, they're hungry, and they have to choose something from the menu), but in others, they can simply decline the offer in question altogether. Exotic jam is probably not an essential purchase; nothing bad will happen if the customer does not bring it home today. Under such conditions, limiting the number of options available to the subject may make it easier to decide to choose one of them. "More" in this case therefore does not mean "better." On the contrary: it means "much worse."

Technique # 50 *Forbid, but carefully!*

Idea

Let's imagine that we want to teach people to stop engaging in some behavior, like putting bread in bags in the supermarket with their bare hands. We can do this in a variety of ways – either positive or negative. In other words, we can tell people to do something (use disposable gloves) or forbid them from doing something (don't grab bread with your bare hands). We can also express a prohibition/command (as in the examples above) or a descriptive norm in a positive version (e.g., "many customers use disposable gloves, this is for our common good") or in a negative version ("many customers grab bread with their bare hands – this is unhygienic"). As we can see, each of these messages is different in terms of length, and of the arguments that they invoke. What about their effectiveness?

Research

Robert Cialdini and colleagues (2006) decided to test the effectiveness of appealing to various social norms in the process of discouraging tourists from destroying nature. The study was of an experimental nature, performed under natural conditions in the Petrified Forest National Park in the US state of Arizona. This park, located in the Maw Desert on the border of Apache and Navajo Counties in northeastern Arizona, is famous for its numerous petrified specimens. Because the park encompasses about 200 square kilometers of land and nearly 800,000 visitors annually, it is not technologically possible to supervise the entire area and all visitors. At the same time, as the experience of the park administration has shown, some tourists like taking pieces of fossilized trees with them "as souvenirs." It does not take much geological or mathematical knowledge to grasp the serious consequences of this phenomenon: if only 1 in 20 visitors committed such an act, after a time the park could be closed due to a lack of exhibits. That's why Cialdini and colleagues (in consultation with park management, of course) decided to see if it would be possible to influence tourists' inclination to carry pieces of fossilized trees out of the park.

First, they wanted to test whether there would be differences between messages based on an injunctive norm and a descriptive norm. Secondly, their aim was to test the focus on the positive message and the focus on the negative message. Consequently, they created four types of messages.

1. Injunctive norm, positive message: "Please leave petrified wood in the park"
2. Injunctive norm, negative message: "Please don't remove the petrified wood from the park"
3. Descriptive norm, positive message: "The vast majority of past visitors have left the petrified wood in the park, preserving the natural state of the Petrified Forest"
4. Descriptive norm, negative message: "Many past visitors have removed the petrified wood from the park, changing the state of the Petrified Forest"

Obviously, the most serious problem was to measure the effectiveness of particular messages – the researchers wanted behaviors to be natural. At the same time, searching all tourists and seeing how much and what they took out would have been ineffective (in addition, it would have introduced a great deal of confusion and could have influenced tourists' behavior in a specific way). It was therefore decided to leave specially marked pieces of wood in specific locations. After each two-hour session, the experimenter's assistant walked the entire route, counted how many pieces of wood had disappeared, replaced the missing pieces, and the session resumed again (but with a different message).

A total of 2655 people participated in the study. It turned out that if the message was positive, it did not matter which norm was involved. For the descriptive norm, exactly 5% of the scattered pieces of trees disappeared, while for the prescriptive norm 5.1%. However, the situation was completely different when the message was negative in form. This time, fossil theft was particularly common for the descriptive norm (7.8% of tree pieces were lost) and particularly infrequent for the prescriptive norm (1.5%).

Mechanism

Note that although the experiment described above clearly showed that using a negative example in combination with a descriptive norm produces terrible results, these are precisely the messages that can often be found in many places (e.g., national parks). Cialdini and colleagues cite one emblematic example: "Your national heritage is being destroyed. Every year 14 tons of petrified wood are lost from the park, carried away in small pieces." They point out that although the overall number of tourists who commit theft is small (estimated at 5%), putting up such a sign essentially makes things worse by invoking a descriptive norm. Thus, a descriptive norm is not very well suited to discourage people from behaving in a certain way (especially if it is combined with a negative example of such behavior). Some people perceive such a message in terms of "since many people behave this way, it can't be particularly bad." We need to be very careful how we forbid things!

Technique # 51 *To be exceptional*

Idea

One day, one of the authors of this book was having lunch at a restaurant in the town of Agia Pelagia, on the Greek island of Crete. The lunch was, like all Greek cuisine, excellent: the octopus soft, the squid juicy, and the retsina (a white wine with characteristic resin) properly chilled. This taverna also, it could be seen, adhered to the wonderful Greek custom of adding a small treat to the bill – usually some fruit, like watermelon, but in this case, the owner, who doubled as the waiter, poured everyone a glass of aniseed-flavored ouzo. He was also extremely friendly in the manner most desirable for a waiter, that is, without a trace of humility. During the meal, a delicate bond of friendship was formed and expressed in observations about the Poles from the Greek perspective and about the Greeks from the Polish perspective, primarily about soccer. When the time came to pay the bill, as expected, a bottle of ouzo and shot glasses appeared on the table. But something was wrong: there were two people sitting at the table, but three glasses. After a while, everything became clear – the owner not only poured his guests a glass of ouzo, but also one for himself, which he drank with them! No other guests were treated this way! Need we add that the waiter received a very generous tip?

Research

One very simple way to observe the influence of how guests are treated on their tendency to return the favor in some form is to study the value of tips left by guests in restaurants. The way waiters and waitresses behave (whether they are polite, friendly, sincere, or suggest avoiding a certain dish) can immediately translate into a customer's gratitude, and in the most tangible and easily quantifiable way: in money. It must, of course, be kept in mind that cultural norms about tipping in different countries can differ wildly. In the US, tipping in a restaurant is culturally mandatory – if you don't tip, you can expect to be asked what was wrong with the meal. In contrast, in some restaurants in Japan, tipping can be considered offensive – the authors of this book, unaware of this rule, decided after enjoying a delicious meal at a small restaurant in Tsukiji, Tokyo, to add a tip to the amount due. What happened next felt to us a bit like the introduction to a kung-fu movie – the diner owner, shouting in Japanese, rejected the money, and it took an English-speaking guest to explain that we had offended an elderly lady. We were informed that she considers the preparation of a delicious meal as a matter of honor, and giving a tip for doing so suggests that she is in it for the money. Naturally, we immediately apologized to everyone present for this unfortunate incident. Not surprisingly, however, in a world where tipping is not considered an insult, psychologists have experimented by giving smaller and larger tips to see how the rules of social influence work. This is what researchers David B. Strohmetz, Bruce Rind, Reed Fisher, and Michael Lynn (2002) did. In their study, the waiter added a small present – in the first group, it was a chocolate mint – when handing the customer the bill. The customers who received the chocolate mint tipped 3% more on average than those in the control group, who did not receive any of the mint chocolate. Well, you might say, 3% isn't that much. Probably not, but in turn, we would point out that in many restaurants there are glass bowls of candy just sitting on a table by the door, not having any impact at all on tip sizes, so maybe handing out those candies differently is worth a shot after all? But let's go back to Strohmetz and colleagues – they didn't stop at one experimental group but added another in which the waiter served not one, but two chocolates with the bill. In this group, the customers, apparently positively surprised by two chocolates, left significantly larger tips – 14% higher than in the control group. However, Strohmetz designed yet a third variant in the experiment, crucial from the perspective of the technique described here. In this one, the waiter exhibited a level of generality similar to the one in the Greek taverna. He would walk up with the bill, leave one candy for each guest at the table, and then walk away. However, after taking a step, he would turn around, go back to the table, and with the words "just for you, because you were so nice…" he would add another piece of candy for each guest. In this group, of course, the tips were the highest, on average 23% higher than in the group without any candy.

Mechanism

What did the waiter at Agia Pelagia and the one in the experiment by Strohmetz and colleagues have in common? In short, they both gave some customers the feeling that they were absolutely unique. That normally customers get the standard – one chocolate, one glass of ouzo. But you, the waiters seemed to say, are special. You (and only you) will be treated differently. Note that the point is not in the amount of "goods" that we receive. After all, in one group, Strohmetz and colleagues' customers also got two chocolates, but their tips were almost half the size. Why was this so? Because the waiter didn't turn it into an exceptional situation; because they might have thought that nowadays (or even always) everyone just gets two chocolates. Similarly, diners at the restaurant in Agia Pelagia always got one glass of ouzo. But to some it was presented in a special way, emphasizing that they were exceptional in some aspect. And they were ready to reward that special treatment immediately.

Technique # 52 *The power of noun: Be a voter*
Idea

Imagine that you, as an ardent supporter of democracy, are pained by the low voter turnout in your country. Far too few people participate in elections. So you are happy when you see public awareness campaigns encouraging people to vote in elections. Whether it's for president, members of Congress, or mayor, people should take advantage of the fact that they can have a say in who governs them. It always annoys you when someone complains about a politician but didn't make the effort to elect another one. You're just out for a walk. Election day is coming up soon. You see a banner with the slogan "Vote!" You walk a few dozen yards and see another one. This time the sign reads "Be a voter!" Almost the same thing, but… "almost" sometimes makes a big difference. Which slogan will be more effective? Which will do more to encourage people to participate in the election?

Research

That was the very question Christopher Bryan, Gregory Walton, Todd Rogers, and Carol Dweck (2011) posed. In a series of experiments, they asked participants to complete a questionnaire about their voting habits. Half of them answered the question "How important is it for you to be a voter in the upcoming election?", while the rest answered the same question but phrased only slightly differently: "How important is it to you to vote in the upcoming election?" In the first experiment, they canvassed unregistered but eligible voters, asking them how interested they were in registering to vote. It turned out that the results differed in the two groups. Among those who read the noun "voter" in the questionnaire, 87.5% answered "very" or "extremely," while among those who read the verb "to vote" it was only 55.6%. More important than verbal declarations, however, are actual behaviors. Psychology is replete with evidence that people often declare one thing and do something very different. In this case, then, real voter turnout is more important than declarations. Bryan and colleagues conducted further experiments to explore this area. They found that among registered California voters in the 2008 presidential election, 95.5% of those who were asked how important it was for them "to be a voter" voted, while only 81.8% of those who were asked how important it was for them "to vote." An analogous pattern of results was recorded among registered New Jersey voters in the 2009 governor election. This time the respective proportions were 89.9% and 79%. The slogan "Be a voter" is a powerful slogan indeed!

Mechanism

People like to think of themselves as responsible individuals. The need to have and maintain one's positive self-image is among our most important psychological needs. "Being a voter" fits more directly into this positive self-image than does "voting in an election." Being a voter is an essential part of our personal identity; it is something permanent, like a character or personality trait. Simple "voting" doesn't give as clear a benefit to our self-image. That's why people prefer to feel like voters rather than to vote, even if, at first glance, they would seem to be the same thing.

Technique # 53 *Be a helper*

Idea

Encouraging people to participate in elections targets a very narrow range of activities. Could using a noun instead of a verb serving as a social influence technique in other areas too? Particularly those that can encompass a wide spectrum of human behavior? Giving people help certainly falls into the latter category. It would be a truism to say that there are many issues in the world that will not resolve themselves. Help is needed for refugees, the homeless, the sick, the hungry. Help is needed for abandoned children, for people affected by natural disasters. Help may also be needed for those who help themselves; for example, some people might not be able to cope emotionally with the trauma they face. We should help endangered species of animals living in their natural habitat and animals abandoned by their caretakers, waiting in shelters for a kind soul to take them home. How can we get people to commit their time, effort, or money? How can we convince them to help?

Research

This time the study conducted by Christopher Bryan, Allison Master, and Gregory Walton (2014) involved children, four and five-year-old preschoolers to be specific. In a specially arranged playroom, the preschoolers met an experimenter who said to them: "Some children choose to help. You could help when someone needs to pick things up, you could help when someone has a job to do, and you could help when somebody needs help," and then handed the child a very attractive toy and encouraged them to start playing. To other preschoolers, the experimenter said almost the same thing at the beginning of the meeting, specifically: "Some children choose to be a helper. You could be a helper when someone needs to pick things up, you could be a helper when someone has a job to do, and you could be a helper when somebody needs help." Of course, in these experimental conditions, the child was also given the same toy to play with. While the child was playing, the experimenter arranged four situations in which she allegedly needed some help (e.g., putting blocks back in their box or opening the lid of a storage bin, which she had trouble doing because both hands were occupied). Thus, for each child, it was possible to determine their willingness to help the experimenter on a scale from 0 (did not help once) to 4 (helped every time). It turned out that children who were addressed with a noun (be a helper) recorded an average engagement in helping of 3.18, while the children who were told almost the same thing but with a verb (help) instead of a noun had an average engagement rate of 2.47. It is amazing how a tiny difference in the wording used translates into a very large difference in people's behavior.

Mechanism

Obviously, we are dealing here with an analogous mechanism to the previous one. Interestingly, this study shows clearly that the need to construct a positive identity based on thinking about oneself in terms of permanent psychological characteristics applies even to young children. Both children and adults begin to exhibit positive behaviors when verbal categories that emphasize human subjectivity are used in conversations with them. A helper is someone who helps, someone who has these characteristics. Helping is not a matter of chance or coincidence, but is in a way a natural consequence of what a person is. It should be emphasized here that the abovementioned rule also applies to negative behaviors and traits. In this case, of course, the opposite is true: no one wants to feel like a selfish person, a thief, or a psychopath. Imagine that someone is trying to persuade you to become a liar. Would you agree? Almost certainly not! What if someone attempts to convince you to lie to someone else for a certain purpose? Now that is probably more likely. After all, everyone lies from time to time for some reason.

5

TIME AND SPACE

This chapter is devoted to social influence techniques related to distance. To be more precise, we focus here on both time-related and physical distance. As far as the former is concerned, we may, for example, when asking someone for a favor, stress the fact that a long time will have to pass before the provided help yields tangible results or that the goal we want to achieve is very close. We may also emphasize the fact that we need someone to act on our request immediately or, on the contrary, ask for something that will require the subject to take action in a few months. As far as physical distance is concerned, we may, for example, touch the arm of the person we are asking for a favor or refrain from doing so; we may also lean towards this person to direct our words into their ear or not. And if we choose to lean over toward this person's ear, we get to choose between the right and the left ear. This is how distance is used in social influence techniques studied by social psychologists. What is more, we suspect that many readers will be surprised by the effectiveness of many such techniques. Would you indeed be surprised? You will find out only after reading this section of the book.

DOI: 10.4324/9781003296638-6

Technique # 54 *Goal progress*
Idea

During high-mountain expeditions tragedies happen relatively often. Mountain climbers die from lack of strength to reach the base camp, from cold, from lack of oxygen. Symptomatically, deaths are especially frequent just before the ascent to the top of the mountain, or during the descent from the summit, reached with superhuman effort, to the nearest camp. Apparently, if the goal, i.e., reaching the summit, is close, the climbers' motivation is so strong that despite being terribly tired they go up, and at some point the rest of their strength evaporates. If, on the other hand, the summit is far away, it is easier for them to accept the fact that their goal will not be reached, to liquidate the camp and end the expedition. What happens in the highest mountains is of course an extreme situation. All of us, however, have experienced situations in which our motivation to reach a goal increased when the goal was close. And, interestingly, this holds true for activities as diverse as finishing your master's thesis, renovating your apartment, or digging up your garden in the spring. If so, then from a social influence perspective, the obvious question is whether this regularity can be used to get people to perform certain activities.

Research

Ran Kivetz, Oleg Urminsky, and Yuhuang Zheng (2006) conducted their experiment at a chain of coffee shops located on the sprawling East Coast Campus of Columbia University. People (mostly students, of course) who visited the café were given a special loyalty card to encourage them to visit again. Each time they drank a coffee, they earned a special stamp on that card. Of course, the first stamp was given at the very beginning, when paying for the coffee. If there are ten stamps on the card, the customer gets another coffee for free. The researchers measured the time that elapsed for each customer between the first and second visit to the coffee shop, the second and third, the third and fourth, etc., etc. They found that the closer coffee lovers got to their goal (i.e., getting the tenth stamp on their card, entitling them to another free coffee), the shorter the time between their visits to the coffee shop. The average difference between the first and second visits and the eighth and ninth visits was about 0.7 days, a time reduction of about 20%. The researchers also showed that people enrolled in the "loyalty program" described here were significantly more likely to come to the coffee shop than participants who were not given such cards. From a social influence perspective, then, the following simple directive can be formulated: If you want to motivate someone to do something, create conditions in which the goal to be achieved is within reach.

Mechanism

Many years ago, behavioral psychologists investigated the behavior of laboratory rats. They observed, among other things, that a rat that moves toward food accelerates markedly as it approaches the food (Hull, 1943). This turned out to be an exemplification of a broader regularity, which states that motivation increases as one approaches a goal. This, of course, does not only apply to rats, and the approach can be understood both as a reduction in physical or temporal distance and in terms of the proportion of work already done (vs. still needed). Then, when people perform an activity that involves them in some way, they also feel a specific unpleasant emotional tension that is only relieved when the activity is completed. That's why, while we might usually be happy to receive an unexpected visit from friends at our house, we won't feel joy when they drop by just before we finish something subjectively important to us. And it doesn't really matter whether we're finishing a long email, cleaning the windows, or knitting a sweater.

Technique # 55 Just one more
Idea

We work at a university that has five campuses in different Polish cities. Most of our research and teaching activities take place in Wroclaw, but we travel to the other four locations relatively often. We mostly travel by train, and at Polish train stations, it is relatively easy to meet various beggars and petty swindlers. On one occasion, a young girl approached one of us and in a shy voice (it's hard to tell if it was genuinely shy or shy to build the right impression) said: "I was robbed, I don't have enough money for a ticket home. People have already given me some, but I am still missing two zlotys, could you please give me just that much?" The girl's request was granted. (It was not, after all, a big expense – two zlotys is not much, more or less the equivalent of 50 cents). However, one can ask the question: would the girl have received two zlotys if she hadn't said that she was short of the ticket? This, of course, we cannot know. We can, however, trace the results of experiments that check what happens when people, while asking for something, at the same time emphasize that a given request has already been fulfilled by many people and they are missing just one more person who will agree to do it.

Research

Christopher Carpenter (2014) conducted an experiment in which individuals walking alone on a university campus were queried. (Those who were clearly in a hurry somewhere, wearing headphones on their ears, or talking on the phone were not approached). The experimenter introduced himself by name and explained: "I'm conducting a survey for my Communication Research Methods Class," after which he asked: "Would you be willing to take a ten-minute survey?" It turned out that 60 percent of people agreed. However, if after making this request the experimenter added "I just need one more person to take my survey," the rate rose to 80%. Carpenter also decided to see what would happen if the requester kept the subject informed of how far along he was. This time, the experimenter said his task was to complete 100 surveys. It turned out that 82.5% of the participants agreed to complete such a survey. However, if the experimenter added that in order to achieve the goal of 100 questionnaires, he only needed to interview one person, all participants agreed to take the survey! Let us add that the "just one more" technique did not work when the experimenter stated that his task was to complete five questionnaires. One might argue that in this case it is difficult to speak of getting any closer to the goal because, even if the experimenter has not yet surveyed anyone, he is still close to completing his work. After all, he is only five surveys short!

Mechanism

When introducing the mechanism underlying the goal progress technique presented previously, we talked about motivation that increases the closer the individual gets to the goal. Although many psychological studies show that people are primarily interested in pursuing their own personal interests and well-being, it is certainly not the case that we are completely indifferent to the fate of other people. In many cases, we "cheer" for other people, wishing them success in achieving various goals, as long as their actions do not diminish our own chances for success. They do not have to be our family members or our friends. When we find out that people who are complete strangers to us and who, for various reasons, arouse our sympathy, are striving to achieve a goal, we also wish them good luck. If we empathize with such a person – we "step into their shoes" – then we have a clear feeling that if the goal they want to achieve is close, they must particularly care about achieving it. We know this because we ourselves have experienced such states many times in our lives, in a myriad of situations. What if that person makes a request to us, saying that our fulfillment of that request will result in the aforementioned goal being achieved? (Note that at the same time this means that if we refuse to fulfill the request, it will not happen, or at least it will not happen now. The person will have to ask someone else, and it is not at all certain that this next person will agree.) In the situation when our agreement will mean the achievement of this person's goal, we will be especially inclined to help them; in fact, we will feel obliged to react in this way!

Technique # 56 *Ask for it well in advance*
Idea

Imagine that you are an undergraduate (perhaps you are one and there is no need to imagine anything) and your professor tells you the date of your exam. It will take place in four months, let's say on June 17th. What would you say if someone asked you how much you are willing to pay for postponing the exam by three days? Well this is an absurd question, is it not? What difference does it make if the exam is on June 17th or 20th? Obviously, you would not pay a single dollar or a single euro for such a change. And now, imagine that the date is June 16th. You are sitting at your desk and, with horror in your eyes, you are looking at a pile of books you have not had a peek at. How much would you be willing to pay to push back the date of the exam by four days? Still nothing? Do you still consider the question to be absurd? This rather trivial example clearly demonstrates that we take a different approach to events that are to happen in the near and in the distant future. When someone asks us to do something on the following day or the day after tomorrow, we often refuse, as we believe that we are very busy. And yet, when someone asks us for virtually the same favor but says that they would like us to do it in a few months' time, we are naive enough to believe that at this remote point in time, we will not be as busy with everyday responsibilities as we are right now. Consequently, we agree. The following section describes an experimental study regarding the differences in one's willingness to agree to perform a time-consuming task depending on whether this task is to be performed in the very near or in the distant future.

Research

Wojciech Bialaszek, together with a group of his associates (Bialaszek et al., 2022), conducted an experiment involving first-year psychology students. In October, i.e., at the beginning of the academic year, they were told that in order to get a credit, they would have to conduct a psychological study. They could choose between the following: a brief survey regarding cleaning up one's garden involving a few tens of individuals selected by the student or a time-consuming laboratory study designed to examine the feasibility of affecting the attitudes of people under parahypnosis. It should be noted that even the individuals conducing this experiment did not exactly know what parahypnosis was; it was simply meant to have a mysterious and attractive feel to it. (An earlier study demonstrated that the first of the above-mentioned two topics was considered boring but easy and the second one interesting but difficult). All of the students knew that there was a set one-week time frame for the performance of each of the activities; however, half of the students were told that they needed to begin their studies on the following day and the others were told that the studies would start in January (in a few months). Bialaszek and his associates were interested in learning how many of his students would choose the attractive but very time-consuming task in the close vs. distant start date conditions. It turned out that if the activity was to start on the following day, only less than 18% of the students chose the laboratory study and the rest decided to conduct the survey. However, if the study was scheduled to start in a few months' time, the option of a difficult but interesting task became much more popular. This time, as many as 44% of the students declared their interest in conducting the study designed to examine the feasibility of affecting the attitudes of people under parahypnosis.

Mechanism

As described above, it was difficult to persuade people into engaging in a time-consuming (even though very interesting, cognitively) activity if the work was to start on the following day. If, however, this task was scheduled to be worked on in the distant future, the number of individuals willing to take it on increased sharply. It should be noted that in both cases the task had to be performed within one week and required devoting the same amount of time. How can we interpret the results? One may assume that if we are asked to perform a task in the very near future (broadly defined "now"), we focus on whether we can do what is required of us. Therefore, we, first and foremost, take into consideration our current commitments and plans, which clash with the potential activity. But if the task we are asked to carry out is to be performed in the distant future, we are more likely to consider it in the "is it worth doing" category. At the same time, we fail to account for the fact that in the future, we may be overwhelmed with responsibilities that will make it extremely difficult for us to perform the task in question. For this reason, if you want to ask someone to engage in a difficult or time-consuming activity, formulate your request well in advance. Let the addressee of your request play the illusion, in their head, that even though they have no time on their hands at the moment, they will surely have lots of it in a few months' time…

Technique # 57 Good location – bad location

Idea

Anyone who moves to another city must learn his or her way around it. They must learn which sites are more or less interesting, which areas are safe or where it would be unreasonable to walk after dark with their wallet in their hand or their back pocket. We all know this very well – even cities that are exceptionally well managed have areas that should be avoided.

This is how "mental maps" of a city look from the perspective of one's safety – but can we think of a place (whether it is a village or a metropolis) from the perspective of how easy (or difficult) it is to make people act on our request? Can we assume that an identically formulated question will evoke a different response depending on where we ask it? Or in other words, are there places where people, when asked to act on a small request, will, by default, refuse to do so?

When we think of a main square in an average city – regardless of its location on the globe – we will most likely have similar images in our heads. Lots of people, lots of motion, many places where various services are rendered, perhaps small kiosks or larger restaurants. And one more typical element: people asking us for something. Sometimes they want us to make a donation, to answer questions from a survey, or simply to buy something (flowers or a balloon). When we enter similar spaces, we usually put on some sort of a coat or invisibility cloak, which should protect us from all forms of pestering. And in the event we are still approached by someone, we, by default, say "no" without even giving this person a chance to explain the details. But what would happen if the same request were formulated in a different location – for example in a park or at a location that we associate with care or charity. Would the outcome be different then?

Research

In one of our experiments, we checked how the same, standardized request is responded to in various locations within the same city (Grzyb & Dolinski, 2022). We created a fictional situation where a person gets robbed and has no money to buy a ticket back home. Each time, the request was formulated in the same manner: "Excuse me, I am sorry to bother you but I have a problem. My wallet and my documents got stolen and I do not have the money to get back home. I would rather not hitch a ride and I was wondering if you could buy me a ticket or give me some change so that I could buy one."

We intentionally chose a scenario that could happen anywhere – after all, our wallets can get stolen anywhere. At the same time, we picked four locations that were notably different from one another. The subjects could associate three of those locations with some form of care and concern for other people. The first one was a church (St. Joseph's Care Church at that), the second was a hospital and the third was a florist (a number of stalls offering flowers, to be precise). While the choice of the first two locations should not surprise anyone, the florist may require some additional explanation. According to research conducted in France, it was precisely the requests made near flower stalls that were granted particularly often. According to the authors of the research, this was caused by the connection between buying flowers and caring for another person – after all, we often purchase flowers for someone who is sick or close to us and we do so to express our good intentions and in memory of this person. The fourth location, which, according to our expectations, should not be associated with any form of care or concern, was the vicinity of a medium-sized discount store (the parking lot in front of the store entrance to be precise).

Needless to say, we were predominantly interested in the differences in the frequency of donations given to the "robbed person" depending on the location where the request was being made. Let us start with the overall results. In general, almost 54% of the subjects decided to help the person in need and gave her (or him, as the experimenters switched in order to eliminate the effect the sex of the person asking for money might have had on the results of the experiment) small amounts for the ticket back home. Yet, the results were different in all four of the locations. People were most willing to help when they were asked to do so near the church (78%). The request was slightly less effective in the vicinity of the hospital (72%) and still less effective near the flower stalls (56%). Yet the most surprising outcome was observed near the discount store – less than 10% of the subjects decided to donate their money in this location!

Mechanism

What is it about the vicinity of a discount store that makes us so distrustful of requests made at this location? It seems that the low outcome may be due to the fact that we frequently meet people asking for change in specific locations – by railway stations, main city squares as well as discount stores or supermarkets. It is there that we often meet people asking for various things – mainly small amounts of money. It could be the case that if we meet somebody asking us for change in certain locations, we tend to believe that this person is trying to wangle cash out of us and we are not really interested in the reasoning behind this person's request. Perhaps we will not even give this person a chance to finish his or her sentence, we will simply wave our hand in a gesture resembling an attempt to chase away a pesky fly and keep on walking. Therefore, it is not just the arguments we present or the story we want to share, the person we ask for help that determines the success of our request. Even if we are perfectly prepared, choose the most suitable words and smile in the most elegant way, we may still fail if we choose a bad location. It may also be the other way around: the same request, only made in another location of the same city, may prove to be extremely effective.

Technique # 58 *Have a face-to-face meeting*
Idea

Do you have a favor to ask but you are not certain whether you will receive a positive reply? Surely, you find yourself in a similar situation relatively often; perhaps you are going through it at the moment. There are many ways in which you can formulate your request. You can use traditional mail, sometimes scornfully dubbed snail-mail, in contrast to the lightning-fast electronic mail, which you can also opt for. You can connect via Skype to discuss your business or you can simply call and present your problem in the course of a telephone conversation. Lastly, you can simply have a face-to-face meeting with the decision maker regarding your matter. Sending an e-mail would be the simplest solution. You just type your message at your convenience and hit enter to send it instantly. A telephone or a Skype connection requires the other person to be available at the given moment. Whereas using traditional mail is time-consuming. You need to go to the post office, purchase an envelope and a postage stamp, and then send your letter. A direct conversation also requires time. Not only that, but you need to make an appointment at a specific time and location with the other person, and this can be tough. The difficulty of using each of the above-mentioned methods is one of the parameters we are interested in. Another, much more important one is the effectiveness of particular channels. When do our chances for getting things done increase and when do they decrease?

Research

Many years ago, we examined various ways of urging people spending their holidays at a resort to participate in a 15-minute long psychological study (Dolinski, 2016). Some of these people we visited personally by knocking on the door of their hotel rooms, some we called, while some received a special invitation, which we slid through the gap underneath the door of their rooms. What was the recruitment success rate? Well, it depended heavily on the method we used to invite our subjects. As many as 56% of those individuals whom we visited personally to ask to participate in our study arrived at the specified time. Out of those who were invited by telephone, 28% came to participate in the study. The written invitation turned out to be the least effective (by a large margin). Only 6% of those recruited through a written invitation showed up. It should be added that the experiment was conducted at a time when the Internet was not common. Therefore, we do not know how effective an invitation sent via e-mail or an instant messenger would be.

Mechanism

The results of the above-mentioned experiment demonstrated that people were most willing to agree to our request (i.e., to take part in a psychological study) when they were asked face-to-face, and they were least willing in the case of a one-way contact in the form of a written invitation. Why is that so? After all, in all three cases, the request was exactly the same! It appears that the more direct the contact with the person asking for something, the more difficult it is to turn the request down. It is particularly difficult to refuse when someone is maintaining eye contact with us and if we can (and have to) see their face as well as their mimic expression of letdown and disappointment they are experiencing. It is slightly easier to refuse over a telephone. In this case, we cannot see the face of our interlocutor. Still, we can hear their voice and we know all too well that if we say, "No," we will hear or at least detect the sound of disappointment in their voice. For this reason, it is also relatively difficult to turn down a request made by another person in the course of a telephone conversation. At the same time, it is significantly easier if we have no contact with the person making the request at the moment it is being communicated to us.

In such conditions, refusal is an abstract concept and we would have to picture the person asking us for something being worried by our negative decision. Even though said experiment did not test the effectiveness of the use of the Internet, it seems that we could apply similar patterns to the World Wide Web. Therefore, if you really want someone to grant your request, try to arrange a face-to-face meeting. And if you are the decision maker and you do not feel like acting on the request but you feel that you might break under direct pressure, make sure the face-to-face meeting never takes place. Say: "E-mail me the details, I will look into it…"

Technique # 59 *Solicitation call technique*
Idea

Various scientific, social, and business entities, as well as political parties, try to learn people's opinions on all sorts of issues. Researchers, depending on the field of science they represent, want, e.g., to know how many cups of coffee people have each day, what they know about the ancient culture, or if they plan on having children in the near or more distant future. Social organizations may be interested in learning how people feel about refugees or if they are willing to donate their bone marrow. Businessmen want to know people's opinions about their products or if they would be willing to purchase goods that have not been marketed yet. Political parties want to know how many supporters they have, which parts of their manifesto voters feel enthusiastic about and which parts they dislike. The basic method for collecting similar data is to send (via traditional mail back in the day, today – via e-mail) a questionnaire to respondents. The problem is that few of the respondents fill out such questionnaires. It is not only about the fact that you need to send a lot of questionnaires (a small percentage of which will be completed) but mainly about the fact that since only a small percentage of people reply to the questions included in the questionnaire, these may be specific individuals in the sense that they may hold views and represent attitudes that are different from the majority of the society. For example, if the questionnaire pertains to an election manifesto of a political party, its avid supporters may be more than willing to fill it out but other people may ignore it. Meanwhile, political party activists want to learn the opinion of not just their hardcore followers.

What can be done to increase the willingness of a larger group of people to fill out a questionnaire they received?

Research

Chris Allen, Charles Schewe, and Gosta Wijk (1980) conducted studies on consumers' feeling of alienation from the marketplace and their dispositions toward the global energy problem. Under this project, they intended to ask a representative group of adult residents of Malmo, one of the biggest cities in Sweden, to fill out a questionnaire. A few hundred individuals received the questionnaire by mail (via traditional mail, as the Internet was not common at the time the study was being conducted) with a kind request to fill it out and send it back to the address of the entity behind the study. The questionnaire was rather lengthy (it consisted of 92 questions) and pertained predominantly to household energy consumption. It turned out that a completed questionnaire was sent back my merely 22.2% of the subjects. The approach was different in the case of other respondents. Instead of just sending them the questionnaire, the researchers called them and said that they had been randomly selected to participate in a survey; they were told that the questionnaire included 92 questions concerning predominantly household energy consumption and were asked if they would agree to complete it. The majority of the callees (82%) agreed to do so. The researchers sent them the questionnaire and achieved a very high level of effectiveness in this group. With this method, 69.4% of the respondents sent back their completed questionnaires.

From our perspective, i.e., determining the actual effectiveness of the approach consisting first of asking the respondents over the telephone if they would agree to fill out the questionnaire, it would be more appropriate to use the index based on the percentage of people who completed their questionnaires from among all the subjects who were asked to do so (instead of taking into account only those who agreed in the course of a telephone conversation). Based on the data provided by the authors, we determined this index to be approx. 57%. It is apparently lower than the value indicated in the scientific paper discussed herein, but it is still significantly higher than the value recorded in the standard conditions.

Mechanism

As demonstrated above, calling respondents in advance to tell them that they would be asked to fill out a questionnaire generated a remarkably strong effect. More than twice as many respondents completed the rather lengthy questionnaire they received. How does such a simple trick work so well? It appears that there are two patterns at play, which we have already discussed in this book. In the case of the previously described technique, we presented data that illustrates that the probability of having a request granted might depend on whether this request is formulated in face-to-face conditions, during a telephone conversation, or in a letter. Therefore, we already know that it is significantly more difficult to turn down a request formulated by someone with whom we are interacting directly (even if over a telephone) than someone who has written us a letter. Consequently, if people receive a request to fill out a questionnaire by post (and today – more frequently via e-mail), they choose not to comply with this request simply because it is psychologically easy to ignore it. However, it is a different story if they hear a similar request over the telephone. They usually agree to grant the request in such conditions, as it is psychologically more difficult to say, "No." And this is where the second mechanism, i.e., the rule of consequence, comes into play. If someone has already agreed to something in the course of a telephone conversation, they later feel obligated to deliver on their earlier promise.

Technique # 60 *Gaze*

Idea

Why are convicts blindfolded when they go before a firing squad? Is it a humanitarian gesture so that they can die in a more dignified manner? Or perhaps it is not supposed to help the convict but the soldiers forming the firing squad, who have to shoot the condemned? If debating what is easier and what is harder in this context makes any sense at all, it is harder to shoot a person who is looking in our eyes than someone who has been blindfolded. Obviously, an execution is an extreme example but I suppose everyone has, on many occasions and in everyday situations, experienced the magic power of a stare of another person looking straight into our eyes. Let us imagine that a hungry, ragged child holds out their hand asking us for alms. Half a second later, we can see the child's sad eyes looking at us with hope. As long as all we see is a dirty hand held out towards us, we can distance ourselves from this child but when we see those eyes looking at us, we reach into our pocket for change so that the child can get some food. But what if we are asked for help by a friend of ours? To be honest, we do not really feel like helping them, we have already made plans for the afternoon. Yet, it is very difficult to look into this person's eyes and say, "No." If looking in someone's eyes is an effective social influence technique, this must be the easiest one to apply. But is it? Does it really work? Let us take a closer look at some empirical studies.

Research

Chris Kleinke and David Singer (1979) decided to see if looking in the eyes of people whom we want to give a flyer increased their willingness to take it. The experiment was conducted by two women and two men. Each of these persons approached 150 women and 150 men who appeared to be adults and who were walking alone down the sidewalk. It should be noted that flyers were only offered to those individuals, who had at least one of their hands free (i.e., they were not holding briefcases, bags, or other items in both of their hands). The design of the experiment was rather simple. One-third of the subjects were addressed with conciliatory tone: "Excuse me. Would you like one?" One-third was addressed with demanding tone: "Take one!" The remaining one-third of subjects were not addressed at all. In each of these three conditions, in half of the cases, the experimenters looked right into the eyes of the passer-by, while in the remaining cases, the experimenters did not look into the subjects' eyes. It turned out that the fact of looking into the pedestrians' eyes was relevant to the number of flyers people agreed to take. While in the demanding tone conditions the differences were minor (81% of the passers-by took the flyer when the experimenter was looking in their eyes and 76.5% when they were not), in the conciliatory tone conditions the differences were significantly more distinct (the flyer was accepted by 79.5% of the pedestrians if the experimenter was looking in their eyes and by 70.5% if they were not). However, the most marked differences were observed when the person handing out flyers did not say anything. In such conditions, almost all subjects (84.5%) took the flyer when the experimenter was looking in their face, and only 62% of the subjects when the experimenter was not.

Mechanism

Phoebe Ellsworth and Ellen Langer (1976) assume that when we realize that someone is looking at us (particularly looking in our eyes), we experience an increase in emotional arousal. In an interpersonal situation, this is a signal that tells us that we have to act accordingly. But what type of conduct is considered interpersonally correct? Which standards apply in such situations? If we are not confronting a hostile individual, we feel that we should act in a friendly manner. Therefore, we comply with the request of another person, we try to meet their expectations or help them. Additionally, as demonstrated by numerous psychological studies, we perceive the people we meet as nicer and more likable if they look at us than if they do not. In the above-described study, there was only a brief interaction between the flyer distributor and pedestrians, and yet this was enough to make the look in the pedestrians' eyes an important factor. Other experimental studies have demonstrated that looking into the eyes of a partner in an interaction is helpful when we ask this person for a donation to charity (both more people decide to put some of their money into the moneybox and the donation amounts are higher), if we want to ask someone for help because we sprained our ankle while jogging and even if we are hitchhikers trying to get a ride. Thus, a word of advice to you, dear Reader, if you have an important request to make and you are afraid that you may be denied, try to make an appointment with the person in charge and try to look into this person's eyes during your meeting. And if you, dear Reader, are the person in charge and you do not want to yield to a request that you know is going to be made, try to avoid a face-to-face meeting and suggest writing an e-mail instead. It is so much easier to type "no" on our keyboard than to say "no" while looking in someone's eyes.

Technique # 61 Touch

Idea

Even though we do not think about it most of the time, we live in a social distance culture. Particularly when it comes to contacts with people we do not know, we try to keep a certain distance. Obviously, there are exceptional situations (a crowded elevator or a subway car) where keeping a social distance is not possible but whenever it is possible, we know that our face should not be too close to another person's face and that our hands should not be touching another person's body. Making sure we keep this distance is a social norm we try to observe. Imagine that you are walking down a sidewalk and suddenly someone you have never met before asks you to take a letter from them (an addressed letter with a postage stamp on it) and put it in a mailbox. This person cannot do it themselves as they are getting on a bus in a short while, and they would like for the envelope to have a stamp from the local post office. Would you agree? Perhaps yes, perhaps no. Let us say that you might. And now imagine that this person, while holding the letter in their hand and asking you for the favor, is touching your forearm or your shoulder with their hand. By doing so, this person has violated the above-mentioned social distance norm. What do you think, would this gesture decrease or increase the probability of you agreeing to grant the request? If you are a typical person (particularly a woman), you probably think that this minor fact would most likely discourage, rather than encourage, you from doing what is being asked of you. But what are the facts? There are numerous studies that prove the opposite.

Research

David Smith, Joseph Gier, and Frank Willis (1982) conducted their studies in a large supermarket. They wanted to see what effect touching a male or female customers' forearm has on their consumer behavior. To be more precise, the experiment was designed to check if the touch would make the customers more willing to try a slice of pizza. The experimenter (sometimes a woman, sometimes a man) approached subjects who appeared to be adults shopping alone and uttered the following phrase: "Hello, would you like to try a free sample of pizza? It's a new product in this area and it's made with all-natural ingredients." While uttering the above phrase, the experimenter always smiled and, at the same time, gently touched the forearm of half of the customers encouraged this way to try the pizza. If the customer decided to try the product, the experimenter would point to the nearby freezer and tell the customer that this is where the new product could be purchased. It turned out that from among those persons who were gently touched on their forearm, as many as 79% decided to try the new pizza. Among the customers who were not touched, the figure was only 51%. So what were the results as far as buying the product is concerned? Here, the positive effect of the touch was even more evident. While in the standard conditions (i.e., without the touch) 19% of the subjects decided to make the purchase, the figure was almost twice as high (37%) among those subjects who were touched on their forearm.

Mechanism

Why are people who are gently touched on their shoulder or their forearm more willing to do what is asked of them? Let us start our explanation from the perspective we have already addressed in several sections of this book. In the majority of real-life situations, we respond in a rather automatic and habitual manner, which replicates behavior patterns we have acquired in the past. Throughout their life, an average person has been touched almost exclusively by people close to them: members of their family, friends, or lovers. They have not been touched by strangers. And now, when someone they do not know (e.g., a staff member at a supermarket), during a conventional, brief conversation, touches them on their shoulder or their forearm, they automatically start to respond in the manner typical of interactions with people they know, members of their family or people they love. And, after all, when such persons ask something of them or offer something, they usually agree. And thus, they also say "yes" in this case. Not all social influence researchers agree with the above interpretation. The alternative explanation is also based on the assumption that people often act in a habitual and automatic manner and that certain gestures or words trigger previously acquired behavior patterns but this time, we are referring to different types of behavior. Parents touch a child on their shoulder when they try to explain something and tell the child to change their behavior, a boss touches a subordinate when they tell them to be more careful and pay more attention. A person enjoying a higher status touches a person with a lower status when they give orders or instructions. Then, the person with the lower status conforms and follows the instructions, advice, or suggestions. So now, in a completely different context, if someone touches us, we act, to some degree, as if this person were our superior and has the right to direct our actions.

Technique # 62 *Speak into the right ear*

Idea

We know that most of our body parts come in pairs. We have two arms, two legs, two eyes, two ears, etc. We also know that in most cases, people are "right-side oriented," i.e., their right limbs are dominant or their right eye is dominant. This is easily verifiable: ask someone (e.g., your child) to kick a ball, throw you a block, or look through a keyhole. In most cases, the person will perform these actions using their dominant body parts (i.e., most likely right-hand side). If this is not the case, e.g., if the person kicks the ball with their left foot but throws the block with their right hand, we will be facing a higher risk of the so-called crossed laterality. This term is used to refer to people whose limb dominance is not uniformly right- or left-sided, and such a disorder may be related to dyslexia, problems with concentration, and, sometimes, learning difficulties. Yet, can the use of a right- or left-side organ alone be relevant from the perspective of the effectiveness of exerting influence on another person? Can a decision to use our left or right hand to give someone a small gift or to utter a request for a favor into someone's right or left ear have an effect on the effectiveness of our actions?

Research

Danielle Marzoli and Luca Tommasi (2009), Italian scientists, conducted studies related to directing requests to a particular ear. The researchers ventured a very interesting project. As scientists focused on the study of a strictly physiological aspect of human existence (to be precise, on the asymmetry of the cerebral hemispheres), they decided to illustrate this phenomenon not with the typical tool, i.e., functional magnetic resonance imaging carried out in strictly-controlled laboratory conditions, but with a field experiment conducted in real-world conditions. They devised a series of innovative experiments through which they intended to investigate the reactions of subjects to a request (e.g., for a cigarette) directed to their ears. As their focus was on the above-mentioned asymmetry of the cerebral hemispheres, the researchers formulated a hypothesis according to which a request uttered to somebody's right ear would be more effective than the same request directed to somebody's left ear. Yet, the researchers faced a methodologically interesting problem, namely: how to plan the experiment in such a manner as to make sure the request is directed to a particular ear of the recipient in a natural way, i.e., without causing puzzlement on the part of the subject? Marzoli and Tommasi decided to conduct their experiment in noisy locations where the only way to communicate effectively is to speak directly to the other person's ear: at discos. A plan was made to conduct a series of experiments. In one of them, the assistant of the experimenters approached randomly-selected individuals (88 women and 88 men) and, while randomly assigning them to particular experimental conditions, asked them for a cigarette by directing her request to their right or their left ear. The results (unsurprisingly) demonstrated that the girl was given a cigarette more frequently by men than by women. More interestingly, a distinctive "ear effect" was observed: the assistant's request was granted significantly more often when directed to the interlocutor's right ear. The effect was statistically significant both in the case of male and female subjects. When women were asked for a cigarette, the request was granted in 31.8% of the cases if directed to the right ear, and in 13.6% of the cases if directed to the left ear; the figures were 45.4% and 25% for men, respectively.

Mechanism

For quite some time, researchers dealing with verbal communication have been pointing to the dominance of the right ear. This means that stimuli coming from the right ear are directed into the left cerebral hemisphere of the brain as it controls the right side of the body. Yet, due to methodological reasons, the results demonstrating this phenomenon came mainly from laboratory experiments conducted in strictly-controlled environments. Such experiments enable scientists to precisely establish the connection between the variables, but at the same time they are very often "unworldly," e.g., they use procedures that are very rare or unprecedented in real-world conditions. The studies conducted by Marzoli and Tommasi demonstrated that dominance on the right side of our body and the left cerebral hemisphere of the brain is also relevant from the perspective of our ordinary life and the choices we make on daily basis. Therefore, if we want to be more effective in our requests, we should speak into our interlocutor's right ear.

Technique # 63 *Position items on the right-hand side*

Idea

Imagine that you are to choose a candle to decorate your tabletop. You go to a housewares store or to your local supermarket. Perhaps there is a specialized store with decorative products in your neighborhood. Regardless of which store you choose, you will most likely find at least a few candles of the right shape, color, and size to choose from. After some time, you will pick one of them. What would happen if someone asked you why you chose that particular candle? Most likely, you would find some justification. Perhaps you would say that this candle offered a more pleasant scent compared to the others, or perhaps it was the right shade to match the tablecloth you usually use. Or maybe some other, more subtle, factors played a role here. However, you would be surprised if you were told that all of the above-mentioned reasons were essentially irrelevant and that you are using them to make your choice appear rational. In actuality, the scent of the candle or the shade of blue it offers did not really matter. What mattered was its position on the shelf.

Research

Research on the role of the position of a product's display and customers' willingness to choose it has been conducted by Timothy de Camp Wilson and Richard E. Nisbett (1978). Their experiment took place in a large bargain store located in a shopping mall. The authors put up a large sign that read: "Institute for Social Research – Consumer Evaluation Survey – Which is the Best Quality?" and then put four pairs of tights on a rack. The tights were a cinnamon color and were hanging from small hangers so that the consumers could see them from a distance of approximately one meter. Once all the tights had been thoroughly visually examined, the experimenter asked female consumers (as women constituted the vast majority of the subjects) which tights they thought were of the best quality. Upon receiving an answer, the experimenter also asked why they thought so.

The trick used in the experiment was that all tights were exactly the same: the same brand, model, and color. And yet almost none of the subjects (except for 2 out of the 52 subjects) noticed that. The participants in the experiment justified their choice by pointing to the splicing, the shape, or the elasticity of a particular pair, and what they failed to notice was the actual reason, i.e., the positioning of the given pair of tights in the row. As it turned out, the more the given pair of tights was positioned to the right side of the rack, the more inclined the female subjects were to choose this pair. When the tights were positioned to the extreme left side, they were chosen by only 12% of the subjects, the pair positioned as the second one from the left-hand side was chosen by 17%, the pair positioned as the second from the right was chosen by 31%, and the pair to the extreme right side of the rack was chosen by 40%. Therefore, it is not the splicing, elasticity, or fancy gusset of the tights but their position on a shelf or a rack that plays the key role in affecting our choice.

Mechanism

In their description of the observed effect, the authors of the experiment were unusually honest in stating that they were not exactly able to explain the rationale behind it (it should be noted that admitting one's inability to provide an adequate interpretation of outcomes is not particularly common among scientists). Yet they proposed certain possibilities in terms of the reasons behind the choices made by their subjects. They suggested that it is almost certain that the subjects evaluated the tights from left to right (especially since they were labeled with letters from A to D). As the subjects were evaluating the first three pairs and they were moving to the fourth one (labeled as D), they had most likely noticed a certain aspect (or aspects) they did not like in the already examined pairs. They might have had problems with assigning these aspects to a particular pair of tights, though. As they were about to evaluate the fourth and final pair, the subjects most likely found no defects in it and since they remembered that there was something wrong about one of the first three pairs, they decided to point to the final (the fourth, labeled as D) pair as the best one. It was simply the easiest and the most optimal choice. As Wilson and Nisbett put it, regardless of what actually causes this effect to occur, it is undoubtedly effective. Obviously, this is not always the case: if we ask subjects to compare items that differ significantly in terms of their quality, positioning a low-quality product on the right will not make the subjects choose it. However, if the examined products are similar in many respects, it is very probable that the one positioned on the right-hand side will be chosen.

6

SELF AND SOCIAL SELF

The desire to achieve (and then sustain) a positive self-assessment is one of the most important sources of motivation for people. Believing that we are valuable as individuals is not only fundamental for our well-being and good mental health but it also allows us to develop, stay positive as to our chances for achieving goals in our life and even reduce our existential fear of death. Apart from our private self-assessments, we also want other people to think highly of us. Therefore, we want to make a good impression. Depending on the particular situational context, we want to be perceived as competent, responsible, likable, or altruistic. We also belong to various social groups – one's nation, their community, the population of the city where one lives in or student body of the university one attends. The so-called social self – the feeling of community with other people – is more than just a crucial element of people's knowledge of themselves. It also represents our belief that together with a particular group of people, we are, in some way, unique and different from others, i.e., those who do not belong to the "us" group. In this section, we present social influence

DOI: 10.4324/9781003296638-7

techniques that make use of the above-mentioned desires and motivations in humans.

Technique # 64 *Labeling*

Idea

The two techniques described in the chapter *Agency and Freedom* concerned situations that did not explicitly discuss what a person was like. "Be a voter" (see: technique # 53) is a plea to engage in certain behaviors in the future. "Be a helper" (see: technique # 54) is a narrative about what children in general are like and how they behave. But in real-life situations, people don't just hear from others what they are supposed to be, but what they are. Psychologists would say that people are given labels. One person says to another, "you have a great sense of humor" someone else says, "you can always be counted on," or someone learns from a friend, "you're a jerk and a loser." Will such messages also help construct people's self-knowledge (respectively: I have an excellent sense of humor, I am helpful and responsible, I am uncultured)? And more importantly from the perspective of interest to us here: will it be followed by behaviors that are consistent with this formed (or at least reinforced) self-image?

Research

Angelo Strenta and William DeJong (1981) invited students into a laboratory and asked them to complete a survey testing certain personality traits. The 49 questions were displayed sequentially on a computer screen. After answering the last question, participants were given feedback about themselves. The experiment was designed so that regardless of the answers given, some people were told that the answers given indicated that they were kind and thoughtful; some were told that they indicated high intelligence on the part of the person completing the questionnaire; others were told that the results would be available after a week and that one of the traits measured by the questionnaire was kindness to others. There was also a group of people who were merely thanked for their participation in the study and not given any information. Regardless of which group the participant was in, as they left the lab, they witnessed a certain scene that, seemingly random, was in fact carefully orchestrated by the researchers. A large stack of five hundred index cards was dropped by a person walking down the hallway. The idea was to see if participants would spontaneously pick up the cards from the floor and how engaged they would be (this was determined by measuring the time spent helping and counting the number of cards picked up). It turned out that 70% of those who had just learned about themselves that they were kind and thoughtful bent down to pick up the cards scattered on the floor. This was higher than the percentage helping in conditions where people learned nothing about themselves (50%). In contrast, those who had just learned that they were very intelligent (36%) were particularly unlikely to engage in helping. People given the altruist label also spent more time on average helping, and they picked up more cards off the floor.

Mechanism

Beliefs about oneself are an important premise for people to make choices and decisions. If I am tone deaf, I shouldn't study conducting; if I am fluent in several languages, I can apply for a job as a translator at international conferences. The effect of labeling consists in telling people what they are like. If this information seems credible, they are inclined to believe it. And if they do, they will begin to behave in a manner consistent with the knowledge they have just received about themselves. Since I am learning that I am altruistic, when I see a person in need of help, I engage in providing it. Jeśli jesteś rodzicem, to być może zdarzyła ci się próba zawstydzenia twojego dziecka. If you are a parent, you may have tried to shame your child. Seeing a mess in their room, you may have said something like "you're terribly messy," hoping, of course, that your child will demonstrate that you are wrong. It didn't help? Or worse yet, did the mess in the room grow even bigger? You probably already know why....

Technique # 65 *Self-labeling*

Idea

If someone tells you "you're an idiot," will you start acting like one? Of course not! You will recognize that the person who says this is not credible and is only insulting you because he doesn't like you and wants to make you feel bad. The credibility of the source of information is therefore one of the key factors for the effectiveness of the labeling technique discussed above. Note that the vast majority of people consider themselves to be the best experts on themselves. This should come as no surprise: who knows us better than we know ourselves? The self-labeling technique takes advantage of the fact that people consider knowledge of themselves to be authoritative. If we ask people whether they are morally upright, whether they have sensible political views, or whether they think about getting value for money when shopping, the answer will almost certainly be yes. Let us note, then, that whereas in the case of the labeling technique, people learned from others what they are supposed to be like, in the case of the self-labeling technique, people say it themselves when responding to the question. In addition, they say it with conviction!

Research

In a simple but ingenious experiment, San Bolkan and Peter Andersen (2009) asked participants if they considered themselves helpful people. Each of them answered this question in the affirmative! After hearing this answer, the experimenters asked if they would agree to participate in a 30-minute survey. They would not receive any gratification for doing so but would help the researchers collect scientific data. It turned out that 77% of people asked in this way agreed to help. In the control condition, in which people were asked without the aforementioned initial question to take part in a survey and informed that it would take 30 minutes, more than twice as many people agreed (29% to be exact). In another experiment, some participants were asked the following question: "Do you consider yourself to be somebody who is adventurous and likes to try new things?", while others were not asked this question. The participants were then allowed to provide their email addresses to receive detailed information about a soft drink being marketed. Of those who were asked the aforementioned question, 75% provided an email address, compared to only 33% of those who were simply asked for their address. If you yourself respond that you are helpful, then you will help; if you yourself answer that you are open to new experiences, you will behave in a manner intended to demonstrate that fact! As we can see, this extremely simple social influence technique, which is based on asking people simple, not to say trivial, questions is in fact very effective!

Mechanism

As in the case of the previously discussed techniques, the key here is the appearance of information about oneself in the individual's conscious- ness. The fact that in the case of the self-labeling technique the in- dividuals themselves are the authors of this information boosts its subjective credibility on the one hand, while on the other hand, it produces in them a particularly strong obligation to engage in behaviors consistent with this self-image. Of course, this technique takes advantage of the fact that people like to respond to certain types of information so as to build or strengthen their positive self-image. If we consider how many of the people we know can actually be described as helpful, we certainly wouldn't say "all of them." And yet, in the experiment de- scribed above, it turned out that all the people who were asked con- sidered themselves to be helpful. It could be said that, sometimes, what people are really like is less important than what they think about themselves.

Technique # 66 *Expert snare*

Idea

If you are an expert in some field, you should know everything (or at least almost everything) about it. What happens if a conversation is about that particular area of expertise, but you have absolutely no idea what your interlocutors are on about? Of course, you can say "I don't know," but then it may turn out that you aren't an expert. It's probably better to remain silent, nodding slightly and giving off the air of someone lost in thought. You're not lying to anyone, and people are convinced that you know what is being discussed. You are, after all, an expert. But sometimes it's impossible to stay silent. You have to react in some way. And this is the essence of a very specific social influence technique.

Research

Anthony Pratkanis and Yigal Uriel (2011) conducted their experiment in the beautiful confines of the beaches of Santa Cruz and Santa Monica, California. Surfers coming out of the water with a board under their arm were asked to sign a petition. The petition was about introducing a rule that would require beginning surfers to use only boards that are painted yellow and bear purple polka dots. Four signatures were already on the petition. Before it was presented to the surfers to sign, in some cases they were given a compliment, hearing that they were obviously great surfers and knew everything there is to know about surfing. It turned out those who heard this compliment from their interlocutor signed the extremely nonsensical petition more than twice as often (46.7%) than those who did not (20%). Perhaps the compliment made them positively disposed toward the person asking for their signature, which explains why they behaved as they did? To test this idea, the experimenters introduced one more condition into the study design. This time, the request to sign the petition was preceded by a compliment referring to the surfer's suit and asking where a suit like that could be bought. It turned out that under these conditions, only 20% of those approached agreed to sign the petition. Thus, we see that the tendency to sign a completely nonsensical petition was not a product of being complimented, but was rather a consequence of the interlocutor treating the surfer as an expert in the area related to the request. To complete the picture, the surfers who were treated as experts were far less likely to ask any questions about whether the new rules made sense. They were also less likely to express any doubts.

Mechanism

The original and creative "expert snare" technique is also based on mechanisms related to self-esteem. Most people are happy to find out that other people think highly of them. This happens even when they realize that such an opinion may not be fully justified. It's nice to hear that someone thinks you are an expert in something. However, people who hear this are motivated to maintain the image of an expert, to behave like one. They may not be able to admit that they don't know or don't understand something. A real expert knows these things and understands them perfectly! And if this is the case, then sometimes you just have to do as you are asked, without posing any questions. Let's face it: the expert snare technique takes advantage of the fact that people can be hypocrites.

Technique # 67 *Induction of hypocrisy*

Idea

We all probably remember a situation from our childhood when we did something wrong. We gobbled up some candy despite being clearly told not to, got in a fight at school, or were caught lying, for example. The reactions of our teachers or parents in these situations may have been different – sometimes they were angry, sometimes they threatened us with consequences or other times they may have had educational conversations. These conversations often followed a similar pattern – when we were caught stealing something that belonged to someone else, for example, they usually began with questions. Is stealing ok? Is it good behavior when someone takes someone else's toy? Would we be happy if someone did that to us? This was usually followed by the fundamental question – if you say that stealing is bad and that you would feel bad if someone stole something from you, then why did you behave that way yourself? People applying such educational techniques perhaps do so unconsciously, but they are using a social influence technique called hypocrisy induction. It involves provoking statements from someone that openly endorse some attitude, opinion, or behavior and then demonstrating how their behavior directly contradicts them.

Research

Chris Dickerson, Ruth Thibodeau, Elliot Aronson, and Dayna Miller (1992) engaged in research on this phenomenon. They asked students to fill out a survey that focused on their attitudes towards wasting water. The survey itself asked students to recall situations in the past when they had wasted water needlessly. The following questions were asked in the survey: When showering, do you ALWAYS turn off the water while soaping up or shampooing? When you take showers, do you ALWAYS make them as short as possible, or do you sometimes linger longer than necessary? In your view, about how long does it take an average person to shower and shampoo, without wasting any water? As we can see, practically everyone was forced to respond to some of the questions by indicating that they could do more to save water. It should also be noted that the whole situation took place at a swimming pool, that the participants were exclusively women, and that the questions were asked just before they entered the locker room after a swimming class. It was thus natural that the participants would make a beeline for the showers. The second experimenter, pretending to take a shower, recorded the showering time of the participants who had been made aware of their hypocrisy (and, of course, of those in the control group). It turned out that participants from the hypocrisy group took shorter showers (221 seconds on average) than those from the control group (302 seconds).

Mechanism

Probably the most salient mechanism responsible for the reduction in shower time in the above-described study (and for the effectiveness of hypocrisy awareness in general) is the phenomenon of cognitive dissonance. In the simplest terms, it can be described as discrepancy between two elements – in this context, a stated attitude (saving water is important) and a behavior (sometimes I waste water). The way to rid oneself of this state of disequilibrium (as it was termed by Leon Festinger (author of the original version of dissonance theory) is to change one of the two elements – either the attitude or the behavior (see: Aronson, 1969). In Dickerson and colleagues' study, it was difficult for participants to conclude after completing the questionnaire that saving water was not as important as they had previously declared, so they were left with no choice but to change their behavior and cut back on their shower time.

Technique # 68 *Flattery*

Idea

One of our colleagues told us about how he once drove his mother to the mall and went with her to a women's clothing store. His mother was trying on a dress and looked at herself in the mirror for a long time, apparently unable to decide whether or not to buy it. A salesman came over, looked at her, and said: "You look perfect in that dress," and then said aloud to our colleague: "Wouldn't you agree that this color suits your wife very well?" Our colleague's mother was convinced: she purchased the dress immediately. Did she really believe that she looked like her son's wife? Did she really believe that she looked fantastic in this particular dress? Our colleague, of course, did not fail to ask her about this on their way back home. She responded that no, she's not an oblivious moron! What's more, she said, the sales staff probably have explicit instructions about complimenting customers. But despite this awareness, the sales-person's compliment inspired her to purchase the dress. Can compliments be an effective tool of social influence? Can they increase the probability of people fulfilling our requests? Let's take a look at experimental research devoted to this very subject.

Research

Back in the days when there was no Internet (there really was such a time!), psychologists also conducted various survey studies. However, this was more difficult than it is today. If, for example, they wanted to gauge the opinions of the residents of some town, they could either use the telephone (but this was only feasible for very short questionnaires), or go door-to-door and ask for answers to a series of questions, or (which, for a variety of reasons, was a common practice at the time) send surveys to randomly selected residents of that town. In these cases, along with the survey, the package contained a self-addressed stamped return envelope. The respondent was expected to put the completed survey in it and then drop it in the mailbox. The problem, however, was that the percentage of people who complied with the request to complete and return the survey was usually very low. Clyde Hendrick, Richard Borden, Martin Giesen, Edward Murray, and B.A. Seyfried (1972) set out to see if people's willingness to complete surveys would increase if a letter asking them to do so was peppered with compliments about their qualities such as goodness, kindness, and generosity. The researchers sent letters to residents of Akron, Ohio, introducing themselves as the Committee for the Study of Population Behavior Patterns. In the control conditions, the letter consisted of phrases such as: "We are asking for your help in completing two questionnaires which are enclosed. (…) We realize that this request for your help is something of an imposition. (…) Therefore we ask your support in this endeavor." It was further explained that the first of these surveys is a so-called "metric" containing questions about basic bio-graphical data of the respondent, while the second survey, seven pages long, deals with feelings, attitudes, preferences, and ideas that the respondent may identify with. Both completed surveys were to be placed in the enclosed, addressed envelope, which was to be dropped in the mailbox. The letter ended with the phrase: "Your assistance will help promote the advance of the behavioral science. (…) We thank you for your assistance." In the alternative conditions, the content of the letter was only slightly different. Simply, whenever the word "help" or "assistance" appeared, it was always preceded by the adjectives "generous" or "kind," and the word "support" was preceded by "gracious." It turned out that, while in control conditions the surveys were completed and returned by 10% of respondents, in the compliment conditions this rate was significantly higher, reaching 29%.

Mechanism

Numerous psychological studies show without exception that people like those who give them compliments. This effect occurs even when they know (or at least suspect) that the person giving the compliment is not sincere. The mechanism underlying the technique analyzed here – so simple, after all – may be the very arousal of sympathy for the person making the request. Alternatively, we can assume that the rule of reciprocity, which we have previously discussed in several places here, comes into play: "someone is nice to me, giving me compliments, I should return the courtesy by fulfilling their request." However, it is possible that the mechanism underlying complimenting as a social influence technique is not interpersonal in nature. Anthony Pratkanis (2007,a) describes a field experiment in which one experimenter complimented the participant's attire, and then either he or a completely different experimenter formulated a request to join a "stop junk-mail" campaign. They found that, compared to the control condition, complimenting increased the propensity to comply with this request in both situations mentioned above. Thus, at least in some cases, the psychological mechanism underlying the effectiveness of compliments may be intrapersonal. Hearing something nice about oneself, for example, may put people in a positive mood or dispose them to be more friendly toward other people.

Technique # 69 *"This is what intelligent people do"*
Idea

One of the authors of this book was once visited by an insurance salesman. His offer included a vast range of all kinds of insurance: property insurance against fire, water, snow, ice, and even insurance against a collision between a building and an aircraft — let us be honest, an event that is unlikely to happen but surely produces vivid imagery. The salesman described the advantages of the offered products in a very vivid manner, he painted a bleak prospect of all sorts of disasters that might potentially occur, only to calm a member of his audience with a soothing awareness that the insurance he offers will free us from any concerns regarding their consequences. Yet, his arguments were of little avail, which the door-to-door salesman could clearly tell by the bored look on the face of the customer, whom he was evidently losing. Finally, the salesman decided to deliver the finisher: he presented a very complex offer for a sophisticated insurance package (basically it covered everything except for losses caused by aliens) and he concluded his presentation with the following words: "You know, ordinary, slow-witted folks will not buy this product but you, being an intelligent person…" A meaningful silence and an effective pause were, obviously, designed to produce what seemed to be the only possible ending to this scene ("YES! I'll take it!"). Admittedly, the door-to-door salesman failed to sell the insurance policy, but he got us thinking — can similar, seemingly simple tricks, help increase our chances for success when we want to ask someone for a favor?

Research

We decided to verify this through a simple experiment (Dolinski et al., 2022). We persuaded our undergraduates to approach people waiting at bus and tram stops with a rather typical request (that is, typical in the case of undergraduates of social sciences). Yet, the request was difficult enough (as we had tested it previously in the course of pilot studies) for people to be rather reluctant to act on it. The request was formulated in the following manner: "Excuse me, I am a university student and I need to conduct a study to get a credit for one of my courses. Could you help me? The thing is, I need to have this questionnaire filled out, it contains

142 questions. Would you agree to fill it out?" Obviously, this is how the request was phrased in the control group – in the experimental group, we decided to use the technique that the insurance salesman set us on the trail of and make sure the subjects felt flattered: "Excuse me, I am a university student and I need to conduct a study to get a credit for one of my courses. Could you help me? The thing is, I need to have this questionnaire filled out, it contains 142 questions. It so happens that we need to elicit answers from intelligent persons and you simply appear to be one of them. Would you agree to fill it out?"

Of course, what we were truly interested in was the difference in the number of people who agreed to grant this request in both the control and the experimental conditions. A total of 1060 people were surveyed. As it turned out, the difference was very distinct: while only 32% of the subjects agreed to act on the request in the control conditions, the percentage was as high as 52 when the subjects were referred to as intelligent.

Mechanism

Why does such a minor change in the way a request is formulated increase its effectiveness so markedly? There are at least several potential explanations.

The first one is the reference to the reciprocity rule, which we have described in another section of this book. It should be noted that our compliment (identifying the subject as an intelligent person) may be considered as a nice gesture, which should be reciprocated with another nice gesture. In this particular situation, simply granting the request, which is important for the nice young man who has just said I was an intelligent person. Sure, there are 142 questions to be answered but since this person did something for me, it would be impolite to refuse. Another possible interpretation would refer to curiosity. Since the questions are meant for intelligent people, perhaps the questions are also very intelligent? Perhaps they are interesting and the time spent on answering them, since I am wasting anyway while waiting for the bus or tram, will be enjoyable. It is also possible that, in this particular situation, the liking rule is at play. After all, as demonstrated by many studies, we like physically attractive people, people who are similar to us as well as those who flatter us (which applies to our case). A situation where someone tells us that we are exceptional in some way (exceptionally intelligent, endowed with vivid imagination, remarkably brilliant) produces warm feelings towards this person. Even if we suspect that this person is, to some extent, making it up to endear themselves to us, we appreciate their effort (at least a sufficiently large percentage of us would have to, to make using this technique worthwhile).

This technique is a typical example of a phenomenon that is difficult to characterize by referring to only one psychological mechanism (but see also mechanism we present to explain the effectiveness of technique # 70). Sometimes, such attempts are futile, as each of the known mechanisms has its partial effect here and, by synergy, affects our behavior – and, ultimately, this is exactly our goal in most cases.

Technique # 70 Sensible people would do it

Idea

The previous technique we discussed consisted of using words referring to one's intelligence. The message addressed to a particular individual suggested that if this person were to comply with the request, it would prove their intelligence. Needless to say, intelligence is a very desirable quality in people and probably everyone would like not only to be intelligent but also to be more intelligent than they actually are. Better yet, they would like to be more intelligent than they believe they are! In various situations, though, other qualities may also be considered important and desirable – e.g., being determined, consistent, honest, loyal, brave, responsible, or sensible. Let us dwell on the last of the above-mentioned adjectives for a second. In certain situations, e.g., when choosing a homeowner's insurance policy, having a chest X-ray scan, taking a flu vaccination as a preventive measure, or changing your tires to winter ones before the winter actually comes – being sensible can play a decisive role. Being sensible is definitely a positive thing and it is pleasant to believe that we have this quality. Will referring to this quality in a situation, while asking for a favor or offering something, when it is explicitly related to the nature of the decision to be made by the subject turn out to be an effective social influence technique? Let us take a look at a study devoted to this problem.

Research

One of our female undergraduates works at a car showroom of a Japanese manufacturer. Apart from selling vehicles, the showroom also offers car repair and maintenance services and the responsibilities of our students include calling customers to offer inspection services for their cars. Since the inspection should be carried out annually, she called car owners a few weeks prior to the deadline for their next inspection. In the case of those customers who had purchased their cars within the last three years, the conversation was very straightforward. They agreed to use the services offered by the showroom (the only official dealer for this manufacturer in our town), as otherwise their three-year warranty would be voided. But it was a very different story with those customers who had purchased their vehicles earlier. Even though they knew that the official showroom offered high-quality services, they were also aware of the fact that these services were offered at significantly lower prices at independent car repair shops. For this reason, many car owners chose not to accept the invitation to the showroom. In the course of the experiment (Dolinski et al., 2022), our female undergraduate, in half of the cases, simply called customers and offered to make a car inspection appointment. As it turned out, approx. 42% of the subjects accepted the offer. Her conversation with the other customers was almost identical. The only difference was the casually added sentence: "Studies show that sensible customers have their cars inspected at official service stations." As it turned out, with this single and short sentence, the percentage of customers who decided to make a car inspection appointment at the showroom increased to 72%!

Mechanism

As regards the underlying psychological mechanism behind the effectiveness of the previously described technique, we provided several alternative explanations. All of them are hypothetical in their nature, as studies on this technique are in their early stages. All those interpretations may just as well be applied to the technique described in this section. Still, we will add one more interpretation here (which, let us remember, also applies to the previously described technique). The psychological mechanism that may be at play here is the specific trap set for the person we are addressing. If we tell this person that sensible people (or "intelligent" as in the case of the previously characterized technique) do exactly what we are offering, turning down our offer would mean… that this person is not sensible (or intelligent). And, after all, nobody wants to be perceived as foolish or unintelligent by themselves or by their interlocutor. In order to avoid it, all we need to do is say, "Yes."

Technique # 71 *We are looking for people like you*
Idea

Let us start with a personal confession. Once in a while, journalists call us and want to know our opinion on topics related to social psychology. This usually happens directly after an incident − a fight involving soccer hooligans, a publication of survey results demonstrating an increase in the dislike of immigrants, or after silent street demonstrations by employees of the school system demanding raises. Yet, we are quite busy and it is not always that we can find time between classes with our students and our research work to discuss these issues with journalists. When we refuse to comment, we think to ourselves that it could be literally any social psychology lecturer who could talk to the journalist about the underlying psychological mechanisms for the above-mentioned incidents (respectively: aggression, prejudice, or the importance of the sense of justice). However, we have noticed that if a journalist asks about issues related to social influence, we hardly ever refuse to comment on those. Why? Presumably because if the question pertains to "social psychology in general," we know that if we refuse to comment, the journalist will call one of our colleagues, who will be just as competent as us to answer their questions. Yet, if the question pertains to social influence, i.e., the area in which we have specialized for a number of years, we feel obligated to give the interview. We feel (even though it is uncertain if rightly so) that the journalist must be looking for interviewees like us − experts in this particular field. We figured that this phenomenon might be much broader. If we approach someone with a request and we explain that we are not just looking for "any person" but someone like them, this person may feel, in a way, obligated to act on the request.

Research

Our studies (Dolinski, & Grzyb, 2022) were conducted during the pandemic and, to be more precise, during the period when everyone was expected to wear face masks inside public buildings (e.g., in stores, offices, or movie theaters). Some people wore standard (white and gray) masks, others chose more vivid colors (such as green or red), while still others wore masks embellished with all sorts of designs (e.g., flowers or checkered). Some people disregarded the rules and did not wear a face mask. The study was conducted in a shopping mall. The researcher (sometimes a woman and sometimes a man) asked an apparently adult lone passer-by to answer several questions from a questionnaire regarding wearing face masks. In the control conditions, the researcher simply said: "Excuse me, I'm a psychology student and I need to conduct a survey regarding wearing face masks"; next, the researcher asked the subject if they would agree to participate in the survey. In the experimental conditions, the request was formulated differently, as first the experimenter suggested that they were looking for a specific group of people to include them in their study. The message communicated to the subject was therefore different depending on whether or not the subject was wearing a mask and, if so, what type. And so, if the person was wearing a patterned mask (e.g., with flowers, a camouflage, or a checkered pattern), the message was formulated as follows: "Excuse me, I'm looking for people who are wearing a patterned face mask just like yours. I am a psychology student and I need to conduct a survey regarding wearing face masks." If the lone passer-by at the shopping mall was wearing a single color, usually gray, mask, the experimenter would start the conversation as follows: "Excuse me, I'm looking for people who are wearing a single-color face mask just like yours" and if this person was not wearing a mask, the experimenter would say: "Excuse me, I'm looking for people who are not wearing a face mask just like you." We made sure that the exact same numbers of people wearing patterned, conventional masks or no face masks at all were examined in both the control and the experimental conditions. While 45% of the subjects agreed to answer the questions from the questionnaire when they were approached in the standard manner, the percentage was markedly higher (63%) when the "We are looking for people like you" technique was used.

Mechanism

When we are faced with a request, a business offer, or a suggestion to perform a specific task, our decision is often not that obvious. There are many reasons to say "yes" and a number of reasons to say "no." One of the arguments in favor of turning the request down is our conviction that even if we refuse, it will be easy for the person formulating the request to find someone else. This argument will often cross our minds, e.g., when we are in a hurry, when we feel tired or when we simply have other, specific plans. However, if the person approaching us with the request also explains to us that they are looking specifically for people like us, the situation becomes very different. At this point, we know that our refusal will put this person in a difficult position, as finding people like us is not an easy task. As a consequence, we may have a specific sense of being under an obligation to comply with the request. It is somewhat similar to a situation when a crowd watches someone drowning: within this crowd of people, no one feels personally responsible for what will happen to the drowning person. This is because people tend to think, "there must be someone who is a stronger swimmer than me here" or "someone must have already called the coastguard." However, if a single person sees someone drowning, they jump into the water, as they know that otherwise this person will die.

In our studies, it was the face mask (sometimes a unique one) or the lack thereof that made the subject special. Obviously, in other situations, the subject may feel similarly obligated to grant the request because the person asking for a favor is looking for exceptionally tall people (like them), people wearing a jacket with golden buttons (like his) or with a Michael Kors purse (like hers).

Technique # 72 *A witness to an interaction*

Idea

Medieval traveling troupes of actors usually consisted of several people. However, the scripts of the plays they performed usually required the participation of more characters. This problem was solved with the help of masks, which the actors wore on their faces. Thus, the same actor was a beggar in one scene, then became a merchant in the next. Another was a young man, only to become an old man a moment later, or even a middle-aged woman if need be. Each of us is such an actor to some extent. We don masks – we behave differently toward our superiors than toward our friends, and we behave differently still when we talk to our children. One difference, in particular, is striking. We behave differently when we are alone and when we are with someone we want to make a good impression on. Can this be used to increase the effectiveness of social influence? It may be worth making a request when you are with someone whose opinion you care about. Especially if fulfilling that request will be a good opportunity for them to gain approval in that person's eyes.

Research

Bruce Rind and Daniel Benjamin (1994) conducted their experiment just before Christmas. It took place in the food court of an American suburban shopping mall, and the design of the study was extremely simple. The experimenter, a 16-year-old male student, approached a man sitting at a table alone or, alternatively, in the company of a woman, and offered to buy him lottery tickets. He explained that the grand prize in the lottery was a weekend for two people in Bermuda. The value of this trip was over $1,000. He also explained that the proceeds from the raffle would go to benefit social causes (the United Way was the beneficiary of these funds). Of interest to the experimenters was the number of tickets purchased by the male respondents in each of the two conditions. This turned out to be almost twice as high in the condition in which the man was accompanied by a woman (2.41) as in the condition in which the man sat at the table alone (1.31). It also turned out that half of the men sitting alone at the table did not even want to listen to the raffle ticket salesman's story until the end. In conditions where the man sat with a woman, it was only in 6% of cases that he was not allowed to finish speaking and to present the offer in detail.

Mechanism

This technique takes advantage of the human propensity for self-presentation. As social beings, we care about how others view us. We care that other people (especially particular people) think that we are moral and intelligent. Sometimes we want to arouse fear or even apprehension (this motivation drives, for example, professional boxers or some bosses), sometimes sympathy or jealousy. Rind and Benjamin's experiment highlighted the role of self-presentation, which manifested itself in a very specific behavior. Apparently, the men sitting with the woman wanted her to think of them as: generous (they are not stingy and buy lottery tickets), inclined to altruism (the proceeds from the lottery will go to important social causes. After all, United Way primarily funds initiatives related to health and education) and cultural (they do not interrupt a person who is trying to make a point). However, one can easily imagine that the human propensity for self-presentation can be exploited in many other social situations as well. The technique of using the presence of a witness offers a wide range of possibilities. The key issue, however, will always be to whom the people we intend to influence wish to present themselves positively and what this self-presentation will consist of. The latter is important, as in some cases not fulfilling a specific request (rather than fulfilling it) can be the best way to make a positive impression on someone… When trying to optimize social influence it is therefore always necessary to consider whether the presence of outsiders is desirable or not in a given situation.

Technique # 73 *Make your commitments public*

Idea

The life of a media expert on psychology-related matters is rather predictable – all you need is a glance at the calendar and you will be able to predict, with almost 100% accuracy, the questions journalists will be asking on particular days. Around February 14, questions will be about love and how people fall in love (and recently, increasingly often, how single people should spend Valentine's Day). In September, journalists will ask experts how to cope with returning to work after the summer holiday season; prior to Black Friday they will ask about the sale frenzy ("why do we keep buying things we do not need?"); and several weeks later it will be a Christmas survival guide for families. But the most clear-cut of them all is probably the question asked on January 1 – why do we make New Year's resolutions (and why do we fail to accomplish so many of our goals, which does not prevent us from setting identical ones the following year)?

The changes we want to see in our lives are a fascinating topic. Most of us would welcome some changes in our lives – we would like to lose a few pounds (more like a dozen or so in the case of the authors of this book...), learn to properly use a foreign language, become better at separating our private and professional lives, or devote more time to physical activity, i.e., sports. Most likely, we adopt the following approach – I will try, I will do my best and I will change (doing one or more of those things or something completely different)! Yet the vast majority of us have also failed miserably in this area – I really tried, I truly wanted this to happen, it just did not work out. What can I do to make it work next time?

Some try the methodical approach. When he was still an undergraduate, one of the authors of this book, while observing walls in a female dorm (where he was for reasons no one should be interested in now), noticed a poster that read, "Goals I want to accomplish," on a wall in a shared room. The poster included resolutions regarding exercises (at least four hours of running per week!), learning a foreign language (reading at least one article in English per week!) as well as maintaining family relations (call mom at least once every two days!). These goals had the form of a commitment made publicly – one of the girls living in this room had put up the poster so that all her roommates could see it. Was she right and did she, by doing so, increase her chances for success?

Research

There have been numerous psychologists who have conducted studies designed to verify if making one's commitments known publicly increases our chances for success and the conclusion is quite clear: yes, it does. Yet not every piece of information about the commitments we have taken on and made public has the same effect. This was cleverly demonstrated by Prashanth U. Nyer and Stephanie Dellande (2009). In order to conduct their studies, they went to a location where one can find many people who are motivated to change their lives: a weight loss center. At the center, women (as all subjects in the experiment were females) were subjected to very thorough diagnostics prior to joining the program – they were weighed, asked about their eating habits, the level of their physical activity, and other parameters that could affect their body weight. In the next step, the goal was determined (i.e., how many pounds the person wanted to lose throughout the 16-week program) and a suitable diet was re-commended, along with a change in specific eating habits. At this stage, the actual experiment commenced. The female participants were randomly assigned to one of three groups: one control and two experimental groups. No non-standard elements were added in the control group, the progress being made was simply monitored in the course of the program. In the experimental groups, there was a public presentation of the set goal (obviously, subject to the consent of the participants). The presentation consisted in putting up the names of the participants along with their goals (i.e., the number of pounds they wanted to lose) in a showcase that everyone could see. The difference between the two experimental groups was the time frame over which said information was put out for public display. In the first condition, the names and the values in pounds were displayed in the showcase for the entire duration of the program (i.e., 16 weeks), whereas in the second condition, they were only displayed during the first three weeks of the program.

The results were measured in percentages, simply indicating to what degree the set goal was accomplished. Generally speaking, all of the groups did rather well, even though, as expected, there were significant differences among them. In the control group (without the public declaration), the success index was close to 89%. In the group with the public, but short-term, commitment the outcome was better – almost 97%. Yet, the best results were achieved by the subjects whose declarations were made public throughout the entire duration of the program – they managed to accomplish their goals in over 102% (i.e., they performed better than expected!).

The researchers decided to test one more aspect. As they knew the participants would stay in touch with the center once the program had come to an end, they decided to weigh the participant one more time, i.e., eight weeks after their bodyweight reduction program had been completed. And here, the results were even more interesting: in the control group, the success index was slightly above 81%, in the group with the short-term commitment, the value was 89.10%, whereas in the group with the long-term commitment, the index was 97.46%. Therefore, it should be concluded that the effect was sustained even after their participation in the program and that individuals from the long-term commitment group were "losing the effect" at a relatively slower rate.

Mechanism

We as humans like to be considered reliable. We believe that it should be the norm to meet one's commitments, and some even know the meaning of the phrase *pacta sunt servanda* (Latin for "agreements must be kept"). And even though, as provided by the laws applicable in many countries, a verbal agreement is equivalent to an agreement in writing, we know all too well that what has been written down is more important. And this was exactly the case in the study by Nyer and Dellande. If you have made a commitment – and, additionally, it was made public, or perhaps still remains so, as it was written in the form of a document – you are significantly more motivated to follow through.

It should be noted that this is something we have been taught from an early age. If you walk into any classroom (particularly in a primary school) you will see all kinds of posters with rules put up on the walls, which pupils and teachers agree to comply with. Sometimes, there will be a list of chores, along with a list of individuals responsible for these chores (who waters the flowers in the classroom or who feeds the class fish or the class hamster). Obviously, this is not to say that without the list the hamster would starve to death but making the list public certainly makes the individuals who have agreed to perform these tasks more motivated.

There is also one more aspect that is not insignificant here – the awareness of the risk of publicizing a potential failure. If I have set a goal for myself and I have failed to achieve it but I am the only person who knows about it, it is not that big of a deal. After all, we have mastered the art of finding all kinds of excuses to take responsibility off of ourselves for lack of the desired result. If, however, everyone learns about our failure, the situation is very different. In order to avoid this, we are willing to make significant sacrifices – even if it means refraining from having a slice of cheesecake or a burger.

Technique # 74 *Using the name of one's interlocutor*

Idea

The human name has something magical about it. Imagine attending a cocktail party – you can concentrate on a conversation taking place in a tight circle of a few people in such a way that all the powerful noise of ingling conversations going on in other such groups becomes a uniform, contentless hum. But if your name comes up in this noise, spoken even by someone standing very far away, you immediately register it and focus on overhearing what this person is saying about you. Will the magic of our own name also make us more inclined to carry out the request of a person who uses it? Supposedly, Julius Caesar possessed a phenomenal memory and very often addressed his legionaries by name. Whether it was for this reason (but perhaps precisely because of it) that they adored him is not known. From the perspective of interest to us here, it can be said that they tended not only to carry his orders out with diligence, but even to anticipate his every wish, including those unspoken, and see they went fulfilled. Does this rule that applied to the ancient Roman world also apply to ours today? Will someone who makes a request of us increase their chances of seeing it done if they say our name?

Research

That was the question posed by Daniel Howard, Charles Gengler, and Ambuj Jain (1995). On the first day of a new semester, students were greeted by a professor who introduced himself as the chairman of the Marketing Department, which was true. The students were then asked to introduce themselves again and say a few words about their expectations for the upcoming classes. The next day, they were to appear individually in the professor's room to register for a multiple-choice evaluation study concerning their classes, for which they were promised extra credit. When a student entered the professor's office, the professor did not ask them their name but said he would quickly try to recall it. After all, he had just heard it yesterday! In half of the cases the professor would say that he already knew (and would say the student's real name), and the other half would say, with an air of resignation about him, that he could not remember and would ask the student to introduce himself again. The professor continued by explaining to the student what the study was about, and when the student was ready to leave, he said that he wanted to make a suggestion. The marketing secretary is selling some cookies for a departmental bake sale. The cookies cost a quarter each, and if the student wants them, he can buy them. The professor pointed to a table located behind him that had some cash on it as well as the cookies. It turned out that in conditions where the professor "could recall" the student's name, almost everyone (almost 92%) took advantage of this offer. However, for the group of students that had to introduce themselves, the cookies were bought by exactly one of every two. Why was this the case? Perhaps it was simply that the students in the former group concluded that the professor had a great memory, and if so, it was better not to risk getting on his bad side by refusing to buy some cookies. However, there were other conditions in the experimental scheme. This time, the professor also mentioned cookies being on sale, but there weren't any in his office. The student, if she wants to, has to go to another room where the cookies are on a tray next to some cash... It probably comes as no surprise that interest in the cookies was generally lower than in conditions where the professor was in the room; but most importantly, again, those who heard the professor say their names were more likely to buy them (over 64% of participants) than those who had to introduce themselves (slightly more than 21%). It is indeed the magic of the name that does the job, not the fear of the professor's good memory.

Mechanism

Most people admit to having trouble remembering other people's names. What's the name of that blonde woman I met last month at my friend's birthday party? What's the name of the bald guy in the oversized jacket I spoke to at a conference in the spring? How do we feel when someone we barely know, someone we've seen once or twice a long time ago, addresses us by name? If it's not because of our infamy for drunkenly bumping into a cake at a wedding reception or because we started a brawl in public, we feel good. Probably we made a very positive impression on that person since they remembered our name. We feel better now, we feel appreciated. We also feel better about the person who used our name, and we are more inclined to fulfill that individual's requests.

Technique # 75 Similarity

Idea

People can be similar to one another in many ways. They can be physically similar (e.g., hair color, eye color, height, weight, or foot length). They may have similar views on global warming, the value of various invest-ment schemes, the chances of humans landing on Mars, or LGBT+ rights. They may also have similar life experiences — going to the same high school, learning dance in their youth, getting with mumps, or coming from the same town. Finding these similarities — in addition to exciting social events — can also be a factor exerting social influence. Many studies show that if we are similar to someone, the chances of our fulfilling that person's request are significantly higher. (And, of course, vice versa: the chances of that person fulfilling our request also increase).

Research

A series of studies on the role of similarity in the exertion of influence was carried out by Jerry Burger, Shelley Soroka, Katrina Gonzago, Emily Murphy, and Emily Somervell (2001). They were curious as to how willingness to help in a social situation would be impacted by the fact of a shared name between the person being asked and the person doing the asking. Experimenters staged a situation in which people leaving a building where they had been taking part in a creativity experiment (they were supposed to think of different uses for different objects) were asked to make a donation to help a person suffering from cancer. The volunteer asking for the donation had a name tag pinned to her clothing. She was also holding a picture of one cancer patient, labeled with her name as well. In the experiment, sometimes the name of the volunteer and sometimes the name of the cancer patient was the same as the person being asked to donate. The average sums of the donations made by each participant in the experiment were recorded carefully, and it turned out that it made little difference whether the cancer patient had the same or a different name than the person being asked to donate. However, if the person being asked for money had the same name as the volunteer asking for it, then the average donation amount increased by over 100%!

Mechanism

People who are similar to us seem more like "one of us," so there is a certain social obligation to help them. Evolutionary psychologists would perhaps even say that this is associated with the desire to help people who are related to us to some extent. In the past, when people lived in clans and small groups, helping "one's own" was even a legal obligation – hence the idea that if someone is somehow similar to us, has something in common with us, we should help them in some way. That is why we often want to identify similarities to person we are meeting at the very beginning of a relationship. That is why we wear T-shirts bearing the name of the university we graduated from, and in some countries class rings are popular, showing not only the university we graduated from but also the year we received our diploma. After all, when someone notices this kind of similarity, they may be more eager to help a fellow graduate of the same alma mater than a different person who graduated somewhere else.

Technique # 76 *Incidental similarity*

Idea

When we think about similarities between people, we must consider not only whether they actually exist (i.e., whether people support the same hockey team or were born in the same city), but also the chances of a similarity occurring. Two men named James or two women named Mary who run into each other in the US are nothing special – these are the most popular names in the country, with nearly 5 million men and over 3 million women bearing them, respectively. But if one Arantxa (a Basque female name, given to 46 people in the US in 2014) meets another, this is clearly something exceptional, because this name is exceptional. So, can the rarity of some similarity determine the potential for social influence to be exerted?

Research

Research in this area was conducted by Jerry Burger, Nicole Messian, Shebani Patel, Alicia del Prado, and Carmen Anderson (2004). In an ingeniously designed experiment, they invited two students into the laboratory. In each case, one of them was a real participant in the study, while the other was a confederate (someone who behaved like a participant, but in reality was the experimenter's assistant and who followed his pre-defined instructions). The pairs of students were informed that the purpose of the study was to determine the relationship between biological and personality traits. Participants were first asked to give their thumbprints. When their thumbprint had been taken, the confederate behaved in one of three possible ways. In the control group, he did nothing. In experimental group one, he said "It turns out you both have Type E fingerprints. Of course, that's not too surprising. About 80% of the population has Type E fingerprints." In experimental group two he also mentioned the "Type E fingerprints" (a category completely invented for the purposes of the study), but in a slightly different way: "This is interesting. You both have Type E fingerprints. That's very rare. Only about 2% of the population has Type E fingerprints." Following this procedure, the students were asked to complete some questionnaires; the procedure was then concluded (at least it seemed like it) and they were sent on their way. However, as the students were leaving the building, the confederate would address a request to the real research participant – he would say that he had written an essay for the class and he needed to attach a short review of it, roughly a page or so in length. He needs it in about 24 hours, and he asks that you help him by reading the essay and writing the review. It turned out that study participants' decisions were strongly related to the experimental group they were placed in. The control group and the frequent similarity group (where it was reported that 80% of people have type E fingerprints) were not particularly different: 48.3% and 54.8% of respondents agreed to comply with the request, respectively. However, when the purported similarity was rare (2% of people with Type E fingerprints), things looked quite different: as many as 82.1% of respondents agreed to comply with the request in this condition.

Mechanism

The mechanism that Burger and his co-workers highlighted can also be presented in another context. Imagine you have a regular job that requires you to be there at the same time every day. It may be that the most convenient way to get there is by bus or bicycle. If you leave at the same time every day, you are likely to see the same people around – for example, the slightly overweight, balding man you always spot at the fruit stand. After a while, you get so used to the sight of him that you even start to grasp time based on him (oh, I see he's leaving the fruit store, so I'm probably late). At the same time, it's unlikely that you think of him as particularly close to you. Imagine, however, that you're on vacation, standing in line at some tourist attraction, where you meet the same man – but this time thousands of miles away from home! Perhaps you won't leap into each other's arms right away (however, stranger things have happened), but you will surely draw attention to yourself; you will express surprise at how small the world is and what a strange coincidence it is that you have run into each other in such a random place. If he asks you for a small favor, for example, to borrow a guidebook to the island you are on, you'll do it no questions asked – after all, how small were the chances of meeting in such a place!

Technique # 77 *The Chameleon effect: Behavioral mimicry*

Idea

Imagine that you have been invited to participate in a psychological experiment. You are sitting in a laboratory with another subject you have just met. Your chairs, even though not directly opposite, are positioned in such a manner that you can see each other very well. You are asked to describe consecutive pictures being shown to you by the person conducting the experiment. There is a video camera recording your actions. The experimental session comes to an end. Now, as you are joined by yet another subject, you are asked to recall the pictures you were shown during the initial session. Your actions are still being recorded with a video camera. You are clueless as to the actual goal of the experiment. You did not notice (and even if you did notice, you did not think it was important) that your first companion rubbed his face every now and then and that the second one was shaking his foot. There was nothing odd about it. People perform various gestures in similar situations. Some will be fiddling with their pens, others will adjust their glasses every minute or so, and others still will be playing with their wedding ring by taking it off their finger and putting it back on. What you do not know is that Tanya Chartrand and John Bargh (1999), who had invited you to participate in this experiment, wanted to know how often, during both sessions, you would be rubbing your face or shaking your foot. The experiment demonstrated that you displayed the former behavior more frequently during the first session, as compared to the second one, and that you were shaking your foot much more frequently during the second session, as compared to the first one. In other words, you were performing the same movements as the other subject in the room. There was no way for you to know that these were not actual subjects but assistants of the experimenters, who were investigating the so-called Chameleon effect: one's tendency to emulate the gestures of other people we interact with. In the course of the above-mentioned experiment, it was the subject who, unknowingly, was imitating the movements of other people. But what would happen if it were the other people who were mimicking the subject's gestures? And, this being of particular importance for us, can it be connected in any way with exerting social influence on the subject?

Research

Wojciech Kulesza, Zofia Szypowska, Matthew Jarman, and Dariusz Dolinski (2014) investigated to what extent mimicking a customer, while she is shopping in a cosmetics store, can affect how much money she spends there. The sales clerk was a 20 years old woman wearing an elegant, black two-piece suit, who had been adequately trained in subtly mimicking customers' gestures. As the authors were interested not only in the consequences of the mimicry but also in the consequences of the physical attractiveness of the person selling the cosmetics, in half of the cases the sales clerk was wearing very carefully prepared make-up, while in the other half of the cases her face was plain and not subject to any beautification procedures. Depending on the experimental conditions, the woman would either simply sell the cosmetics requested by the customer or she would mimic some of the customer's gestures. For example: if the customer brushed her hair aside, the sales clerk would do the same approximately two seconds later, and if the customer rested both of her hands on the counter, the sales clerk would do the same. In those cases where the sales clerk was not made to look particularly attractive, mimicking the customer resulted in a significant increase in the average amount spent by the customers (from 31.04 Polish zlotys to 51.44 Polish zlotys). The difference is quite impressive, isn't it? However, the effect of mimicking the customer was truly astonishing in those experimental conditions where the sales clerk was wearing carefully prepared make-up. With the make-up, customers spent, on average, 50.12 Polish zlotys in standard sale conditions, and as much as three times more (an average of 151.24 Polish zlotys) when the sales clerk was subtly mimicking their gestures!

Mechanism

Mimicry is a common phenomenon among both animals and humans. Copying the behavior of adult individuals by the younger ones is a key element in the process of learning which reactions are appropriate in a given situation and which are not. Mimicry enables animals to avoid poisonous foods and choose those that are good for their health and life, hide from enemies, find a mating partner, etc. As far as humans are concerned, mimicry can be observed as early as in infants, who open their mouths or put their lips together when the person playing with them performs these gestures. Adults also mimic one another spontaneously and, in most cases, completely unknowingly. Literature on psychology refers to mimicry as social glue. Numerous studies have demonstrated, explicitly, that people who mimic each other start, as a result, to like each other more, they are more willing to help each other, they reach agreements easier during negotiations, they think better of each other, and they find it easier to think about themselves and the other person in the "we" category. In normal social situations, such mimicry is performed unknowingly by both parties. When an intentional attempt is made to exert social influence, the mimic is, obviously, aware of their actions as well as the purpose behind them. This way, they will be more popular, they will win more affection and trust, and consequently, they will increase the chances of having their request (even if it is not expressed directly) granted.

Technique # 78 The Chameleon effect: Verbal mimicry

Idea

Needless to say, people perform all kinds of gestures with their upper and lower limbs, they stand erect and stoop, they also stretch particular parts of their face in mimicked expressions. When interacting with other people, we also (perhaps more importantly) communicate verbally.

We all speak with a particular pace (most people utter 120–180 words per minute but everyone probably knows someone who drawls out their words and speaks at half the standard pace, as well as someone who produces words like a machine gun at speeds reaching twice the standard pace), specific volume, and pitch. Apart from the above-mentioned formal characteristics of human speech, there are also the contents. Our speech is a medium for specific messages we communicate. We have already demonstrated that by copying the behavior and gestures of an individual, we can make this individual more susceptible to social influence. Does this hold true when we mimic what the other person is saying? Numerous studies in the field of social psychology have been devoted to this problem. A description of one such study can be found in the following section.

Research

Wojciech Kulesza, Dariusz Dolinski, Kinga Szczesna, Mariola Kosim, and Tomasz Grzyb (2019) decided to investigate how waitresses' mimicking the verbal utterances of customers in a restaurant affects their tipping patterns. In the control conditions of this experiment, the waitresses served the customers in a standard fashion. When a customer said something, they reacted with a nod and replied: "OK, right away." In other cases, the waitresses repeated the phrase uttered by the customer. Additionally, these experimental conditions varied, as the researchers wanted to check how significant the moment of verbal mimicry was. Therefore, in some cases, the waitress would repeat after the customer at the time of placing the order (e.g., "OK, one beer, tea, and a pizza"), in some cases she would repeat the customer's words as the customer was asking for a check (e.g., "OK, you would like to receive the check"), while still in other cases she would repeat the customer's utterances consistently in both situations. The researchers wanted to see if the customers would tip the waitress (in Poland, where the experiment was conducted, tipping is not that common) and if so, how much would they tip her. As it turned out, the verbal mimicry was very profitable for the waitresses. While 12% of the customers tipped the waitresses in standard customer service conditions, the figure was 23% when the waitress was verbally mimicking the customers. The timing of the mimicry was irrelevant. As far as the average tip amount is concerned it was approximately 5.20 Polish zlotys in standard conditions and the amount was significantly higher in the verbal mimicry conditions. Here, however, the moment when the waitress mimicked the customer was, in fact, relevant. In those cases, where the customer's words were repeated at the time of placing the order, the average tip amount was approximately 6.25 Polish zlotys, whereas in those cases where the customer's words were repeated as they were asking for the check, the tip amount was approximately 7.04 Polish zlotys. However, the highest tips were given in those situations where the waitress mimicked the customer both at the beginning and toward the end of their visit to the restaurant. The average tip amount earned by the waitress in such conditions was as much as 10.12 Polish zlotys.

Mechanism

Verbal mimicry is a very common and natural phenomenon in social exchanges. When greeting one another and saying their goodbyes, people tend to utter the same words as their interlocutors. Nevertheless, there is a lot of space between the greeting and the goodbye for uttering a huge number of words and sentences. These may be a repetition of what the other person has said or something completely different. We have learned about the positive results of copying other people's gestures. As it turns out, the outcomes of psychological studies of verbal mimicry are also unambiguous. It is believed to be as equally strong a social glue as behavioral mimicry. Therefore, it should come as no surprise that we are more inclined to grant a request made by a person who repeats what we have said. At the same time, one can assume that perhaps there is something more to it than just social glue, something more than the sheer liking that occurs in the case of behavioral mimicry. For if someone restates what we have said, it is very often synonymous with agreeing with us, with informing us, verbally, that they believe that we are right. By the same token, the person mimicking us is helping us believe in our competence and our high value. At this point, it becomes difficult for us to turn down a request made by someone who has made us feel so good and so positive about ourselves!

Technique # 79 *Two-in-one: Behavioral and verbal mimicry*

Idea

If mimicking the gestures of a person as well as repeating what they have said makes them more susceptible to social influence techniques, and we already know this to be true, the following question arises: will a simultaneous application of both behavioral and verbal mimicry produce a similarly positive effect? The answer seems to be obvious, but not everything that does turns out to be actually true. Gardeners know that a particular fertilizer can induce growth in plants and that using another fertilizer will yield a similar outcome. Yet, using both fertilizers at the same time may inhibit the correct growth of the plant. It may be a similar case with mimicry. It cannot be excluded that a mimic overdose, resulting from a simultaneous application of both behavioral as well as verbal mimicry, can lead to a decline of its positive effects. Therefore, let us examine the results of an experiment consisting of mimicking both the gestures and the verbal communication of certain individuals who were subsequently tested for their susceptibility to social influence.

Research

Celine Jacob, Nicolas Gueguen, Angelique Martin, and Gaelle Boulbry (2011) conducted their experiment at a store offering consumer electronics in the section with MP3 players. The offer included over 80 models of the device in question and the price range was very broad (from 15 to 580 euro). At the time an MP3 player was a common birthday or Christmas gift. Many customers (especially those over 40 years of age) typically ask the sales clerks for advice as to which model to choose. The subjects in this experiment were lone customers who appeared to be within the 40–70 age group and who asked a sales clerk for advice. At that point, the sales clerk would ask them about the maximum amount they were willing to spend on an MP3 player and subsequently would bring them two different models. In some instances, the following interaction between the sales clerk and the customer would proceed in a standard fashion, while in other cases the sales clerk would subtly mimic both the gestures of the customer (e.g., brushing one's hair aside or scratching one's head) as well as their verbal communication. If the customer said, "I want to buy an MP3 player for my grandson," the sales clerk would reply with, "An MP3 player for your grandson," followed by, "How old is he?" What is more, the sales clerk would repeat the terms used by the customer to describe the offered piece of equipment (e.g., "It's funny," or "It's light"). As it turned out, customers whose behavior was copied by the sales clerk decided to make their purchase more frequently (78.8% purchased an MP3 player) than the customers who attended in a standard fashion (61.8% purchased an MP3 player). Another aspect worth noting is whether the customers who purchased an MP3 player chose one of the models suggested by the sales clerk or whether they decided to buy another one. The suggestion of the sales clerk was followed more frequently by the mimicked customers (71.7%) than by those whose gestures and verbal communication were not being mimicked.

Mechanism

For mimicry to be effective, when used as a social influence technique, the person being mimicked must not be aware of the fact that the person mimicking their gestures and verbal communication is doing it intentionally. Otherwise, the mimicked person may become concerned and even, in extreme cases, convinced that they are being mocked and jeered at. Therefore, there were valid concerns as to whether intense mimicking (which is exactly the case here, where both the behavioral and the verbal channels are being used) would cause the mimicry to lose its potential for making subjects compliant. The above-mentioned experiment demonstrates that such concerns are not necessarily valid. People who were mimicked both in terms of their gestures as well as their verbal communication complied with requests more frequently than those who were not being mimicked. Therefore, the double-compound social glue turned out to be a strong adhesive!

Technique # 80 Synchrony

Idea

Imagine that you are standing in front of a large mirror. You slowly lift your right arm and touch your nose with your index finger. The image in the mirror is doing the same. Now, you jump and, of course, the image in the mirror jumps with you. There is nothing odd about it; after all, this is how mirrors work. Now, imagine that there is no mirror and that you are facing another person. Imagine that this person is following your every gesture as you are making it. It should be noted that in this case we are dealing with something other than the mimicry we discussed earlier. In the case of mimicry, a person is mimicking another individual by performing certain movements (or uttering certain words) over some time. In the case of synchrony, the phenomenon addressed in this section, people behave identically at the same moment. Examples of synchrony include singing in a chorus or dancing, or when people perform identical movements at the same time, such as a military parade or a sports discipline aptly referred to as synchronized swimming. Some instances of synchrony went down in history as extremely negative (e.g., thousands of hands raised simultaneously as the Nazi salute), while others were seen as extremely positive (e.g., thousands of citizens of the Czech Republic jumping on Wenceslas Square in Prague in 1989 during the period when their country was fighting for freedom and independence). Can synchrony be used as a social influence tool? Let us examine one of the very few experimental studies devoted to this problem.

Research

Scott Wiltermuth (2012) came up with a very original method for creating a state of synchrony. In the initial part of his experiment, subjects were told to walk the university campuses with the experimenter. Some subjects received instructions to walk in step with the experimenter, left foot with left foot and right with right. Other subjects were instructed to do the opposite: to take a step with their right foot when the experimenter stepped with his left foot and to take a step with their left foot when the experimenter stepped with his right foot. Others still were simply told to go for a walk at the university campuses with the experimenter. All subjects received the same explanation as to the purpose of their walk. They were told that the experiment pertained to the connection between movement and memory. Therefore, the subjects were not surprised when they were asked a few questions after they had returned to the laboratory, for example: "How many restrooms did you pass on your walk?" or "How many stairs did you climb on your walk?" Officially this concluded the experiment even though the participants remained in the laboratory. At that point, the experimenter would tell them that they would participate in a study pertaining to physiological reactions that occur while performing a task that people in some parts of the world may find objectionable. The subject was presented with a device resembling a coffee grinder, referred to as "the extermination machine," and 20 clear plastic cups. There were sow bugs in each of the cups. The experimenter would tell the subjects that their task was to put as many sow bugs in the grinder as they could within 30 seconds. Subsequently, after 3 more seconds, the extermination machine was supposed to start automatically. Would you be willing to kill any forms of life in this manner, even organisms that are as hostile to humans as sow bugs? Surely not. Well, the subjects who had simply taken a stroll with the experimenter were quite sluggish in carrying out their instructions. On average, they managed to put the contents of 4.92 plastic cups in the grinder. A similar result (5.50 cups on average) was recorded among those subjects who were instructed to take a step with their right foot when the experimenter stepped with his left foot and to take a step with their left foot when the experimenter stepped with his right foot. The subjects who synchronized their walking with the experimenter performed much more eagerly. They managed to put, on average, the contents of as many as 7.57 cups in the deadly grinder.

Mechanism

As we have already explained in the initial section of the description of this particular technique, unlike in the case of mimicry, in synchrony, analogous reactions of (at least two) individuals take place at the exact same moment. There is one more vital difference between mimicry and synchrony. In order for mimicry to be an effective social influence tool, the person whose behavior is being mimicked must not be aware of it. If, however, the person becomes aware they are being mimicked, they will not be willing to grant the request made by the mimic. This reservation does not apply to synchrony (and anyway, it would be very difficult for a subject not to notice that another person is copying their movements at the exact same time). What makes synchrony an effective social influence technique? If another person has been performing the same gestures as we are, shouting exactly what we have been shouting, or chanting the same slogan, it means that we both belong to the same group of people: we share certain values, ideas, and goals. Even if there are only two of us, we tend to think about us as "we" rather than "I" and "he/she." We experience positive emotions resulting from belonging to the same group and from the observation that we are not alone in our views and in the way we perceive the world around us. Now, if this person, who has become a member of the "we" group through their synchronized behavior, asks us for a favor, it is only natural that we would be willing to grant the request. Obviously, the requests, suggestions, or instructions do not have to be as surprising or, at the same time, ethically controversial as those referred to in the description of the experiment conducted by Scott Wiltermuth.

Technique # 81 *The "We" rule*

Idea

"We the people," reads the initial line of the American constitution. "We Are the Champions" – this song by Queen is enjoyed by soccer fans at stadiums all over the world when their team wins a national championship. "We": a magic word that expresses unity, shows that we stand united with other people, people with whom we feel connected by something, which both we and they consider important. This "something" goes beyond just the similarity we discussed earlier in this book. We might consider some people "we" even though we might feel that almost everything sets us apart from them! But, at the same time, there is something subjectively significant that unites us. This could be having been born in the same country or the same city, being a hardcore fan of the same soccer team, a regular supporter of a given political party, or a follower of the same religion. This suffices for us to perceive them and ourselves as "we." Now, will a person being asked to grant a request be more willing to comply with it when they learn that the asker also belongs to the "We" group?

Research

Kelly Aune and Michael Basil (1994) decided to verify this while collecting donations for charity. The collection took place on the campus of a major

Hawaiian university. Collecting money at this particular location meant that, most likely, university students would constitute a vast majority of the people asked for money. In the control conditions, a young woman conducting the experiment simply held out her hand with a moneybox and asked the subjects to support a well-known charitable organization conducting a campaign on the campus at that time. It turned out that in those conditions, the majority of the people who asked for a donation decided not to support the charity campaign. Less than 10% of the subjects put some of their money into the box. In the conditions designed to test the aforementioned technique, the experimenter behaved differently. She asked the subjects if they were students at the local university. Obviously, the typical answer was affirmative. At that point, the experimenter said, "Oh that's great so am I," and only then did they ask for a donation. In those conditions, as many as 47% of the subjects decided to put some of their money into the box!

Mechanism

When we are asked to say something about ourselves, apart from talking about our goals, values, or personal achievements, we very often mention certain groups we belong to. For example, we refer to our family or our friends, our nationality, the school or university we graduated from. If we practice a religion, we also mention its name. When referring to such narrations, social psychologists speak of social identity – the feeling of unity with other people, with whom we feel connected by things we consider important. We may have frequent and personal contacts with such people (e.g., our family) or we may be strangers to most of them (e.g., the nation). The feeling of social identity and "We" thinking may take place in both of the above cases. We are proud when our children graduate from universities and when our fellow countryman wins a gold medal at the Olympic games in race walking, even if we did not even know there was such a sports discipline. We are glad to meet a resident of our hometown at a campsite abroad (even more so, if we live in a small town and the campsite is far from the border of our country). A certain social norm makes us support one another within our own group. Therefore, we should help particularly those individuals about whom we think of as being in the "We" category. And even if, objectively speaking, this should be completely irrelevant, as in the case of the above-described experiment, we are more willing to comply with a request if the request is formulated by someone from the "We" group. In this particular case: "We, the students of this university."

Technique # 82 "That's how we do it here"

Idea

Social norms can take many forms. Sometimes we learn them in a very open and clear way – for example, during "onboarding" at work, when we learn about the company's customs concerning the use of a shared kitchen or coffee machine, or that on Tuesdays our whole department goes for a beer after work. Sometimes, however, norms are much more subtle. One of the authors of this book spent a significant part of his childhood in the countryside, where there were quite specific customs concerning keeping one's house in order. Every Saturday you had to sweep very carefully not only your yard and the sidewalk adjacent to it but also the part of the street where the house was located. This meant a lot of work, of course, so the author, while still a young boy, would ask why he had to clean a street that neither he owned nor anyone had hired him to maintain. "Because that's the way we do it here" – was the only answer he received. He did not ask any more questions, just swept "his" section of the street thoroughly. So why do we sometimes follow norms even if we don't understand their meaning? And what happens when we stop following them? Do we change our behavior when someone points the violation of a norm out to us?

Research

Michal Bilewicz and a group of his collaborators (2021) conducted a very interesting study on Reddit – an internet forum for exchanging opinions. We all know that such places are full of hateful comments, and hurling epithets at other users is not rare there. Bilewicz's team decided to check how to reduce the amount of such vulgar or hateful posts by using bots – programs analyzing the content of the entered comments and reacting to a given set of words. So when a post like "go fuck yourself dumbass" appeared, the bot was supposed to respond to it. How? This is where the experiment began. The bot had three possible reactions in its arsenal (and of course no reaction in the control group). The first way to react was to express disapproval – thus a message like "Actually, I kind of get how you feel. but please don't offend anybody." Another way was to draw attention precisely to a general norm: "the ability to imagine a different point of view is a wonderful quality and requires hard work." The last way was to formulate some empathetic message – "What other people are saying or doing can be hard to get for some people but let's keep in mind to be gentle, people are fragile." It turned out that each of the interventions led to an improvement – after such a message from the bot (although it should be noted that the participants in the discussion did not realize they were not dealing with a live person), the number of aggressive or hateful comments dropped. Moreover, this was not a short-lived phenomenon – measurements were taken for 60 days. And although the differences be-tween the effectiveness of particular interventions were not very clear, it was in the case of paying attention to the norm of politeness that the proportion of negative comments decreased the most, dropping from 2.1 to 1.4%. Thus, even in the world of the Internet, stereotyped as a place full of bad behavior, aggression, and hatred, simply pointing things out in-fluenced the participants in the discussion to mitigate and change their behavior.

Mechanism

All of us (or almost all of us) like to think of ourselves as respectable, moral people who behave decently. So if someone points out to us that, in fact, the exact opposite might be true, we cannot be indifferent to such in-formation. Of course, it may happen that we question its sense or even react aggressively towards the person who made such a remark. This was also the case in the described study by Michal Bilewicz and his team – it happened that participants of the discussion made various intriguing suggestions to the bot, suggesting where it could insert its pleasant re-minders… However, even if the bot's attention was initially met with aggression, in the long run the behavior changed. Let's also draw attention to a very important feature of the discussed message – its depersonaliza-tion. It is not that someone says "I don't want you to behave like that,"

"I don't approve of such behavior." A personal message may cause resistance ("what do I care what you want or what you like") and a desire to enter into a direct dispute with its author. A depersonalized message, on the other hand, is difficult to argue with. To sum up: sometimes it is enough to simply attract someone's attention to achieve a goal. To skillfully draw their attention to the importance of a certain norm. This is worth doing even if the change may not be immediate.

Technique # 83 *We are exceptional*

Idea

That norms are important to us seems an obvious thing to say. When we go abroad, find ourselves in a new environment, or even when we go to visit new acquaintances for the first time, we quickly try to figure out what behavior is welcome and what is not. This is an attempt to discover what the norms are – how, according to them, we should act, and what we should avoid at all costs. However, we must remember that different norms apply to us in different ways. There are norms that apply to everyone (or almost everyone) without distinction – for example, that in a restaurant we eat with cutlery rather than with our hands. There are also norms that apply only to certain social groups or people who are "chosen" in some way. Norms regulate, for example, who extends their hand first when greeting someone or who is introduced to another person first. Belonging to a particular group (e.g., "women" or "elderly people") determines what one should do in a given situation and which behaviors one should avoid. But is it possible, by artificially creating a group, to encourage people to behave according to a standard invented for that group?

Research

Hotel regulars know very well that one of the obligatory pieces of hotel bathroom equipment is a hanger (or sticker) encouraging guests to use their hotel towels again. The arguments that hotels invoke are varied – most often they refer to the general notion of ecology (if you use the towel again, you will not have to wash it immediately, and therefore you will save water and will not put detergents into the sewage). It is very likely that the hotel manager has something else in mind – saving money. Fewer washed towels mean less electricity, water, and washing powder consumption, and sometimes also less staff. They are therefore determined to find an argument that will strongly convince hotel guests to reuse their towels. In their study, Noah Goldstein, Robert Cialdini, and Vladas Griskevicius (2008) examined what message resulted in an increased percentage of people choosing to use the same towels twice. In the control group, the hanging tag had a standard text focused on ecology – an appeal to show respect for nature and help protect the environment. In one of the experimental conditions, the researchers decided to create a descriptive standard – they wrote that 75% of the hotel guests choose to reuse towels. Indeed, they found that this treatment effectively increased the number of people who chose to do so. However, Goldstein and colleagues didn't stop there – they created yet another hanger. On it, they reported that 75% of the guests in the room (a number was printed such as "215") decided to use the towels again. Of course, the number on the tag matched the number of the room in which it was placed. Thus, the guests were informed that it was the norm for people IN THIS ROOM to use towels twice. And indeed, in these conditions the message proved most effective – 49.3% of the visitors in this experimental condition followed the request formulated on the hanger. This was significantly more than in the control group, which focused solely on the ecology aspect (37.2%).

Mechanism

As Aristotle wrote, we are social animals – this also means that group identity is extremely important to us. We always belong to some group – women, men, members of some club, residents of some neighborhood or even street. This makes the norms espoused by the people in that group our norms as well. And the people who live on Elm Street can park their cars improperly, while we, from Cherry Street, do it completely differently: more orderly and better. Adherence to the group norm is therefore an important element of social identity. On the one hand, "we" are characterized, among other things, by the fact that we conform to such a norm; on the other hand, "they" do not necessarily do so, and this is what distinguishes us from them. In general, it can be assumed that the smaller the group, the more important the need to comply with its norms seems to be and the more strongly it affects us. Because, after all, in such a small and – let's not be afraid of this word – elite group, we have to care more about it. And following the norms of the group is one of the best forms of caring for its welfare.

Technique # 84 Consensus

Idea

Imagine that we are in a small town that we have never visited before. We have one thing to buy at the local supermarket. We might hope to do it in no time. But it's Friday afternoon, everyone is out shopping, and there isn't a single vacant space in the entire parking lot to leave our car. To be more precise, there is a small lot right next to the store, but there is a sign forbidding cars to stop there. However, the situation is a bit unclear – because although the sign is clear, there are several cars on the square and there is room for one more. Not too big, a truck wouldn't fit there, but our car would. Who will we listen to? The local authorities that put up the sign, or the local residents (the registrations on the cars indicate they are cars from here) who apparently ignored the sign? Which norm will apply to us?

Research

The most classic social psychology study to describe the consensus effect is the experiment by Solomon Asch (1951) in which participants were asked to compare line lengths (and in some cases believed the words of the people around them more than their own eyes). However, it may be better to describe a somewhat lesser-known study that was once conducted by one of the authors of this book (Grzyb & Dolinski, 2022). The participants were men who were informed that they were taking part in a television production. The purpose of the program was to find out the opinions of the townspeople on various topics – this time it was about corporal punishment of children. The men were asked whether they had ever hit their children (the survey was conducted about 20 years ago, when parenting standards were somewhat different). The participants gave their answers in groups of five, where only one person was the real participant, while the others were the experimenter's assistants. The "journalist" said that the sound and all the equipment had to be set up first, so initially, the statements would not be recorded. In this round, all the experimenter's aides admitted that they had spanked a child, although these were incidental cases. The real participant most often (in almost 90% of cases) also stated that such a situation had occurred in his life. After this, the "journalist" informed that everything was already set up and the real recording could begin. Again, he started with the experimenter's assistants, who, however, this time unanimously claimed that they had never hit a child in their lives. As it turned out, almost all of the real participants (18 out of 20 people – 90%) changed their minds compared to a few moments previous, and in full agreement with the other "participants of the recording" declared that they do not apply any physical punishment.

Mechanism

Being in tune with the behaviors and opinions of the people around us is important – in some situations even crucial. This is most often the case when we don't really know what to do (or when the instructions on what to do are unclear). There is an old saying "when in doubt, follow the crowd" – so when you don't know what to do, do what others do. It may not be the best option, but it's certainly the safest in this situation: even if you don't choose well, you're certainly not alone in that choice. And that in itself is a very important reward for us. It is also important that even when we make a mistake or fail (and in uncertain situations the fear that this will happen is considerable), the negative feelings associated with this fact are much weaker when we suffer it together with other people. Every student knows that a failing grade is disheartening when you are the only one who gets it but is of little consequence when the whole class gets it. Shortly speaking: if you eat a lot, you are a glutton, but if everyone eats a lot it just means that the food is very tasty.

Technique # 85 *Show me the list of people involved*
Idea

Imagine that one day, at your workplace, someone comes up with an initiative you have mixed feelings about. Let us say that the initiative is to go out together to a new restaurant specializing in molecular gastronomy. Generally speaking, you do enjoy the company of your co-workers and you do feel like meeting them in a neutral environment of a restaurant to have a relaxed conversation not necessarily devoted to professional matters. On the other hand, you have heard a little bit about molecular gastronomy – about bizarre spheres with sodium alginate or the process of spherification and you are quite certain that if you were to go out with your colleagues, you would prefer a place where food is prepared on a cutting board using a knife and a meat tenderizer, and not in retorts and flasks using a laser. But declining this invitation could be considered impolite and you do not want to be impolite to your co-workers... you are thus in a difficult position. You are not exactly sure what to do and time is pressing. After all, given the social context, even hesitation could be considered impolite. And now imagine that the person inviting you to this restaurant, prior to your final decision, shows you a list of the individuals who have already signed up for the evening of molecular gastronomy. This person flashes the list at you from a distance so that you cannot see who is actually on the list but you can see there are at least a dozen names. Will this make it easier for you to make up your mind? Is the sheer fact that the event will be attended by a considerable number of people a sufficient recommendation and will you therefore decide to participate in it?

Research

Studies designed to verify if this makes sense (i.e., if showing a list of individuals supporting an initiative affects the effectiveness of persuading more people into supporting it) were conducted by Peter Reingen (1978). In his study, he used a public fundraiser organized for the benefit of the Heart Association. The subjects were students of one of the universities in California who were walking, alone, down the paths of the university campus. The subjects were randomly assigned to one of the experimental groups – there was, obviously, also a control group. In the control group, a standard request was made – the experimenter approached a given in-dividual and said that he represented the Heart Association and that he was collecting donations for the benefit of this organization under the annual fundraiser. In the end, the experimenter asked the subject if they would join the fundraising initiative and make a donation.

Apart from that, Reingen created a number (as many as nine) experimental groups. Within the experimental groups, he manipulated three elements. First, even though members of all experimental groups were shown a list of people who had already decided to make a donation, Reingen manipulated the length of the list – in some variants, there were four surnames on the list, while in other variants there were twelve. The amounts indicated in the list of donations varied, too – in some cases these were low (ranging from 15 to 35 cents, on average 25 cents), while in other cases these were higher (ranging from 75 to 95 cents, on average 85 cents). In the course of his experiment, Reingen wanted to verify one more aspect –the effect of inducing a certain social norm on the subjects' willingness to donate money – in certain groups, the subjects were told that their donation was needed in order to support the prevention of heart attacks among people they might know. Reingen assumed that adding this information might improve the effectiveness of the request.

The results were examined in two ways: both the number of subjects who decided to make a donation was verified as well as the amount of the donation. As evidenced by the results, the assumptions were correct. In the control conditions, 40% of the respondents decided to donate money. When the subjects were shown the short list of previous donors, the figure increased to 47%. However, when the list was long, as many as 60% of the subjects decided to make a donation. The figure increased even more when the above-mentioned social norm was being induced – when it was combined with the long list of donors, the effectiveness ratio was 70%. Also, the donation amount increased in these conditions – from 28 cents in the control group up to 68 cents in the group with the long list, a high average donation amount and induced social norm.

Mechanism

If we want to identify a potential psychological mechanism behind the effectiveness of this technique, at least two can be considered. The first is the consensus rule, which we are already familiar with. If we are not certain what to do, we copy the behavior of other people – in this case, even if our decision turns out to be rather poor, at least we are not the only one in trouble. However, this technique also refers to something else – a certain magical effect of a written obligation, the legitimizing power of a list with names. It should be noted that when we talk to a volunteer representing a charity, there is always an element of uncertainty in us. Perhaps he/she is an impostor? Perhaps this is completely unsupervised and my money will be embezzled? Seeing a list with names and donation amounts should eliminate such doubts (or at least reduce them).

Obviously, one should keep in mind that the effectiveness of this technique is not necessarily limited to fundraisers. If you want to assemble a group of friends willing to go canoeing on Saturday or come to Steve's birthday party, or if you want people to sign a list of support for your candidate for the city council, show them a list of names of people who have already signed up. And – of course – make sure the list includes at least a dozen names.

A specific form of applying this technique is the preparation of advertising posters intended for fly-posting. If we want to sell a bicycle or promote our moving services, we can prepare a poster to be put up at various locations in the city. Usually, at the bottom of such a poster, we provide our telephone number on narrow strips of paper, which one can easily tear off and put in their pocket (in order to call at a later time). Fly-posting veterans suggest to always tear off a few strips with the telephone number immediately after putting up your poster – this is a form of virtually creating a list of people who have already expressed their initial interest in the poster. We have no "hard" data that could prove that this method is effective but based on the results of Reingen's experiment, we can conservatively assume that it is highly probable that it is.

Technique # 86 "The group's expanding"
Idea

We have already described how to take advantage of a situation in which a large group of people (or the majority of the population we want to target) behave in a certain way. By appealing to consensus, we can show that a certain behavior (attitude, appearance, way of looking at the problem) is dominant, is the norm. If something is the norm, then other people should also behave in a similar way – and this is the mechanism behind the effectiveness of consensus as a mechanism of social influence. But what can be done if a behavior is not exhibited by the majority of people?

For example, imagine that you want to encourage people to have a preventive annual abdominal ultrasound. According to many doctors, this is
an excellent way to check whether organs such as the liver, pancreas, and
kidneys are functioning properly – and if something suspicious starts
happening with them, you can react quickly and diagnose the disease
while it is fully curable. However, despite these benefits and the pain-
lessness of the test itself, still not many people opt for it – so how do we
inform them about it? After all, if we wrote that 4% of the population
performs a preventive ultrasound every year, it would be counter-
productive – people would consider it rather evidence that the test is
unnecessary and ineffective, since almost no one does it. We also don't
want to lie and claim, contrary to fact, that most people do these preventive screenings. So what can we do? In such a situation, it is better not
to focus on absolute numbers, but on an upward trend. So not "4% of
adults had an abdominal ultrasound last year," but rather "twice as many
people had an abdominal ultrasound last year as the year before."

Research

Research demonstrating this mechanism was conducted by Chad
Mortensen and colleagues (2019). It should be noted that the procedure
itself was remarkably ingenious and precise in the way it was measured.
The participants were students who were first informed that they were
taking part in a study on the relationship between personality traits and
drafting ability. They were given a popular science text to read that described the results of a study on students' attitudes toward water conservation. In one group, it appeared that a minority of students (48%)
engaged in at least some form of water-saving activities (such as turning
off the faucet while washing hands, using aerators – shower head at-
tachments that reduce water consumption, etc.). In the second group,
another sentence was added to this information: although now it is 48% of
students, two years ago it was only 37%, so there has been an increase.
There was, of course, also a control group in which the respondents were
asked to read a text about architecture. When the students had paraphrased
and edited all of the texts, they were informed that the study was over, but
that they could participate in one more study taking place in the next
room. Once participants entered the room, they were shown a tube of

toothpaste and a toothbrush and told that the purpose of the study was to test consumer preferences for toothpaste. They were asked to brush their teeth over a sink located in the same room and describe their impressions (about the toothpaste) in a questionnaire. However, they did not know that a device had been mounted under the sink to measure the amount of water used while brushing their teeth (which was the real purpose of the study). The results confirmed that it was the "growing trend" information that was a strong motivator to reduce water use – it was the people in this group who most often turned off the water while brushing their teeth, and this group had the lowest average water use (0.34 gallons). The worst group was the one that was only informed that students who conserve water were in the minority. The participants reading this text were those least likely to turn off the faucet while brushing their teeth and consequently had the highest average water use (0.49 gallons).

Mechanism

There is no doubt that our own behavior is significantly modeled by the behavior of others (although, of course, we don't particularly want to admit this). However, we should remember that the behavior of others is also subject to change. This means that in certain situations it may be diagnostic for us not only how many people are doing something, but also how this number changes. This can be seen very clearly when we observe fashion – for example, the wearing of a particular type of shoe. If it can be observed that more and more women are wearing emu shoes, then even if the absolute value of the number of pairs of such shoes in the female population oscillates around 10–15%, there will be no doubt about what will be fashionable this season. The number of women wearing emu will increase. Thus, in certain situations, it is the minority that can clearly influence the behavior of the majority – provided, however, that the minority is on an upward trajectory. Therefore, the attitude, behavior, or view presented by the minority will gain more and more followers. Psychological research shows that people, on the basis of two consecutive measurements of a phenomenon, most often acquire a belief about its rectilinear course (if something is increasing, it will continue to increase; if something is declining, it will continue to decline). That's why shareholders often sell company stock when share prices are falling and buy when they are rising. And only sometimes are these decisions correct. Thus, showing that the prevalence of some behavior is increasing is a method of using the principle of emerging consensus. A consensus that does not (yet) exist, but according to the addressees of such a message will exist in the future.

7

WORDING THE REQUEST

It would be difficult to enumerate all the different ways one could word their request to borrow garden shears from their neighbor. One could start by asking if the neighbor is going to do any gardening work in the next couple of days, we could complain to the neighbor that our garden shears have just broken or gotten lost, or we could simply ask if he would not mind lending us his garden shears for two hours. If we go for the last of the above options, we could start by telling the neighbor that we have a favor to ask of him or we could formulate our request without any introduction. Some neighbors would lend us their garden shears regardless of how we phrase our request. Surely, there are some neighbors who never lend their tools to anybody and would not do so this time around no matter how the request is phrased. However, how we choose our words may be crucial in the case of other neighbors we might have. Whether or not we return home with borrowed garden shears may depend on wording nuances, the use of particular terms, saying some things, or choosing not to say others. Almost all social influence techniques are based

DOI: 10.4324/9781003296638-8

on verbal communication, which we are sure our readers have already learned. Nevertheless, this chapter presents those techniques, in the case of which wording plays the dominant role.

Technique # 87 (Don't) say "please"

Idea

In some cultures, young children are taught that there are three magic words: "please," "thank you," and "excuse me." Their use causes the "magician" to be regarded as a friendly and kind person and to meet with the approval of their social environment. From the perspective of social influence, one of these words, in particular, seems very important. It is rather obvious that if we want to address a request to someone, we will increase our chances of having it fulfilled if we use the word "please." While this is probably true for most cases, psychological experiments show that there are some situations in which adding this word to the end of a request can decrease, rather than increase, the chances that it will be fulfilled. In presenting the following study, we do not wish to convince you that politeness does not pay. We're also far from encouraging people to eliminate the word "please" from their vocabulary. However, we cannot help but present something that is completely counterintuitive, namely, to show that there are situations in which it is better not to use this word.

Research

Michael Firmin, Janine Helmick, Brian Iezzi, and Aaron Vaughn (2004) conducted a very simple experiment in which they induced male and female students living in a dormitory to buy chocolate chip cookies. A homemade chocolate chip cookie cost 50 cents, and potential buyers were informed that the proceeds from the sale of these sweets would contribute to a charity to help the hungry. Firmin and his colleagues varied slightly in the way they encouraged the students to buy the cookie in each experimental condition. In half of the cases they simply said: "Will you purchase a cookie?", and in the remaining cases the word "please" was added to this short question. In the first case, 79% of the participants bought cookies. And what about the second situation? As the authors of the study themselves were surprised to see, it turned out that this time the rate was only 65.3%. So we can see that the addition of the "magic" word "please" not only failed to increase the number of people willing to buy cookies but quite significantly reduced it.

Mechanism

It can be assumed that if people learn that engaging in an activity will help other people who are in a difficult situation, they will do it with those people in mind. This is probably also the case in the situation created in the experiment described above. If someone offering a cookie for 50 cents says that the proceeds from the sale of these sweets will go to people suffering from hunger, the message is clear from this perspective. It is the hungry who will benefit from you taking two quarters out of your pocket and buying a cookie that you may not even particularly want. But what if the message contains the word "please"? Well, we can assume that in such conditions it is the asker who is particularly interested in making people buy cookies. So it becomes unclear who the main beneficiary of the action (i.e., buying cookies) will be: starving people or the person making the request. It's not even a question of suspecting that the cookie seller is making a profit from each cookie sold, but rather that they become the person for whom we are to do a favor. And we want to help the starving, not the seller! Of course, the situation created in this experiment is specific. However, it is worth considering under what other conditions the use of the word "please" may cause ambiguity as to who would actually benefit from the fulfillment of the request, and, consequently, significantly decrease the chances of its being carried out.

Technique # 88 Gratitude

Idea

It would seem that saying thank you is simply a polite phrase. It's appropriate to say thank you for certain things: for a birthday present you receive, for someone picking up and returning a pen that fell out of your pocket without you even noticing, for someone helping you put a heavy suitcase on a shelf on a train, or patiently explaining the directions to a certain address. Saying "thank you" completes an action rather than starting it (although sometimes we do say thank you in advance). But there are other situations in which thanking occurs, as it were, in the middle of an activity. We may thank someone who is doing some work well, hoping that they will want to continue doing it equally well. But what if someone is not very zealously engaged in some activity? If we offer our thanks for what they are doing anyway, will their conduct improve? Or, on the contrary, will they see the thank you as a full endorsement of the quality of their work, and therefore not improve their performance one bit? It is obvious that certain activities can be done with different frequencies. For example, you might clean your windows once a week, once a month, once a quarter, or even less frequently. Similarly, we can go jogging daily, every two days, or twice a week. The frequency of certain activities is fundamental to re-education efforts. An example of this might be the frequency with which case managers of social service agencies visit minors who have come into conflict with the law. Will thanking them for what they have done so far make them increase the frequency of contact with their charges in the near-term?

Research

A very important part of rehabilitation programs for minors is the care provided by specially trained case managers of social service agencies. The key to their influence is direct contact, during which they can learn about the problems of their charges. The visits also allow them to see for themselves if their charges are sober or under the influence of drugs. Most importantly, however, face-to-face conversation is an opportunity to build mutual trust. Hewitt Clark, James Northrop, and Charles Barkshire (1988) decided to take a closer look at this issue and found that only 43% of young people in such programs are visited at least once a week. The question thus arises of what can be done to change this situation for the better. Simple psychological interventions included sending all staff a short, standard letter thanking them for their work. This was done after each visit they made. It turned out that this was enough for the frequency of visits to increase significantly! As many as 78% of the young people in the rehabilitation program were visited at least once a week. However, when the letters were discontinued, the frequency of visits dropped again.

Then about 50% of the charges of social service agencies could count on a weekly visit from a social worker.

Mechanism

Receiving a thank-you note for work done, in addition to the satisfaction of the person receiving it, leads to several less-than-obvious consequences. First, the people receiving the thanks learn that what they do is important and noticed by others. Secondly, the received thanks constitute a kind of obligation for them to act in the manner of one who deserves the gratitude. Third, it makes the very actions for which they were thanked more cognitively accessible to them. They think about them more often, reflecting with greater frequency on their course and consequences. It will also be easier for them to perceive the deep sense of the actions they have taken so far. All this together makes people more likely to engage in the activity they are being thanked for. The results of the experiment described above showed that the consequence of receiving the thanks was an increase in the frequency of visits to social service agencies. This is an unambiguous and easily quantifiable indicator. We cannot be sure (though we can hope) that it also resulted in increased care shown by agency staff to troubled young people, as well as their greater commitment to fulfilling their responsibilities. The results of numerous other studies suggest that this is very likely the case. While in the case of the previously discussed technique we indicated that, in some cases, the use of the word "please" may reduce the chances of a request being fulfilled, this time we must state unequivocally that we are not aware of empirical research that suggests that in some situations the use of the word "thank you" may reduce the power of social influence. So let us not refrain from thanking people for what they do, if they are doing good things.

Technique # 89 I hope I'm not disturbing you

Idea

The technique *service request* described at the beginning of this book (# 4) has the advantage of being extremely simple to apply while appearing quite universal. Its essence consists in preceding the main request with a basically meaningless phrase, like "could you do me a service?" or "could you help me?" We can ask ourselves whether we will achieve a similar effect by using other linguistic phrases, which also evoke an automatic tendency in the addressee to give a polite, conventional answer. Just as when we hear "Good morning" we reply "Good morning," when we hear "I hope I'm not disturbing you, am I?" we usually reply in the negative. Of course, there are exceptions to this rule. We won't say yes when we are really very busy with something or when we don't like the person speaking to us and want to conclude the interaction as quickly as possible. But what if we give a conventional answer to the question? How will we react when we are then asked to do something? French social influence researchers decided to find out.

Research

Sebastien Meineri and Nicolas Gueguen (2011) were tasked with conducting a telephone survey on the opinions that residents of the South Brittany (France) region have about their local newspaper. The questionnaire consisted of 32 questions and answering them required at least a few minutes. The main problem with such surveys is the typically high percentage of people who refuse to participate. The researchers decided to take advantage of this assignment to test the effectiveness of a social influence technique that could reduce this refusal rate at least somewhat. They asked themselves whether this effect could be achieved by using the phrase: "I hope I'm not disturbing you, am I?". Within the framework of this survey, which is – as we already know – at the same time an experiment devoted to this question, 1791 telephone numbers were randomly selected from the phone book. (These were still the days when people usually had landline phones in their homes, and the phone books gave their names and phone numbers.) The people calling the respondents always politely introduced themselves first, after which the conversation was directed down slightly different paths in each of the three experimental conditions. In the first one, the control condition, they were simply asked to spend a few minutes talking about the newspaper Le Telegamme. It turned out that in this situation only 17.3% of people agreed to take part in the survey. In the second condition, the person calling the respondent said: "I hope I'm not disturbing you, am I?", then listened to the answer, and only then (regardless of its content) made a request to talk about the newspaper. Of the 587 people who were asked whether the caller was bothering them at the moment, only 12 (i.e., about 2%) said that they were. They said, for example: "I'm in a hurry," "Yes, I don't have time right now," or "I have to leave." Not surprisingly, only one of them subsequently agreed to talk about Le Telegamme. The others who were questioned usually answered politely: "No," "Not much," or "No, not really." Of all those interviewed in these conditions (and thus including those who said the caller bothered them), 25.2% agreed to talk about the local publication. This is thus a significantly higher rate than that obtained in the control conditions discussed previously. And how was it in the conditions in which the caller did say, "I hope I'm not disturbing you, am I?", but did not wait for the caller's response and proceeded straight to asking for participation in the survey? It turned out that this time the percentage of those consenting was 19.1, which was similar to that achieved in the control condition.

Mechanism

It seems that, as in the case of the previously discussed technique, the psychological mechanism underlying the effectiveness of the influence presented here is people's tendency to exhibit consistency in their own behavior. If someone answers the polite question "I hope I'm not disturbing you, am I?" in the negative, they are at least implicitly declaring that they have free time and are not doing anything important or urgent at the moment. If this is the case, then we should expect agreement to comply with the request, which requires at most 10–15 minutes of activity. Consistent with this assumption is the result that the technique ceases to be effective when the person who says "I hope I'm not disturbing you, am I?" does not wait for an answer, but immediately begins to formulate a request. Let us note that in such a situation the person being approached will not find themselves in a consistency trap. After all, they did not say that the caller did not interrupt them in some activity. However, one can also accept an alternative interpretation of the recorded results pattern. Perhaps the key here is the perceived politeness of the person calling us. Starting the conversation with a polite question: "I hope I'm not disturbing you, am I?", waiting for an answer and only making a request, according to the rule of reciprocity that we have already written about, should result in politeness. It materializes as an agreement to fulfill this request. However, making a similar statement without waiting for a response is not so polite (or perhaps it is just plain rude!). Not surprisingly, it does not increase the propensity to comply with the request that follows.

Technique # 90 *Legitimization of a paltry contribution: Even a penny will help*

Idea

You, the Reader, are probably often asked to make a donation to a charity. If your reaction in such situations is typical, you may or may not make a donation. What does it depend on? You will probably answer that it depends on many factors: what the money is being collected for, who is collecting it, whether the collector is neatly dressed, what your own financial situation looks like at the time. You will probably also agree that it depends on what mood you are in and whether or not you have just made a donation to something else. Other factors may also be relevant: are you alone at the time or with your friends, and if with friends, how did they behave: did they donate or not? Or did they give, saying loudly "this is on behalf of all of us?" We could probably go on at length with a list of such factors potentially contributing to your reaction. But instead, let's focus here on an entirely different issue that may be relevant: how a donation request is phrased, or more specifically: exactly what words the person making the request uses.

Research

Robert Cialdini and David Schroeder (1976) conducted an experiment on the effectiveness of collecting charitable donations. In their study, representatives of the American Cancer Society went door to door and asked for donations to fight this terrible disease. They found that 28.6% of the people approached gave them money. We note, by the way, that this is quite a good rate, indicating high generosity among the people being asked! However, when the researchers added a few seemingly meaningless words to their request – namely, "even a penny will help" – the frequency of donations was even higher! This time every second person gave money to them! Let us also add that if we consider only the people choosing to give money, the average donation amounts were almost the same in both conditions ($1.44 and $1.54, respectively). This means that by adding just the few words mentioned above, almost twice as much money was raised!

Mechanism

Cialdini and Schroeder pointed out that people find it relatively easy to refuse difficult requests. If someone asks us for something that is materially expensive, requires a lot of time from us, or is in any other way troublesome, we are able to give many reasons why we will not fulfill this request. What is more, the reasons for such a refusal are then socially accepted – other people would consider them sufficient to refuse to help. What if someone asks us to donate to a charitable cause? By refusing, we might explain to ourselves that we don't trust the person making the request, and we're not sure the money will go where it should. Usually, however, we have no cause for such suspicions. Why would we, even if just in our head, insult a volunteer! So we find another, very serious and rational argument: "I am not rich enough." I am not rich enough to help everyone in need, I am not rich enough to help in a situation such as this. But what happens when the requester uses the phrase "even a penny will help?" By saying that, they negate the opportunity to use this argument, which seemed so great just a moment ago. After all, I don't have to be rich to give a penny. I'm not so poor that I can't afford to give a single penny! So we reach into our pocket. But once we've already put our hand in there, we're not going to pull out one penny. We're going to pull out as many as are usually given in these situations. So we see that a few simple, seemingly meaningless words can bring about a big change in the behavior of the people we ask to donate to a charitable cause.

Technique # 91 *Legitimization of a paltry contribution: Beyond collecting money*

Idea

The social influence technique described above concerned the possibility of significantly increasing the funds raised during charity collections. However, the technique of legitimization of a paltry contribution can also be used in other activities and does not only apply to fundraising. One can imagine, for example, that while looking for volunteers to devote their time to tidying up an abandoned cemetery or cleaning the cages of animals in a shelter, we would use the formula "even a few minutes would help." When organizing demonstrations to protest against threats to democracy, we may be interested in getting the largest possible turnout for our event. So we appeal to various people to come, but we also tell them to try to persuade their friends to come as well. What is the best thing to say then? Perhaps something like "every single person will count." There are, of course, many more examples of this type. So, does the legitimization of a paltry contribution technique work for more than just raising money? Below we present an experiment whose results quite clearly answer this question.

Research

Many years ago Wroclaw, the city where the university we work in is located, was a candidate to organize the World Expo. The city's authorities decided (rightly so) that it was necessary to gain the full acceptance of the residents for this idea. So they prepared, among other things, leaflets that provided reliable information on what the World Expo is and what benefits the city organizing the event can expect. Of course, the goal was to distribute these flyers as widely as possible. Along with several colleagues we decided to combine "the pleasant with the useful," and thus to do an experiment concerning a technique that would effectively make people not only take individual leaflets from the hands of volunteers but also take additional informational materials for other people (Dolinski et al., 2005). Our experiment was designed like this: students distributed said flyers in the city center. Any person who reached out for a leaflet was, of course, handed one, but at the same time was told that it would be great if they took a pile of those leaflets for their neighbors and friends. In half the cases, at the same time, we added the phrase "every single distributed leaflet will count." It turned out that, while in the control conditions, 31% of people took the additional leaflets, in the conditions where the message contained the additional phrase, this rate was significantly higher – it reached 43%.

Mechanism

The mechanism underlying the effectiveness of this technique is, of course, very similar to the one we described when presenting the "even a penny will help" technique. After all, almost everyone has a person in their social circle to whom they can hand out a single leaflet without any effort or waste of time. So it is hard to refuse to get involved in the distribution of such informational materials, it is hard not to take one extra leaflet. But if one agrees to act as a leaflet distributor, one does not have to limit oneself to a single leaflet. We can take at least a few, and maybe even a few dozen leaflets (after all, almost no one has just one neighbor or one friend). The power of the technique discussed here (as well as the technique discussed previously, of course) is that we tell a person that we would be satisfied with even their minimal help, but at the same time we don't explicitly tell them that we are asking them to get involved only to a minimal degree. As it turns out, people in such situations usually do not limit themselves to the minimum as described.

Technique # 92 *Metacommunication bind*

Idea

Imagine you are walking quietly down the street. You meet a stranger who asks you for something. The request seems a little strange to you. Actually, why would you do that? You will probably say: "no, thank you, goodbye" and go on your way. Or you might say nothing at all, just shake your head in response, or shrug your shoulders, give a perfunctory smile, and move on. But what if the person asking you to do this ends the story more or less like this· "I am not pressuring you with this request. If I am, please tell me," or says "but tell me if this seems inappropriate between strangers." You probably don't think this will change your decision in any way. After all, it's just a few meaningless polite words. But... read the description of the experiment below. When you see the results of this study, you may not be so sure that the few extra words mentioned are of no significance.

Research

Michael Patch, Vicki Hoang, and Anthony Stahelski (1997) approached their participants on a university campus. In the control condition, the message directed to a person walking alone was: "I'm part of a student group concerned with student interests such as campus social events and parking. We need to conduct some in-depth interviews with a few students to help us define where the most serious problems are. Would you be able to give us 20 minutes of your time some afternoon this week?" It turned out that 18% of those questioned agreed to comply with this request. In other conditions of this experiment, before asking the participant to spend 20 minutes, they heard: "This is kind of awkward. There is something I'd like to ask of you, but tell me if this seems inappropriate between strangers." It turned out that then the number of people who agreed to fulfill this request more than doubled, going as high as 41%.

Mechanism

If a stranger asks us to fulfill a request and we conclude that we don't feel like doing it, we refuse. However, the reason why we refuse is our private matter, and we have no intention of disclosing it. The person making the request may, however, use the so-called metacommunicative bind: namely, they may insert into their short speech a suggestion that perhaps we do not feel comfortable in this specific situation, and that is why we would like to refuse the request. However, they add a particular incentive: if you want to refuse, tell me directly and explain the reasons for your refusal. The problem is that explaining to a stranger that we feel pressured to do something we don't feel like doing, or explaining that we find their request inappropriate for some reason, would make us even more uncomfortable than granting the request! Psychologically, such a seemingly exceptionally polite message somehow neutralized our ability to refuse a request without explaining the reasons for our decision. So it renders impossible a behavior that we very often exhibit. Now we only have a choice: either to agree or to refuse and at the same time explain why we are not going to fulfill the request. As you can see, many people in this situation prefer to comply with the request, rather than get involved in an unpleasant discussion about the reasons for their refusal.

Technique # 93 *The only request*

Idea

What does one feel upon being asked to grant a request? Let us imagine a scenario – it is a pleasant and sunny afternoon – perhaps you are getting home from work or maybe you have simply decided to go for a short walk. You are contemplating the world around you, considering your dinner options (perhaps you are also thinking about the person with whom you would like to have your dinner), you are strolling in a leisurely manner when, suddenly, a young woman holding a clipboard approaches you and asks you a question. Let us assume that she is asking you to fill out a four-part questionnaire regarding your holiday plans.

What can you do in such a situation? After all, you are really tired of all those calls from telemarketers asking all sorts of questions only to offer a once-in-a-lifetime opportunity to purchase a luxury alpaca quilt or invite you to a demonstration of medical devices. You may suspect that the question regarding your holiday plans is just an introduction – an attempt to get you involved in a dialogue only to offer you yet another transaction or ask you for a donation for the benefit of a charitable organization. If this is the case, perhaps it would be better to refuse straight away – to tell the young woman that you are pressed for time or that you are not interested in whatever it is that she is offering. Or perhaps, which would be, relatively, the simplest solution, you should walk past the woman and carry on without engaging in any form of conversation. Yes, this seems to be the best option. After all, this way you will save your and other people's time and you can avoid the risk of escalation of requests. But what would happen, if the young woman added, "this is the only request I am going to make," at the end of her utterance?

Research

In our studies, we decided to verify if the argument pointing to the fact that the request being made is going to be the only one and that it will not be followed by any other requests affects one's willingness to make a donation for the benefit of a charitable organization Grzyb & Dolinski, 2017). In order to do so, we decided to cooperate with a local children's hospice, which regularly collects money for its operation at various public events (fairs, concerts, and all sorts of trade fairs). It should be noted that such cooperation is always mutually beneficial – we, as researchers, collect data for our calculations but all donations collected in the process are, obviously, handed over to the charitable organization we cooperate with.

In the case of this study, two female volunteers approached randomly selected passers-by in the vicinity of an open-air concert organized by the hospice. The volunteers assigned lone passers-by to the experimental or the control group. In the control group, subjects were addressed in the following manner: "Good day, I'm collecting funds for a local children's hospice to improve its functioning, would you join our cause and make a donation?" In the experimental group, the same utterance was supplemented with "this is the only request I am going to make."

The results confirmed our assumptions. In the experimental group, a markedly higher number of subjects decided to donate some of the money they had in their wallets to the charity. In the control group, slightly over 15% of the subjects decided to make a donation, whereas the percentage was almost 55% in the group where the volunteer added, "this is the only request I am going to make," at the end of her utterance. By the same token, the addition of a simple piece of information translated into an over threefold increase in the number of subjects willing to support the charity!

Mechanism

We would all like to live in a world governed by clearly defined rules (or at least we often declare so). We are not particularly fond of uncertainty – as to the intentions of our interlocutor or as to the further development of a situation we have found ourselves in. Therefore, sometimes we "play it safe" – we withdraw from a situation that – in our opinion – might develop in an undesired direction. We choose to pre-emptively say "no" rather than get involved in a conversation with an uncertain outcome. "The only request" technique is based on this type of fear or – to put it more precisely – it is designed in such a manner as to reduce this fear. Hence, if you intend to ask someone for something in particular (a donation for charity, signing a petition, or answering questions included in a questionnaire), you may try to eliminate this fear straight away by stressing that the favor you are asking is going to be your only request and that it will not be followed by anything else. This way, you will increase your effectiveness and as demonstrated by the above-described studies (as well as many other studies which confirm their outcomes), this method is effective. But what will happen if you choose to formulate another request once the subject has acted on the initial one? This does not have to result from a cold calculation or a previously prepared scenario – sometimes, one request simply stems from another, and thus we choose to formulate it. Is this method doomed to failure? The subject might think, I thought we had an agreement, and terminate the interaction. Yet the techniques described in other chapters of this book (the meta-technique of dialogue as well as the rule of involvement and consequence) suggest that it would be unlikely. Therefore, even if it turns out, in the course of our conversation, that the only request is not actually the only one, it does not mean that the subjects will necessarily withdraw from the situation we have created.

Technique # 94 *Dialogue involvement*

Idea

Several years ago, one of the authors of this book conducted a study commissioned by an appliance store chain. The purpose of the study was to identify the traits of the most effective members of the sales staff. The findings of the study were to be used as the starting point for the training of all staff members. It should be an easy guess that one's competences should be of crucial importance here. A good sales clerk is someone who can answer all questions asked by a customer in an exhaustive and competent manner. Meanwhile, it turned out that the most effective sales clerks not so much answer questions but... ask questions themselves. For example: if a customer walks into a store and wants to buy an iron, a good sales clerk asks if the iron will be used frequently or rather occasionally. Will the iron be used to iron everyday clothes or perhaps curtains or heavy bedspreads? Will it be used solely at home or will it travel with its user to various places, etc.? It is only after a short conversation that the sales clerk nods and brings over three or four irons and says: "we should be able to pick something optimal from these." In other words, the best sales clerks talked to the customers and engaged in conversations with them instead of just attending to them. Leaving selling irons, coffee machines, or juicers aside, does engaging in a conversation with someone make this person more willing to grant our request or accept our offer? Or, to put it differently, can involving someone in a dialogue be regarded as a social influence technique?

Research

The experiment (Dolinski et al., 2001) was conducted by young people (university students) at the main pedestrian precinct in Wroclaw – one of the biggest cities in Poland with 700,000 residents. The individual conducting the study approached apparently adult lone passers-by. In the control conditions, the experimenter said that they were a university student and that together with their friends, they were raising funds for a trip to Nepal. To this end, they are selling Indian incense sticks. The price for a pack is very attractive. Will the subject decide to make the purchase? It turned out that only 6% of the subjects decided to use this opportunity. In the alternative conditions of the experiment, the dialogue involvement technique was used. In this case, the experimenter approached a subject and asked the following question: "Who do you think is more sensitive to scents: women or men?" Regardless of the answer, the initial question was followed by another: "Why do you think so?" Having listened to the arguments provided by the subject, the experimenter said that together with their friends, they were raising funds for a trip to Nepal, and to that end, they were selling Indian incense sticks at an attractive price. It turned out that this time around, exactly 20% of the subjects decided to purchase the incense sticks. At the same time, additional analyses demonstrated that the frequency of purchasing the incense sticks was not related, in any way, to the sex of the subjects, the sex of the experimenter, or the answers provided by the subjects to the questions asked by the experimenter.

Mechanism

A monologue and a dialogue are two basic modes of communication. It should be noted that a monologue is typical of a situation where the communicating individuals do not know each other. We turn on the radio and we can hear the monologue of a weather forecaster. We enter a railway station and we can hear messages about delayed trains. We do not know the radio announcer or the lady working at the railway station. But what happens when we run into an acquaintance? We first greet the person and then we ask them either a more general question (e.g., "how are you?" or "how have you been?") or a more precise one (e.g., "did you attend the lecture yesterday?" or "do you know the score of yesterday's game?"). When we hear the answer, we comment on it or refer to it. Therefore, a dialogue is typical of interaction with people we know. Presumably, everyone will agree that we are more willing to grant and that we more frequently grant requests made by people we know than those made by strangers. Especially if acting on the request is not difficult or particularly problematic, refusing someone you know would be considered tactless and even impolite. Therefore, if a stranger asks us for something in the form of a monologue, they behave like a typical stranger. Yet, if the same person manages to first involve us in a dialogue, they act as if they knew us. Since, as we already pointed out several times in this book, people often act in a rather automatic manner by initiating ready-made patterns of behavior developed in the past, a stranger who involves us in a dialogue triggers the pattern of behavior that we developed in the past and that we apply to interactions with people we know. This pattern of behavior consists of agreeing to act on a request or accepting an offer. In the experiment discussed above, the initial conversation (dialogue) was thematically linked to the offer made towards the end. The conversation pertained to one's sensitivity to scents and the commercial offer of purchasing incense sticks. Other experiments clearly demonstrate that this is not necessary. Even dialogues on weather, one's mood or a conversation with a university student about the end-of-term examinations: all of them make people, immediately after, more willing to comply with all kinds of requests (not necessarily related to the topics of the conversations). Nevertheless, the topic of conversation should be trivial, conventional. For if we initiate a conversation on a topic that is important for our interlocutor, this person will cease to act automatically and will become more critical and thoughtful. If, in the course of such a conversation, it becomes apparent that our views on this critical issue are different than those of our interlocutor, not only will the chances for them to act on our request immediately after this conversation not increase but they will even decrease.

Technique # 95 *Dialogue and LPC*
Idea

The dialogue involvement technique is easy to apply, as starting an interaction with a person, whom we intend to exert influence upon, with a conversation on a trivial topic is perfectly natural. In this case, conversation means asking a few questions, listening to the answers, and perhaps answering the questions asked by our interlocutor. The above-mentioned natural character of the dialogue involvement technique and the fact that it initiates our contact with another person make it easy to imagine this method being combined with another social influence technique. When we ask someone for help, the act of which may vary significantly in terms of the degree of its difficulty (e.g., an activity oriented towards helping us may take from one minute up to several hours, a donation for charity may range from a penny to a mind-boggling amount, etc.), it is easy and useful to apply the legitimization of paltry contributions technique, which we have already discussed here. Let us briefly remind our readers that this refers to a situation where we inform our interlocutor that even the smallest help would be appreciated. We already know that this technique is effective. But will it become even more so if we use it on someone whom we involve in a dialogue beforehand?

Research

The authors of this book, together with a few associates (Dolinski et al., 2005), conducted a field study in Opole (a city of approx. 100,000 residents). The students impersonated volunteers of a charity raising funds for Afghan refugees staying in Pakistan. The subjects were apparently adult lone passers-by. In the standard conditions, students simply said, "Good morning/afternoon," held out their hand with a box of coins jingling inside and uttered the following phrase: "Would you like to contribute a donation to a charity supporting Afghan refugees?" It turned out that in such conditions, as many as 16.7% of the subjects decided to put some of their money into the moneybox! In other experimental conditions, the subjects were first involved in a dialogue and only afterwards asked to make a donation. For some reason, the researchers decided to use two different topics of conversation with the subjects. Some subjects got involved in a conversation on the subject of refugees. First, they were greeted and then they were asked the following question: "Have you heard about the conflict in Afghanistan?" Obviously, the answer to this was affirmative. At that point, the experimenter asked another question: "Do you think it is necessary to somehow help refugees who got stuck in camps on the Pakistani border?" It turned out that in such conditions, as many as 50% of the subjects decided to put some of their money into the moneybox. As we can see, again, dialogue involvement is a highly effective social influence technique. But what do you think happened when, in the above described experimental conditions, the experimenter, while holding out their hand with the moneybox, added the phrase "even a penny will help?" In such circumstances, as many as 63.3% of the subjects responded positively to the request for a donation. When thinking about the above results, one may have doubts as to whether the dialogue itself was actually of key importance. It should be noted that most of the people who were asked if it was necessary to somehow help the refugees replied affirmatively. If they refused to make a donation, they would, in a sense, contradict their own words. And if they did, we would be dealing with a variant of the four walls technique, which we addressed in the initial sections of this book. For this reason, the other subjects were not involved in a conversation about refugees, instead, they were simply asked the following question: "How are you doing today?" The experimenter listened to their answer and commented accordingly by asking if, perhaps, the weather influenced their frame of mind. Again, the experimenter listened to their answer and then told the subjects about the fundraiser for the benefit of Afghan refugees and held out their hand with the moneybox. This dialogue also proved to be effective. In such conditions, the number of individuals who decided to make a donation was over two times higher than in the standard conditions (precisely speaking: 36.7%). And what was the result of adding the "even a penny will help" phrase? As many as 53.3% of the subjects put some of their money into the box!

Mechanism

Two social influence techniques have been combined in such a manner as to make sure they appear to be a normal conversation, which ends in a normal way. There is nothing strange, unusual, or unexpected in the interaction with the person whom we want to influence and yet, as evidenced by the results of the above-described experiment, the power of the influence is quite remarkable. It should be noted that the technique described in this section requires virtually no time input or precise preparations. It is a bit of a paradox but this is exactly why it is so effective. The person being the target of this influence technique may fail to see any reason for rejecting the request being formulated. What is more, both influence-exerting components are based on different psychological mechanisms that work in synergy. Thanks to the dialogue involvement technique, one begins to treat a stranger as someone they know, and the following phrase, making use of the legitimization of paltry contributions technique, makes it even harder to say "No."

Technique # 96 *Dialogue and labeling*

Idea

When combining social influence techniques in order to increase the probability of someone granting our request, following our suggestion or instruction, we have to make sure this combination appears natural. In the previous section, we described the example where a dialogue that preceded a request for supporting a charitable campaign and holding out a moneybox toward the subject was combined with the phrase "even a penny will help." All of this seems coherent and the interaction proceeds, uninterrupted. One could also imagine other verbal phrases that are effective social influence techniques in themselves and that may be particularly powerful when used on a person involved in a dialogue. The use of the labeling effect may be one example. We might simply communicate to the person whom we want to ask for help that we have reasons to believe that they are someone who is willing to help others. Will a combination of the dialogue involvement and the labeling technique prove to be effective? Well, social psychologists rarely formulate statements without first empirically verifying their suspicions. Let us take a look at studies devoted to this problem.

Research

The experiment, which the authors of this book planned together with Wojciech Kulesza, was conducted on the streets of Wroclaw on a sunny day (Grzyb et al., 2021). In half of the cases, the experiment was conducted by a woman in her twenties; in the other half, the experimenter was a man also in his twenties. The experimenters approached people who appeared to be adults and who were walking alone. In the control conditions, the experimenter introduced themselves by stating their first name and explained that they were a volunteer at a pediatric ward of the local hospital. The problem is that not all of the young patients are visited by their parents. Therefore, volunteers are needed, who would agree to pay a visit to the hospital and read a book to the kids. Would the subject agree? It turned out that 26.7% of the people declared their willingness to come to the hospital. In the dialogue involvement conditions, the person was first asked if they lived in Wroclaw. Once they had replied, the following question was asked: "What do you think, how is life for young people in Wroclaw?" Once the subject presented their view on this topic, they were asked the following: "Do you think there are young people who have it (even) worse? Maybe because of a difficult family or economic situation?" And again, the experimenter listened to the opinion expressed by the subject. Only at that point did the experimenter say that they were looking for people willing to devote some of their time to reading books to young patients at the local hospital. Again, it turned out that dialogue involvement was an effective social influence technique. In these conditions, 38.3% of the subjects agreed to act on the request. But when the experimenter, once the subject had been involved in a dialogue and was asked to join the group of volunteers, added: "You look like someone who really cares about the well-being of children," i.e., used the labeling technique, the percentage of people who agreed to join the group of volunteers was markedly higher. This time around, every other subject agreed to comply with the request!

Mechanism

It should be noted that the labeling technique applied in the above-described experiment consisted of suggesting, to the subject, that they are altruistic individuals. One might expect that if the dialogue, which precedes the labeling effect, makes the subject treat their interlocutor as someone they know, the combination of these two techniques should be effective only when the person making the request is the beneficiary of the help being provided. This is because the person being influenced should, at that point, start to think, "I'm an altruist," and, specifically, this person should be willing to help people they know (or those who act as acquaintances). Yet, a totally different situation was created in the experiment. The person who first involved the subject in a dialogue and, subsequently, labeled the subject did not ask for help for themselves, instead, they asked the subject to join an initiative for the benefit of a completely different group of people. It should be noted however that this is what our willingness to help people we know is all about. It is not necessary for such persons to ask for something for themselves, it suffices that they (and not strangers) are doing the asking. Therefore, this is where the power of the dialogue involvement technique comes from, as well as its potential for being combined with other social influence techniques.

8

MISCELLANEOUS

Letters can be easily assigned to one of two categories: vowels and consonants. It is a more difficult task with numbers, as these can be positive or negative, even or odd, rational or irrational... oh, and there is zero. Therefore, if we had, let us say, a set of thirty different numbers, we would need to think really hard which categories we need to distinguish to make sure all the numbers are assigned to the correct one. This task will become even more challenging if we want to keep the number of these groups or categories relatively low. As authors of this book, we also wanted to assign particular techniques to one of several chapters. The problem is that even though we tried, again and again, to create all sorts of categories, we were never able to accommodate all the social influence techniques we described. Finally, we decided to give up and proceed as a pedantic individual would, who keeps various items in separate drawers of his desk (bills in the first one, insurance policies in the second, documents related to the inheritance left by his uncle in the third, letters exchanged between his grandmother and a famous painter in the fourth, and so on and so

DOI: 10.4324/9781003296638-9

forth) but who also has one last drawer, where he keeps all "other" items. The content of this last drawer results from the fact that the items kept in it do not match the categories represented by any of the other drawers. This chapter is "the last drawer." Therefore, it includes descriptions of those techniques that failed to match any of the above-mentioned seven categories we distinguished.

Technique # 97 1-in-5 Prize Tactic

Idea

It is rather hard to find a person today who hasn't been informed by email that - for reasons that are difficult to pin down - they are incredibly lucky. Some woman with an exotic name is the widow of a billionaire who bequeathed her a fortune. However, she is having trouble getting it out of her bank account. She would be willing to transfer all that money to us as long as we pay a small percentage of it for the transfer. At other times, we may find out that a computer working for a chain of stores has picked us as the winner. Well, actually, *almost* the winner, because we've made it to the semi-final, but if we do a lot of shopping in this chain of stores, we'll automatically be entered in the final. And there the win is a done deal. A special variant of these exceptional opportunities that – in the end – turn out to be an ordinary loss is the so-called 1-in-5 Prize Tactic. It consists of a telemarketer calling whoever's in possession of a phone, introducing himself, and announcing in an enthusiastic voice that they have just become a lottery winner. They're now certain that they have won one of five prizes! The telemarketer begins to list them one by one. Let's assume that these are: a new car, a weekend stay in a luxury hotel in an attractive location, a summer house in the mountains, an autographed book by a Nobel Prize winner with a personal dedication, or 100,000 dollars in cash. Of course, the winner is to be congratulated, but in order to take part in the drawing of one of these prizes they only have to pay a small amount (usually several dozen dollars, pounds, or euros) to a designated account. This is necessary because of the regulations concerning this type of lottery. Someone who makes this payment will either never get any prize, or they will get a so-called gimme prize – an almost worthless item listed in one breath with the actually very valuable items by the dishonest telemarketer.

In this case, it would be a book by a Nobel laureate with an autograph and a personal dedication. The dedication is indeed personal, as the name of the "laureate" is mentioned, but it's not handwritten by the Nobel laureate themself, and the autograph turns out to be a scanned reproduction. The book, on the other hand, is printed on poor-quality paper, and its covers are a little harder than toilet paper.

Research

Todd Horowitz and Anthony Pratkanis (2002) set out to demonstrate the efficacy of this, admittedly fraudulent, technique in their experiment. They engaged students who had just finished participating in another study. They were told that an initiative had been launched as part of the University's effort to get more people participating in psychological research. A computer had randomly selected people to receive one of five prizes and they themselves were the ones chosen! As for the prizes involved, they are as follows: a television, a portable CD player, a multicolored university mug, or a $50 mall gift certificate. To receive one of these prizes, all they have to do is spend two hours writing an essay. It turned out that all of the participants (100% to be exact!) accepted the offer. In conditions where no prize was promised to the students, only one in five agreed to give up two hours of their time. It is easy to surmise that if this was not an experiment, but a real situation, a gimme prize would be drawn for the winner of the lottery, which in this case was the multicolored mug. To complete the picture, let us add that when, in another study, Horovitz and Pratkanis asked students if they would agree to spend two hours writing an essay in exchange for such a mug, only 10% of those indicted responded affirmatively.

Mechanism

The authors of the study presented above perceive a phenomenon called phantom fixation as the primary psychological mechanism underlying the effectiveness of the thieving 1-in-5 Prize Tactic discussed above. The possibility of winning fabulous prizes engages the subjects' attention so much that they cease examining the details of the offer itself. At the same time, they most likely assume that the probability of winning any of the five prizes is the same at 20% (although this is not said in the offer), and thus greatly overestimate their chances of winning the most attractive items. Finally, the important thing is that if they do not continue, they will lose what they in fact already have (although it is not clear what, exactly, they have, but certainly one of the five prizes!). All this makes this technique, used by telemarketer thieves, operating mostly via the telephone or the Internet, extremely effective. If you find yourself in this situation, dear reader, keep in mind that the most serious victory you can achieve in this situation is… the satisfaction of not having been fooled. And this will only happen if you don't let yourself get sucked into this game.

Technique # 98 *An authority figure (wearing a uniform) says so*

Idea

Have you ever called a plumber? For example to fix a leaky tap or toilet that decided to develop a mind of its own and started to, rather arbitrarily, at random times and for reasons known only to itself, run. You surely have. Perhaps you searched for a specialist among suitable advertisements or maybe you decided it was a better idea to call a friend of yours who had recently had her bathroom refurbished and seemed satisfied with the quality of the service. And so let us imagine that, one way or another, your bathroom is visited by that guy, a man wearing a checkered shirt and cargo work pants with a leather tool bag slung over his shoulder, a bag that has witnessed hundreds of threading and screwing operations and that is no stranger to patching pipes with nuts. The pivotal moment comes. The plumber takes a critical look at the plumbing system and utters the sacramental phrase, which we assume they are taught at the Hogwarts School of Plumbing ("Mate, who botched it up so bad?"), then he states, in an authoritative manner, that "you need to tear it all down and redo it using white PE pipes. Threaded steel pipes are not used anymore." Then he states that there is no point in starting the job that day but that he will come tomorrow to fix it. At the same time, he warns that the job will not be easy or cheap.

How do you respond? Most likely, you conclude that since an expert said it needed to be done, there is no other option. But what actually made you believe that Mario is an expert? A recommendation from a friend, his stereotypical outfit, or a discrete scent of WD-40 mixed with a gentle aroma of cup grease? And is it any uniform that can make us believe someone (and follow their instructions) even if we have no other tools to verify their reliability, professionalism, or competence?

Research

There is a large body of research to demonstrate the effect of an authority figure on the behavior of subjects participating in experiments – a significant portion of such studies also examine the role of the outfit worn by the authority figure (and in some cases, it is the outfit that actually gives the authority). Let us discuss a study that is remarkably simple in nature. The study in question was conducted by Leonard Bickman in 1974, and the scheme he proposed was used later on in numerous replications and always provided very similar results. The authors of this book also use this scheme often as an exercise for their students, as the idea Bickman came up with is, on the one hand, very simple and, on the other hand, extremely impressive.

In the study, a natural situation consisting of parking a car and paying for a parking ticket was used. As the original study by Bickman (1974) was conducted in the era when payment cards were not that common (not to mention payments made with a smartphone or a smartwatch); cash was virtually the only available payment method used when purchasing a ticket at a parking meter and, unfortunately, this required change. For this reason, sometimes one could see people standing next to a parking meter and frantically searching for a dime in their pockets in order to purchase a ticket. This is exactly where Bickman took his advantage. He chose a parking lot in a small American town and acted out a situation such as the one described above. Then, he randomly assigned his subjects to one of the following three groups: first the experimental group, in the case of which the experimenter was wearing a guard's uniform, second the experimental group, in the case of which the experimenter was wearing a milkman's uniform, and the control group, in the case of which the experimenter was wearing plain clothes. Regardless of his outfit, the experimenter approached randomly selected individuals and said, "This fellow is over-parked at the meter but doesn't have any change. Give him a dime!"

It should be noted that none of the characters, regardless of the outfit, were authorized to require this sort of behavior from the subjects. This is obvious in the case of someone wearing plain clothes. A milkman, albeit wearing a white uniform and holding a basket full of bottles in his hand, also had no right to require this of the subjects. Even the intriguing guard, wearing a uniform similar to that of a police officer (although with no insignia or a side arm), is not authorized to ask us for this kind of thing and certainly has no right to order us to do it. Taking the above into consideration, the outcome was more than interesting. In the control conditions, one-third of the individuals agreed to act on the request of the person wearing plain clothes. When the request for a dime was formulated by the milkman, its effectiveness increased to 57%. The subjects were most willing to act on the request of the experimenter when he was dressed as a guard. In those conditions, as many as 89% of the subjects agreed to give the ten cents to the person in need.

Mechanism

There are at least a few ways to interpret the outcome of the experiment conducted by Bickman (and many of his followers). First of all, one may claim that we obey authority figures because we were brought up this way. From an early age, many of us have been told to do as a police officer, a doctor or a fireman tells us. Textbooks often present characters in uniforms as authority figures who instruct children on important matters (from brushing one's teeth to looking both ways before crossing a street). Therefore, it should come as no surprise that upon hearing an instruction characterized by a relatively low level of harmfulness (a dime is not a lot of money), we act in a rather automatic manner. We do not reflect on whether the authority figure has the right to do something or not. The figure has a uniform and thus has the right (even if it is only a milkman's uniform!).

Another important aspect is that, in actuality, we are, to a large extent, unaware of how this mechanism works. Once he had conducted his experiment (or to be more precise, his series of experiments, as he investigated this phenomenon in a number of ways), Bickman decided to describe, their procedure in detail and to subsequently ask people about their predictions as to the behavior of the subjects in the course of the experiments. To his surprise, it turned out that people were not particularly taking the fact of wearing a uniform into account. To be more precise, even though the subjects believed there would be differences among the three groups, they thought the differences would be significantly smaller than in reality (the subjects concluded that half of the participants would give a dime in the control conditions, 54% in the conditions with the milkman and 63% in the conditions with the guard). The above figures also demonstrate how significantly we can underestimate the effectiveness of underlying psychological mechanisms of our behavior.

Finally, it should be noted that one does not need a guard's uniform to elicit a similarly high level of obedience. In one of the exercises, we asked our students to conduct, they were instructed to make various requests while wearing not a uniform but a high-visibility vest, similar to those we keep in the trunks of our cars. As it turned out, such an inexpensive vest, available at any gas station, allowed our students to elicit a level of obedience similar to that elicited with the guard's uniform in Bickman's studies. Hence, if you are wearing a uniform and you ask for something, most people will not call your request into question.

Technique # 99 *Cognitive exhaustion*

Idea

Have you ever felt like you have no energy at all? Like you are so exhausted that any activity seemed absolutely beyond your power? Surely you have — these episodes happen to us more frequently that we would like them to. Sometimes it is physical tiredness — a result of an exhaustive excursion, a training session, or perhaps hard manual labor. Sometimes it is quite the opposite: sometimes we feel tired because we have been sitting and staring at the computer screen all day. In some cases, we can experience cognitive exhaustion, which is a state where, to use a comparison, our brain resembles a sponge that has been completely wrung out and, no matter how hard we try, will not give a drop of water more. At that point, all we want is a cup of tea or a glass of wine and complete isolation from the stimuli that our reality has been providing us with all too much. It may come as a surprise, but this state may cause us to take on new commitments. Yes, this seems counter-intuitive, but the results of experiments demonstrate it quite clearly: the state of exhaustion, particularly cognitive exhaustion, paradoxically, increases the probability that we will agree to things that would be otherwise very hard to accept. It appears that the prior intellectual effort (or simply the state of tiredness caused by the same) deprives us of the energy required to decline another request.

But is it actually that hard to imagine? Think of a child who is being very persistent at persuading their parent into buying a dentists' nightmare: cotton candy. After the seventeenth time when the child says "Pleeeeeeease…," even the firmest parent will probably give in regardless of their beliefs about the hygiene of the oral cavity or the nutritional value of sugar.

Research

Research into the effect that the state of exhaustion has on one's willingness to comply with requests was conducted by Bob Fennis, Loes Janssen, and Kathleen Vohs (2009). In one of their very simple and yet ingenious experiments, they invited university students to participate in studies allegedly conducted by the Dutch Tax and Customs Administration. The participants were randomly assigned to one of two groups. In both groups, the subjects were asked to carry out a certain task, yet in the first group, the task was very difficult and exhausting, while in the other group it was easy and required no substantial intellectual effort. For example, subjects from the first (exhausting) group were asked to answer the following question: "One of the problems of the Tax and Customs Administration is the fact that many people tend to submit their tax returns after the annual deadline. What steps can the Administration take to prevent this without giving citizens a fine?" As one may expect, providing a reasonable answer to such a question may be cognitively exhausting. Now, imagine answering ten similar questions! Meanwhile in the "cognitively easy" group, the participants were asked to, e.g., say what comes to their mind when they hear the name "Tax and Customs Administration." Having answered ten questions, the subjects from both groups were asked to declare their potential willingness to participate in future studies conducted by the Tax and Customs Administration. They could make said declaration by stating (from 1 to 10, even though they could, of course, refuse altogether) the number of studies they would like to participate in. As the authors of the experiment expected, there were differences between the two groups: when the participants were cognitively exhausted, they were willing to participate, on average, in 2.28 studies, but if the prior questions were not intellectually challenging and answering them was not particularly exhaustive, the figure was only 0.95.

An attentive reader could ask the following: but how can we know that the subjects from the first group were cognitively exhausted and those in the second group were not? Perhaps thinking about taxes alone makes people tired regardless of the phrasing of the questions? Fennis, Janssen, and Vohs verified this with the so-called Stroop test. It is a quite interesting experiment, in which you are required to say the color of the word, not what the word says (e.g., the word "blue" is written in yellow). Contrary to what one could expect, it is a rather complex task, as you have to ignore the obvious answer ("blue") and say "yellow" instead, and in practice, this is much more difficult than it seems. Based on other research, we know that cognitively exhausted individuals find it more challenging than "fresh" individuals who are not tired. It was a similar case with the experiment conducted by Bog Fennis and his associates: the individuals from the group with difficult questions did worse on the Stroop test.

Mechanism

Why is that so? What is it exactly that makes us more compliant when we are cognitively exhausted? Let us try to analyze it by "starting from the end," i.e., from the expected consequences of our acceptance or rejection of someone's request. What will happen if someone asks us to do something and we refuse? Most likely, they will say, "But why?" Consequently, we will have to explain ourselves ("I would really like to help you, unfortunately, I cannot because...") and what is more, it may become necessary to justify our decision, negotiate and perhaps defend it. Not only that, but a refusal brings forth "social" trouble – someone will feel bad, perhaps they will not admit it but they will pull a long face, grumble... All this makes it necessary for us to involve our cognitive resources in order to explain the reasons behind our decision or to regain a positive self-assessment after we made someone feel bad. Let us make it clear – we are referring to cognitive resources we already lack as these have been depleted! Now, let us compare the above with an expected response to our agreement – a happy face of the asker, smiles on both sides, mutual satisfaction, and agreement. Therefore, let us try to decide which decision is more optimal for us (at least in the short-term perspective): the one that brings about more cognitive load or the one that ends the conversation immediately and with no problems? After all, we don't want problems, we just want everyone to leave us alone...

This is precisely why we have to stay alert when we are exhausted (this applies to physical, cognitive, as well as emotional exhaustion). When exhausted, we are easily persuaded into doing things we would rather not do simply because we are too tired to defend ourselves (i.e., refuse). And you need to stay alert because otherwise you may end up participating in yet another fascinating research endeavor by the Tax and Customs Administration.

Technique # 100 *Do not hesitate, just ask*
Idea

Just ask! And this is supposed to be a social influence technique! And where is the trick, or any psychological trick at all here??? What is this advice to simply ask??? Despite appearances, things are not so simple. Imagine that you need to ask someone for help. And it's not such a trivial thing as asking someone what time it is at the moment or asking them to show you the way to the train station. For example, let's say you need someone to climb a ladder to the roof of your house and check the gutters for leaves. You can't do it yourself because you have a fear of heights. Oh, there goes someone! Will you ask him? No, I don't think so, he doesn't look like the kind of person who would want to go up a ladder. What about the person walking down the street now? Mhmm... why should he help me? He doesn't even know me! As Francis Flynn and Vanessa Lake's (2008) research shows, people consistently misjudge the likelihood that others would comply with their requests. Whether it is borrowing a cell phone for a moment, making a donation to a charity, or escorting someone around a university campus, people believe that few of those being asked would in fact comply. However, if you actually ask people, it turns out that they give their consent much more often. So it's highly likely that you too are not asking favors of other people simply because you assume in advance that it's pointless because they won't comply with such requests anyway. The do not hesitate, just ask technique is therefore about not thinking that the probability that someone in particular will agree to fulfill a request is too low to try to ask them at all. So don't play around thinking about the odds that your request will be granted (especially since you're making the mistake of underestimating the probability here) – just go up to that person and ask them.

Research

Of the several published studies addressing this issue, we chose to describe perhaps the most spectacular one here, because it involved fulfilling a request for a clearly unethical behavior - namely, an act of vandalism. Vanessa Bohns, Mahdi Roghanizad, and Amy Xu (2014) asked their students to imagine that they were walking up to a person sitting in a library and, holding out a book and pen toward them, saying to them: "Hi, I'm trying to play a prank on someone, but they know my handwriting. Will you just quickly write the word 'pickle' on this page of this library book?". Students were asked how many people they thought they would have to approach sitting in the library for three of them to agree to this unusual request. The same students then actually visited the library and approached people sitting there. The student would pull out a pen and a book whose cover looked just like a library book (it was properly labeled and stamped), but was actually just prepared by the experimenters who had bought it for research purposes. He would open this book to some page and make the statement described above. Then he would go up to the next person and do the same thing, then to the next person, until three people had written the word "pickle" in the book. What were the results of this experiment? Well, the participants thought that you would have to ask more than 10 people (average 10.7) to get agreement from three. In reality, however, the average number of people necessary to get three acts of vandalism was only 4.7. So there is no doubt that people utterly miscalculated the probability that someone would comply with this type of request. To be more precise: they underestimated it.

Mechanism

Of course, we are not urging anyone to encourage other people to commit acts of vandalism. Our point was simply to show that even in the case of bizarre (and, in the study presented here, unethical) requests, they are agreed to by clearly more people than we expect. Effective social influence, then, is about not wrongly assuming at the very beginning of an interaction (or even before it) that there is no point in making a request because we will almost certainly be met with a refusal. Why do people comply with requests much more often than we think? First of all, when they are politely asked for something, they cannot refuse, even if they think that for some reason they should not fulfill a certain request. In fact, since childhood, we have learned that if someone asks us for something, a polite person agrees to the request. And we are polite people... From the perspective of the technique described here, however, another question is more important: Why do we refrain from making requests, mistakenly believing that people will not agree to them? We are dealing with an interesting mechanism here. For it is not only the belief that someone does not fulfill our request that makes us withhold it. It is also the case that if we decide not to make a request, we immediately convince ourselves that we did the right thing because the person would certainly not have complied. From here it is only a small step to the belief that if people do not comply with such requests, then there is no point in making them, and if there is no point, then we do not ask. So our beliefs affect behavior, behavior affects beliefs, beliefs affect behavior, and so on and so forth.

The do not hesitate, just ask technique is the last one presented in this book because using it increases the chances that others will comply with our request or suggestion, but it is also a condition for the effectiveness of all the other techniques we have described. After all, these techniques can only work in the conditions in which we apply them. If we assume from the outset that we have no chance of influencing other people, we will not use any of the techniques presented in this book. Thus, the do not hesitate, just ask technique is the most important of all social influence techniques!

CONCLUDING REMARKS

Once they have read the descriptions of social influence techniques included in this book, our readers might want to put one of them to a practical test. They may use it on a friend, from whom they would like to borrow some money, on a spouse, whom they would like to persuade into going for holidays to a place which their partner is not particularly fond of, or on a business partner, with whom they have been conducting lengthy negotiations. It may happen that, despite using a particular technique, the subject will not agree to do what is being suggested to or asked of them. To be perfectly honest, it would not surprise us at all if that were the case. It should be noted that none of the techniques we presented in this book made <u>all</u> subjects comply with the requests they were approached with. The techniques only increased the chances for success – in some cases by a few, a dozen or so and only in a few cases by a few tens of percentage points. What is more, each of the presented techniques proved to be effective only in a given situational context. Some techniques could be effectively put to use when the goal was to collect donations for charity, while others when the objective was to boost the sales of certain products. Only a few of them were truly universal.

There is also one more aspect we should bear in mind: social influence psychology is, undoubtedly, a science. It uses empirical methods, our cognitive apparatus as well as statistical tools – sometimes extremely advanced ones. Nevertheless, it belongs to the field of social sciences; one might even describe it as probabilistic. This means that, based on the knowledge of its achievements, we can increase the probability of someone acting in a particular way but we will never have 100% certainty in this respect. We will try to illustrate it using an example. Imagine that you are holding a pencil in your hand – what will happen if you release your grip? It will most likely fall on the ground – you can verify this instantly if you wish. Since science requires results to be replicated, we can repeat the experiment – did the pencil fall? Probably yes. If we were to repeat this activity 100 times, the pencil would fall on the ground or a desk every single time. This is because we would be testing a law from the domain of natural sciences – the one related to gravity. Yet, if we were to imagine testing a social influence technique, our metaphorical pencil would behave as expected (i.e., it would fall) in, let us say, 70% of the cases, in 10% of the cases it would remain in its original position, in 10% of the cases it would fly up and in the remaining cases it would start spinning around its axis. This is exactly why social influence psychology may be considered a probabilistic science – a science that makes a particular behavior more probable but without a 100% guarantee of effectiveness.

The problem is that not everyone is willing to acknowledge it. One of the authors of this book, when his career was just starting, worked in the training line of business – he, among other things, taught people how to be a good salesman. A rather frequent question asked by trainee salesmen was, "which word do I need to include in my request to make everybody comply with it?" The obvious cliché "abracadabra" was not exactly what they were hoping to hear. Why? Probably because some people treat social influence psychology as being on par with "Jedi Knight psychology." Star Wars fans surely remember that Jedi Knights displayed remarkable persuasion skills – they could "cast a spell" on their interlocutors and make them docile by just moving their hand, their voice, or a gesture. It is time to tell the truth – regardless of how tough it may be to accept. Social influence psychology does not offer such "powers." And it may happen that we do not achieve the expected results despite applying social influence techniques.

So what advice can we give to someone who has used a social influence technique but noticed no results? First, you need to use it on a rather large group of people (approx. a few dozen individuals) just to be able to tell if the technique is effective or not in a given situation. Second, you need to think of the psychological mechanism that made the technique effective in the experiment we described and make sure this mechanism is also being activated in the situation in which you are applying the technique in question. Third, it may happen that, due to various reasons, the particular technique does not work in the specific situation you have created. If this is the case... you can always try another technique. But before you do so, think about the passage of time, which plays a specific role in this context. In order to explain our point, let us examine, as examples, two techniques described earlier in this book. In the case of the door-in-the-face technique, the rule is that if we want to present someone with a challenging request, we first have to ask this person for something much more difficult, while expecting them to refuse. Only after they turn down our initial request do we present them with the one we actually want them to act on. However, it turns out that if we wait too long before formulating our actual request (e.g., we do it on the day after our interlocutor refused to comply with the initial request), the technique is no longer effective. To put it differently, the door-in-the-face technique requires that our actual target request be formulated immediately after our interlocutor replies "no" to our initial request. Passing time works to our disadvantage to an even greater extent in the case of another technique we discussed earlier, i.e., fear-then-relief. Even though an individual experiencing a sudden and unexpected relief is willing to perform various tasks (including those that are inconvenient for them), this state lasts for only a dozen or so seconds after the fear-inducing stimulus has subsided. After this time, the technique loses its effectiveness altogether.

It is precisely for this reason that one of the latest works by Robert Cialdini of the University of Arizona, a leading researcher into the problems of social influence, is titled "Pre-suasion." The similarity between the title and the word "persuasion" is both obvious and intended, but Cialdini shows us that the time vector, i.e., what happens before we ask someone for a favor and before we present this person with the arguments supporting a given standpoint, plays a key role. Therefore, one can argue that there is no persuasion without pre-suasion.

When considering social influence psychology and its techniques, we should always try to see both sides of the coin – the person using a given technique and the person being its target (obviously, sometimes there will be groups of people instead of individuals). We also play both roles. On some occasions, we wish to affect the behavior of other people, while on other occasions we want to defend ourselves against the influence of others, e.g., when a female friend of ours is asking us for a favor that is completely and utterly not in our best interest. And yet, if this female friend uses such arguments as, "I have always helped you when you needed me to – could you please do me a favor at least this one time?" it will be extremely difficult for us to refuse. But will it be impossible?

We are frequently asked, by our students or during all kinds of training sessions, how to avoid unwanted social influence. It would appear that having a good grasp of various techniques that could be applied by those who attempt to persuade us, deceitfully, into performing certain actions should be enough. However, the problem is much more complex. The above-mentioned Robert Cialdini, during one of his visits to our university, shared with us the following story. He went to an appliance store to make a trivial purchase but, while looking for the item he was going to buy, he accidentally reached the part of the store with TV sets on display. There, he saw a model he had previously read very positive opinions about on the Internet. What is more, the product was offered at a very attractive price. As Cialdini was going through the product specification label set on the shelf, he was approached by a sales clerk, who said: "I couldn't help but notice that you are interested in this TV set. I'm not surprised: this is a great product at a very attractive price. But you need to know that this is the last unit we are selling at this price. TV sets from the next batch are going to be significantly more expensive. What's more, 15 minutes ago a customer called and I think he is coming to get it." At this point, Cialdini reached for his wallet and bought the TV set, even though he did not intend to do so as he was entering the store. It is important to note who the story is coming from – a leading social influence researcher who, for a number of years, has consistently studied and described the scarcity rule, which was used by the sales clerk.

This personal experience of Robert Cialdini corresponds with the outcome of the experiment conducted by Richard Katzev and Richard
Brownstein. Using press advertising, they recruited over one hundred
adult residents of Portland, Oregon, for the purpose of their laboratory
study. The subjects were informed that they would participate in a study
designed to examine the effect caffeine had on reading comprehension and
were asked, at the onset of the experiment, to drink a cup of coffee or a
cup of tea. Next, the subjects were asked to read a text; some received a
scientific paper on the low-ball technique, some received a text on the
door-in-the-face technique, and others a psychological article unrelated to
the topic of social influence. After ten minutes, the subjects were asked to
complete a reading comprehension test, which was interrupted by the
appearance of another psychologist, who, upon entering the laboratory,
complained to the experimenter about an unexpected issue. He had invited
certain individuals to participate in his study but one of the subjects did
not show up. Would, in such a situation, an individual just finishing their
test agree to also participate in another experiment? At this moment, a
relevant social influence technique was used on the subject. A person who
had just read a text on the door-in-the-face technique was approached by
the psychologist in the following manner: "I just need you to fast for the
next 24 hours, then come in and do 75 push-ups for me while I attach
some electrodes to your arms and head for data collection." Needless to
say, a vast majority of the subjects refused to comply with this request. At
that point, the experimenter concluded that in such a case, he would like
to ask the subject to take a set of math problems with them, to have a go at
them at home for two hours, and send them back to the university. The
approach was completely different in the case of those subjects who had
been asked to read the text about the low-ball technique. These people
heard the following message: "I just need you to answer 25 questions on a
math test. Would you please help me out? It will take only a few minutes."
Just as the subject had agreed to comply with this request, the psychologist
added that it would actually be great if, instead, the subject agreed to take a
set of math problems with them, to have a go at them at their home for
two hours. Those subjects who had been asked to read a neutral text were
simply asked if they would take a set of math problems with them and
solve them at home. It turned out that the percentage of the subjects who
agreed to spend two hours on solving math problems was almost identical

in all three groups. However, more of the subjects on whom the door-in-the-face technique was used, as compared to the other subjects participating in the experiment, sent solved math problems back to the university (as instructed). It should be noted, though, that the former simply proves the effectiveness of this technique and does not prove that by knowing this technique one becomes less susceptible to its use. Why is that so? Well, let us start by stating that in most real-life situations, we react instantaneously. Thus, we activate ready-made, automatic chain reactions created throughout our lives. A rational and cool analysis appears (if it appears at all) only after we have granted a given request, ordered a given product, or purchased a given item. Today, Robert Cialdini knows exactly how to explain his aforementioned decision regarding buying the TV set. At that point in time, when he said, "I'll take it!" he simply activated a reaction pattern typical of a situation where something becomes unavailable and, by the same token, significantly more attractive. So, should Cialdini regret his choice? Was he manipulated? Well, not necessarily! If the sales clerk informed him about the actual state of affairs, if he honestly warned him that unless he decided to buy the TV set fast, soon this model would no longer be available or it would be sold at a higher price, he was actually taking the customer's side. If this was the case, the sales clerk was Cialdini's ally and not his enemy or a manipulator. Obviously, Cialdini could not tell if the sales clerk was being honest or not. Yet, if he learned that the sales clerk was not telling the truth, he would surely never come to this store again. Therefore, our knowledge of social influence techniques may not be enough to tell if we are being manipulated in a given situation, but it can protect us from becoming a victim of the manipulator in the future.

Well, it would be impolite and unfair to describe Robert Cialdini's mishap and omit our own experiences – specifically one incident which is particularly interesting as it happened to both authors of this book when they were spending time together. One could imagine that two social influence experts would be a little too much to handle even for someone with a lot of hands-on experience. Quite the opposite – tricking us was easy, like taking candy from a baby. The incident happened when we were both taking part in a scientific conference. It was being held in Thailand and the incident itself happened in Bangkok. Needless to say, we were perfectly aware of the potential pitfalls waiting for tourists but we were also certain that the locals would not be able to outsmart us. So we went for a walk. At some point, in a completely non-tourist-oriented neighborhood, we stopped at a pedestrian crossing together with an elderly man, who smiled at us and asked what we were doing there, as all sights were located elsewhere. We smiled back and replied that we knew that and that we were not particularly fond of typical tourist attractions, as we wanted to see how Thais actually lived. Having heard that, the man grinned broadly and congratulated us on our choice. He said that tourist attractions were overrated and that real Thais did not go to such places. He told us that if we wanted to experience local attractions, we should see the city from the water level, i.e., from a boat, as this is what Thais would do. We nodded and the man said, "You two look like fine chaps, perhaps I will be able to help you out. There is a floating market today, you know, like those you see on postcards. Only a real one, because it's for local folks. It is not as big as the one intended for tourists but it has a real local flavor. Remember, you always need to say, 'Thai price,' otherwise you will be charged tourist rates!" This was an obvious red flag for us but the Thai man was very resourceful; he hailed a tuk-tuk (a three-wheel open taxi) driving by, he lowered his voice at the driver and started talking to him in a quick and threatening manner in Thai. Once he was done, he said to us, "I told him to treat you as he would treat local folks! 20 bahts and not a single baht more!" We got in reassured, as this was the lowest taxi fare we had ever paid in Bangkok.

A moment later, we arrived at a harbor for boats and, even though we kept saying "Thai price! Thai price!" we paid through the nose. Each of us paid approximately USD 100 for a one-hour cruise along the Chao Phraya River and the channels of Bangkok. At some point, we even got to see the promised floating market. In reality, our "captain" simply hailed another man in a boat, who rowed up to us and tried to sell us all sorts of attractive goods such as a plastic Buddha figure or a lacquer elephant (he, of course, told us that those were offered exclusively to Thai people and that he would charge us "Thai price"). As we refused, several times, to buy anything, he sighed and reached into a small refrigerator for a product we never say no to, and that is beer. We agreed to buy the beverage even though it was one of the most expensive beers we have had. It was not the end of the story, though. When each of us was holding a can of beer, the clever salesman pointed to our "captain" and asked, "Well, what about him?" Our honor was at stake and so there was the only thing we could do, we bought one more beer for the boat operator, who put it into his breast pocket to, most likely, give it back to the salesman during the next cruise to receive his share in the profit.

Generally speaking, the cruise was not that bad (although, it is entirely possible that now we are trying to rationalize our actions to, at least partially, save face). We saw parts of Bangkok that we would not have seen otherwise, we cruised along the city's channels, and we saw monitor lizards and other wild animals. Most of all though, once again, we proved that no matter how smart you think you are, there will always be someone who can outsmart you. And you may be a leading expert on social influence, but once you are faced with a true professional you do not stand a chance.

There is one more aspect that needs pointing out. Some say, with pride in their voice: "No marketing experts and salesmen are fooling me with their tricks. If I see 'an extraordinary bargain' or an 'amazing sale' I don't even consider buying anything from such an offer." As far as we are concerned, we believe this feeling of pride is completely unjustified. To us, this approach seems to be as equally irrational as experiencing a compulsion to get these "extraordinary bargains" only because they have just become available. The common denominator for both of these approaches is a specific rigidity of one's behavior. What should we do then? How should we behave? Let us imagine that a clothing shop window says the following: "Special offer! Only today! Buy one tie and get one free!" Should we take this offer? Well, first we should ask ourselves the following questions: "Do I even wear ties?", "Do I like the ties being sold?", "Would I like to wear this tie if I got it as a gift?" If the answer to these questions is "no," we should not even consider this offer. Paying for one tie to get one free will only result in two completely useless ties sitting around in our wardrobe collecting dust. But what if we wear ties regularly, what if we have only a few and we really like the ones on sale? Well, then why on earth would we choose to miss the chance to get two ties for the price of one? In this case, our only concern should be whether the price of a single tie is not inflated. In other words: if this is an actual bargain. If so, we should definitely take advantage of this special offer, which is clearly beneficial to us. Therefore, the key to being able to move around in an environment where we are subject to social influence virtually all the time is thoughtfulness: we need to refrain from reacting automatically and consider the arguments in favor of and against a particular decision, we are about to make. Needless to say, this refers to more than just buying a tie.

If we manage to move to the thoughtful level of operation, the knowledge of social influence techniques and their underlying psychological mechanisms will become very useful. This has been proven by what happened to both of us on a sunny afternoon in Wrocław, as we were enjoying ourselves in one of the many beer gardens. We were sitting there examining the latest offering of Wroclaw-based microbreweries, debating vehemently, when we were approached by an elderly woman wearing rather simple clothes. She looked at us and said, "Would you help an elderly woman?" We were a bit puzzled, as she did not use any social influence technique, and so one of us asked cleverly, "All right then but how much do you expect us to give you?" The elderly lady took a step back, gave us a critical look, and said, "Dear sirs, I would gladly accept PLN 100, 50, and even 10. But I don't suppose you will give me that much..." Obviously, we burst into laughter and gave her some money, even though it was not PLN 10, 50, or 100, it was way less (even though one should remember that this happened several years ago). Later on, we had a rather lengthy discussion on the validity of the method used by the elderly woman. If it had not been for the fact that she encountered two social influence experts who (at that particular moment) were capable of operating in a thoughtful manner, her income might have been significantly higher.

Social influence techniques can be used for both noble causes (e.g., to persuade people to become volunteer blood donors, sign a petition defending democracy or support, financially, charities) as well as unethical purposes (e.g., to persuade people into committing all sorts of fraud or discriminating against a certain group of people). Regardless of this, the very use, in a given situation, of a particular technique may be ethical (if we are being honest) or unethical (if we are lying by, e.g., pretending to be an authority figure in a given field or misleading someone into thinking that the price of a product we are selling will increase significantly in the next few days). Obviously, we encourage our readers to use social influence techniques exclusively in an ethical manner and, at the same time, to expose those who use such techniques unethically or who use them to achieve unethical goals. Of course, knowledge of various social influence techniques will be very useful for this purpose. After all, this is why we wrote this book. It discusses only those techniques, as well as experiments designed to test them, that demonstrate changes in real and observable human behavior. We did not present methods of affecting attitudes and opinions of other people and, it should be explicitly emphasized, that most psychological studies from the area of social influence pertain precisely to changing one's attitudes and beliefs, not one's behavior. However, our decision to focus exclusively on one section of the social influence area was well thought out. In the field of psychology, there are numerous books on affecting people's attitudes; there are also quite a few books devoted to changing both attitudes and behaviors. Yet, those focused exclusively on people's behavior are virtually non-existent. Surely, there is no other book that presents as many techniques for affecting one's behavior like this one. At the same time, we are aware of the fact that readers who are interested in social influence might also be interested in the methods of affecting one's attitudes and beliefs. They may also want to expand their knowledge of the underlying psychological mechanisms behind effectively influencing other people. For this reason, we encourage you to read also other books that provide reliable information on these problems and are written in an accessible manner, which does not require a degree in psychology from the reader. From our perspective, we would like to recommend several such books (presented below in alphabetical order). We believe that all of them are worth reading. This obviously does not mean that any monographs not included in the list below are not worth reading. Additionally, more in-quisitive readers should be directed also, or perhaps predominantly, toward scientific articles that address selected problems in more detail, but this is not our intention here.

Recommended reading list:

1. Cialdini, R.B. (2017). Influence. Harper Business.
2. Cialdini, R.B. (2017). PRE-SUASION. A revolutionary way to influence and persuade. Random House.
3. Crano, W.D., & Priskin, R. [Ed.] (2014). Attitudes and attitude change. Psychology Press.
4. Dolinski, D. (2016). Techniques of social influence. The psychology of gaining compliance. Routledge.
5. Forgas, J.P., Cooper, J., & Crano, W.D. [Ed.] (2016). The psychology of attitudes and attitude change. Psychology Press.

6. Gass, R.H., & Seiter, J.S. (2018). *Persuasion, social influence and compliance gaining.* Routledge.

7. Goldsmith, E.B. (2015). *Social influence and sustainable consumption.* Springer.

8. Maio, G.R., Haddock, G., & Verplanken, B. (2019). *The psychology of attitudes and attitude change.* Sage.

9. O'Keefe, D. (2015). *Persuasion. Theory and Research.* Sage.

10. Pratkanis, A.R. [Ed.] (2014). *The science of social influence. Advances and future progress;* Psychology Press.

11. Pratkanis, A.R., & Aronson, A. (1992). *Age of propaganda: The everyday use and abuse of persuasion.* Freeman.

12. Vogel, T., Bohner, G & Wanke, M. (2015). *Attitudes and attitude change.* Routledge.

An important quality of our civilization is that people often help one another unselfishly. It should be noted that the percentage of people who, in the control conditions (i.e., without the use of any technique) of the empirical studies designed to demonstrate the effectiveness of a particular social influence technique, agreed to comply with the request they were approached with was not marginal. In most cases, it ranged (depending on the study) from 20 to 60. Therefore, one can claim that acting on various, direct requests is, in a sense, a natural thing to do for a substantial number of people. They see no sufficient reason to say "no." With a relevant social influence technique in place, an even greater number of subjects were willing to comply with the request. In other words, a relevant technique acts as a contributory factor conducive to granting the request and, consequently, an even greater number of people see no good enough reason to turn the request down. But what would happen if, along with said additional factor, which is to make people more willing to comply with the request, there occurs another factor that induces people to say "no"? Konrad Maj conducted studies into the low-ball technique; in their course, he offered undergraduate students an opportunity to purchase teaching materials that might help them prepare for upcoming exams. In the control conditions, the price was approx. USD 20. In the conditions designed to test the effectiveness of the low-ball effect, these materials were initially offered at the price of USD 15, but when it was time to actually conclude the transaction, the experimenter would apologize and explain that he had made a mistake and that the actual price was USD 20. As it turned out, the technique used by Maj was very effective. While 34% of the students decided to purchase the materials in the control conditions, the percentage was almost twice as high (62.5%) in the experimental conditions featuring the low-ball technique. However, the scheme of the experiment conducted by Maj made way for one more set of conditions. This time, the seller initially said that the materials cost USD 15 only to, later on, say that they cost USD 20 without apologizing for his mistake and without explaining the entire situation. In this case, only 25% of the subjects (i.e., even less than in the control conditions) decided to purchase the teaching materials. Noticeable impoliteness (or perhaps even insolence) on the part of the seller was most likely the factor that caused people to no longer feel the need to adhere to their previous declaration.

In real-life social situations, it does not have to be impoliteness on the part of the person asking for a favor or offering something that is the factor making people refuse to comply with a request, despite the use of a social influence technique. It may just as well be the fact that, e.g., the subject is in a hurry, is hungry, or that it has just started to rain cats and dogs. One of the most trivial truths in psychology is that "different people react differently in different situations." Any social influence technique that we use is only one of the factors affecting the behavior of the given individual. Other factors may, at the same time, be working toward the opposite direction by inducing this person to turn down the request.

One should bear in mind that the social influence techniques described in this book were verified in such conditions where the person exerting the influence and the individual subjected to this influence did not know each other and probably had no reason to believe they would become acquainted at any time in the future. Thus, the effectiveness of the presented techniques does not have to be identical in such conditions where individuals who are in a close relationship (e.g., friends, co-workers, spouses) try to influence each other's behavior.

Our readers may also be surprised by the fact that the one hundred techniques presented in this book do not include a technique that they have seen as applied by sales clerks, door-to-door salesmen, or telemarketers. It is obviously possible that we have never encountered this technique and that we do not even know it exists. However, it is more probable that it has not been verified through a reliable and properly controlled empirical study and we have agreed that this book will describe only such techniques that have been verified in this way.

Finally, there is one last aspect we would like to mention. Psychology, as a field of science, is approximately 150 years old. The psychology of social influence is even younger – the first period of its dynamic development corresponds to the 1970s. Various popular books describing social influence techniques come from an even more recent period. But does it mean that nobody took interest in these problems before? Quite the contrary. Just look into old books – but not of scientific nature. Try belles-lettres and you will see how the rules of social influence were described in the past. One of the most prominent books of the Scandinavian people is the "Poetic Edda" – the oldest relic of Icelandic literature from the 9th century AD. The Words of Odin the High One, included in the Poetic Edda, read as follows:

> With raiment and arms shall friends gladden each other,
> so has one proved oneself;
> for friends last longest, if fate be fair
> who give and give again.
>
> To his friend a man should bear him as friend,
> and gift for gift bestow,
> laughter for laughter let him exchange,
> but leasing pay for a lie.
>
> Hávamál
> The Words of Odin the High One
> from the Elder or Poetic Edda
> (Sæmund's Edda)
> translated by Olive Bray

Upon closer examination, we can recognize a clear description of the reciprocity rule in use! And in two variants at that (when we give back the good and when we get our revenge). Similar accounts can be found in the Epic of Gilgamesh, the Aeneid, the Bible, and other relics of literature. Social influence techniques have been present in our life since the very beginning and will most likely stay with us forever. This is precisely why we believe that it is better to know them than to be ignorant of them. This is also one of the reasons why we wrote this book. We hope that after reading it, you will agree with us. After all, any sensible person surely would...

REFERENCES

Allen, Ch., Schewe, Ch., & Wijk, G. (1980). More on self-perception theory' foot technique in the pre-call/mail survey setting. *Journal of Marketing Research, 17,* 488–502.

Apsler, R. (1975). Effects of embarrassment on behavior toward others. *Journal of Personality and Social Psychology, 32,* 145–153.

Aronson, E. (1969). The theory of cognitive dissonance: A current perspective. *Advances in Experimental Social Psychology, 4,* 1–34.

Asch, S.E. (1951). Effects of group pressure upon the modification distortion in judgments. In: H. Guetzkow (Ed.) *Groups, leadership and men.* (pp. 177–190). Pittsburgh, PA: Carnegie Press.

Aune, R.K., & Basil, M.D. (1994). A relational obligations approach to the foot-in-the-mouth effect. *Journal of Applied Social Psychology, 24,* 546–556.

Bem, D.J. (1967). Self-perception: An alternative explanation of cognitive dissonance phenomena. *Psychological Review, 74,* 183–200.

Bialaszek, W., Marcowski, P., Mizak, S., Ostaszewski, P., & Dolinski, D. (2022). *The role of temporal scheduling in task preference.* (Manuscript in preparation)

Bickman, L. (1974). The social power of a uniform. *Journal of Applied Social Psychology, 4,* 47–61.

Bilewicz, M., Tempska, P., Leliwa, G., Dowgiałło, M., Tańska, M., Urbaniak, R., & Wroczyński, M. (2021). Artificial intelligence against hate: Intervention reducing verbal aggression in the social network environment. *Aggressive Behavior, 47,* 260–266.

Bohns V.K., Roghanizad, M.M., & Xu, A.Z. (2014). Underestimating our influence over others' unethical behavior and decisions. *Personality and Social Psychology Bulletin, 40,* 348–362.

Bolkan, S., & Andersen, P.A. (2009). Image induction and social influence: Explication and initial tests. *Basic and Applied Social Psychology, 31,* 317–324.

Boster, F.J., Shaw, A.S., Hughes, M., Kotowski, M.R., Strom, R.E., & Deatrick, L.M. (2009). Dump-and-chase: The effectiveness of persistence as a sequential request compliance-gaining strategy. *Communication Studies, 60,* 219–234.

Brehm, J.W. (1966). *A theory of psychological reactance.* New York: Academic Press.

Bryan, Ch. J., Master, A., & Walton, G.M. (2014). "Helping" versus "being a helper": Invoking the self to increase helping in young children. *Child Development, 85,* 1836–1842.

Bryan, Ch. J., Walton, G.M., Rogers, T., & Dweck, C.S. (2011). Motivating voter turnout by invoking the self. *Proceedings of the National Academy of Sciences of the United States of America, 108,* 12653–12656.

Burger, J.M. (1986). Increasing compliance by improving the deal: The that's-not-all technique. *Journal of Personality and Social Psychology, 51,* 277–283.

Burger, J.M., Hornisher, J., Martin, V., Newman, G., & Pringle, S. (2007). The pique technique: Overcoming mindlessness or shifting heuristics? *Journal of Applied Social Psychology, 37,* 2086–2096.

Burger, J.M., Messian, N., Patel, S., Del Prado, A., & Anderson, C. (2004). What a coincidence! The effects of incidental similarity on compliance. *Personality and Social Psychology Bulletin, 30,* 35–43.

Burger, J.M., Soroka, S., Gonzago, K., Murphy, E., & Somervell, E. (2001). The effect of fleeting attraction on compliance to requests. *Personality and Social Psychology Bulletin, 27,* 1578–1586.

Cann, A., & Blackwelder, J.G. (1984). Compliance and mood: A field investigation of the impact of embarrassment. *Journal of Psychology, 117,* 221–226.

Carpenter, Ch.J. (2014). Making compliance seem more important: The "just one more" technique of gaining compliance. *Communication Research Reports, 31,* 163–170.

Charles-Sire, V., Stefan, J., & Gueguen, N. (2016). Single exposure to the world "loving" and implicit helping behavior. *Social Influence, 11,* 1–6.

Chartrand, T. & Bargh, J. (1999). The Chameleon effect: The perception-behavior link and social interaction. *Journal of Personality and Social Psychology, 76,* 893–910.

Cialdini, R.B. (1980). Full-cycle social psychology. *Applied Social Psychology Annual, 1,* 21–45.

Cialdini, R.B. (2017a). *Influence. Science and Practice.* New York (NY): Harper Business.

Cialdini, R.B. (2017b). *PRE-SUASION. A revolutionary way to influence and persuade.* New York (NY): Random House.

Cialdini, R.B., Cacioppo, J.T., Bassett, R., & Miller, J.A. (1978). Low-ball procedure for producing compliance: Commitment then cost. *Journal of Personality and Social Psychology, 36,* 463–476.

Cialdini, R.B., Demaine, L., Sagarin, B.J., Barrett, D.W., Rhoads, K., & Winter, P. (2006). Managing social norms for persuasive impact. *Social Influence, 1,* 3–15.

Cialdini, R.B., & Kenrick, D.T. (1976). Altruism as hedonism: A social development perspective on the relationship of negative mood state and helping. *Journal of Personality and Social Psychology, 34,* 907–914.

Cialdini, R.B., & Sagarin, B.J. (2005). Interpersonal influence. In: T. Brock, & M. Green (Eds.) *Persuasion: Psychological insights and perspectives.* (pp. 143–169). Newbury Park, CA: Sage Press.

Cialdini, R.B., & Schroeder, D. (1976). Increasing compliance by legitimizing paltry contributions: When even a penny helps. *Journal of Personality and Social Psychology, 34,* 599–604.

Cialdini, R.B., Vincent, J.E., Lewis, S.K., Catalan, J., Wheeler, D., & Darby, B.L. (1975). Reciprocal concessions procedure for inducing compliance: The door-in-the-face technique. *Journal of Personality and Social Psychology, 31,* 206–215.

Clark, H.B., Northrop, J.T., & Barkshire, Ch.T. (1988). The effects of contingent thank-you notes on case managers' visiting residential clients. *Education and Treatment of Children, 11,* 45–51.

Crano, W.D. & Priskin, R. (Eds.) (2014). *Attitudes and attitude change.* New York & Hove: Psychology Press.

Davis, B.P., & Knowles, E.S. (1999). A disrupt-then-reframe technique of social influence. *Journal of Personality and Social Psychology, 76,* 192–199.

Dickerson, C.A., Thibodeau, R., Aronson, E., & Miller, D. (1992). Using cognitive dissonance to encourage water conservation 1. *Journal of Applied Social Psychology, 22,* 841–854.

Dolinski, D. (2011). A rock or a hard place: The foot-in-the-face technique for inducing compliance without pressure. *Journal of Applied Social Psychology, 41,* 1514–1537.

Dolinski, D. (2016). *Techniques of social influence. The psychology of gaining compliance.* London & New York: Routledge.

Dolinski, D., & Grzyb, T. (2022). *We are looking for people like you.* Manuscript in preparation.

Dolinski, D., Grzyb, T., & Kulesza, W. (2022). *The egotistic trap as a technique of social influence.* Manuscript submitted for publication.

Dolinski, D., Grzyb, T., Olejnik, J., Prusakowski, S., & Urban, K. (2005). Let's dialogue about penny. *Journal of Applied Social Psychology, 35,* 1150–1170.

Dolinski, D., Nawrat, M., & Rudak, I. (2001). Dialogue involvement as a social influence technique. *Personality and Social Psychology Bulletin, 27,* 1395–1406.

Dolinski, D., & Nawrat, R. (1998). "Fear-then-relief" procedure for producing compliance: Beware when the danger is over. *Journal of Experimental Social Psychology, 34,* 27–50.

Dolinski, D., & Szczucka, K. (2013). Emotional disrupt-then-reframe. *Journal of Applied Social Psychology, 43,* 2031–2041.

Ellsworth, P.C., & Langer, E. (1976). Staring and approach: An interpretation of the stare as a nonspecific activator. *Journal of Personality and Social Psychology, 33,* 117–122.

Fennis, B.M., Janssen, L., & Vohs, K. (2009). Acts of benevolence: A limited-resource account of compliance with charitable requests. *Journal of Consumer Research, 35,* 906–924.

Firmin, M.W., Helmick, J.M., Iezzi, B.A., & Vaughn, A. (2004). Say please: The effect of the word "please" in compliance-seeking request. *Social Behavior and Personality, 32,* 67–72.

Flynn, F.J., & Lake, V.K.B. (2008). If you need help, just ask: Underestimating compliance with direct request for help. *Journal of Personality and Social Psychology, 95,* 128–143.

Fointiat, V. (2000). 'Foot-in-the-mouth' versus 'door-in-the-face' requests. *Journal of Social Psychology, 140*, 264–266.

Forgas, J.P., Cooper, J., & Crano, W.D. (Eds.) (2016). *The psychology of attitudes and attitude change.* New York & Hove: Psychology Press.

Freedman, J.L., & Fraser, S. (1966). Compliance without pressure: The foot in the door technique. *Journal of Personality and Social Psychology, 4*, 195–202.

Friedman, H., & Rahman, A. (2011). Gifts-upon-entry and appreciatory comments: Reciprocity effects in retailing. *Journal of International Marketing Studies, 3*, 161–164.

Gass, R.H., & Seiter, J.S. (2018). *Persuasion, social influence and compliance gaining.* New York & London: Routledge.

Goldman, M. (2011). Compliance employing a combined foot-in-the-door and door-in-the -face procedure. *Journal of Social Psychology, 126*, 111–116.

Goldman, M., & Creason, Ch.R. (1981). Inducing compliance by a two-door-in-the-face procedure and a self-determination action request. *Journal of Social Psychology, 114*, 229–235.

Goldsmith, E.B. (2015). *Social influence and sustainable consumption.* New York (NY) Springer.

Goldstein, N.J., Cialdini, R.B., & Griskevicius, V. (2008). A room with a viewpoint: Using social norms to motivate environmental conservation in hotels. *Journal of Consumer Research, 35*, 472–482.

Goldstein, N.J., Giriskevicius, V., & Cialdini, R.B. (2011). Reciprocity by proxy: A novel influence strategy for stimulating cooperation. *Administrative Science Quarterly, 56*, 444–473.

Gouldner, A.W. (1960). The norm of reciprocity: A preliminary statement. *American Sociological Review, 25*, 161–178.

Grzyb, T., & Dolinski, D. (2017). "This is my only request" – using the "Omega" strategy to boost the success of charity drives. *European Review of Applied Psychology, 67*, 181–185.

Grzyb, T., & Dolinski, D. (2022). *The field study in social psychology. How to conduct research outside of a laboratory setting?* New York, NY: Routledge.

Grzyb, T., Dolinski, D., & Kulesza. W. (2021). Dialogue and labelling. Are these helpful in finding volunteers? *Journal of Social Psychology, 161*, 63–71.

Gueguen, N. (2016). "You will probably refuse, but...": When activating reactance in a single sentence increases compliance with a request. *Polish Psychological Bulletin, 47*, 170–173.

Gueguen, N., & Jacob, C. (2013). The birthdate effect: Solicitation on birthday affect compliance. *The International Review of Retail Distribution and Consumer Research, 23*, 353–356.

Gueguen, N., Joule, R.-V., Courbet, D., Halimi-Falkowicz, S., & Marchand, M. (2013). Repeating "yes" in a first request and compliance with a later request: The fourth walls technique. *Social Behavior and Personality, 41*, 199–202.

Gueguen, N., Meineri, S., & Stefan, J. (2012). "Say it with flowers" ... to female drivers: Hitchhikers holding flowers and driver behavior. *North American Journal of Psychology, 14*, 623–628.

Gueguen, N., & Pascual, A. (2005). Improving the response rate to street survey: An evaluation of the "But you are free to accept or to refuse" technique. *Psychological Record, 55*, 297–303.

Gueguen, N., Silone, F., & David, M. (2016). The effect of the two feet-in-the-door technique on tobacco deprivation. *Psychology and Health, 31*, 168–775.

Hendrick, C., Borden, R., Giesen, M., Murray, E.J., & Seyfried, B.A. (1972). Effectiveness of ingratiation tactics in a cover letter on mail questionnaire response: *Psychonomic Science, 26*, 349–351.

Hetts, J.J., Boninger, D.S., Armor, D.A., Gleicher, F., & Nathanson, A. (2000). The influence of anticipated counterfactual regret on behavior. *Psychology and Marketing, 17*, 345–368.

Higgins, E.T. (2005). Value from regulatory fit. *Current Directions in Psychological Science, 14*, 209–213.

Hornik, J., Zaig, T., Shadmon, D., & Barbash, G.I. (1990). Comparison of three inducement techniques to improve compliance in a health survey conducted by telephone. *Public Health Reports, 105*, 524–529.

Horowitz, T., & Pratkanis, A.R. (2002). A laboratory demonstration of the fraudulent telemarketers' 1 in 5 prize tactic. *Journal of Applied Social Psychology, 32*, 310–317.

Howard, D.J. (1990). The influence of verbal responses to common greetings on compliance behavior: The foot-in-the-mouth effect. *Journal of Applied Social Psychology, 20*, 1185–1196.

Howard, D., Gengler, Ch., & Jain, A. (1995). What's in a name? A complimentary means of persuasion. *Journal of Consumer Research, 22*, 200–211.

Hull, C.L. (1943). The goal-gradient hypothesis and maze learning. *Psychological Review, 39*, 25–43.

Isen, A.M., & Simmonds, S.F. (1978). The effect of feeling good on a helping task that is incompatible with good mood. *Social Psychology, 41*, 346–349.

Iyengar, S.S., & Lepper, M.R. (2000). When choice is demotivating: Can one desire too much of a good thing? *Journal of Personality and Social Psychology, 79*, 995–1006.

Jacob, C., Gueguen, N., Martin, A., & Boulbry, G. (2011). Retail salespeople's mimicry of customers: Effects on consumer behavior. *Journal of Retailing and Consumer Services, 18*, 381–388.

Johnson, E.J., & Goldstein, D.G. (2004). Defaults and donation decisions. *Transplantation, 78*, 1713–1716.

Johnson, W.B. (1937). Euphoric and depressed mood in normal subjects. *Character and Personality, 6*, 79–98.

Joule, R.V., Gouilloux, F., & Weber, F. (1989). The lure: A new compliance procedure. *Journal of Social Psychology, 129*, 741–749.

Kaczmarek, M.C., & Steffens, M.C. (2017). Mindlessly polite: A conceptual replication of the emotional seesaw effect on compliance and information processing. *Frontiers in Psychology, 8*, 239.

Kahneman, D., Knetsch, J.L., & Thaler R.H. (1991). The endowment effect, loss aversion, and status quo bias. *Journal of Economic Perspectives, 5*, 193–206.

Kahneman, D., & Tversky, A. (1979). Prospect theory: An analysis of decision under risk. *Econometria, 47*, 263–291.

Katzev, R., & Brownstein, R. (1989). The influence of enlightenment on compliance. *Journal of Social Psychology, 129*, 335–347.

Kivetz, R., Urminsky, O., & Zheng, Y. (2006). The goal gradient hypothesis resurrected: Purchase acceleration, illusionary goal progress and customer retention. *Journal of Marketing Research, 43*, 39–58.

Kleinke, C.L., & Singer, D.A. (1979). Influence of gaze on compliance with demanding and conciliatory request in field setting. *Personality and Social Psychology Bulletin, 5*, 386–390.

Konoske, P., Staple, S., & Graf, R.G. (1979). Compliant reactions to guilt: Self-esteem or self-punishment. *Journal of Social Psychology, 108*, 207–211.

Kubala, I. (2002). 420 sekund to mniej niż 7 minut. Eksploracja zakresu efektywności techniki "Dobrze To Rozegraj". [420 seconds is less than 7 minutes. Empirical exploration into Disrupt-Then-Reframe technique]. *Studia Psychologiczne, 40*, 111–125.

Kulesza, W., Dolinski, D., Szczesna, K., Kosim, M., & Grzyb, T. (2019). Temporal aspects of the chameleon effect and hospitality: The link between mimicry, its impact, and duration. *Cornell Hospitality Quarterly, 60,* 212–215.

Kulesza, W., Szypowska, Z., Jarman, M.S., & Dolinski, D. (2014). Attractive chameleon sell: The mimicry-attractiveness link. *Psychology and Marketing, 31,* 549–561.

Lamy, L., Fischer-Lokou, & Gueguen, N. (2012). Priming emotion concepts and helping behavior: How unlived emotions can influence action. *Social Behavior and Personality: An International Journal, 40,* 55–62.

Langer, E.J., Blank, A., & Chanowitz, B. (1978). The mindlessness of ostensibly thoughtful action: The role of "placebic" information in interpersonal interaction. *Journal of Personality and Social Psychology, 36,* 635–642.

Maimaran, M., & Salant, Y. (2019). The effect of limited availability on children's consumption, engagement, and choice behavior. *Judgment and Decision Making, 14,* 72.

Maio, G.R., Haddock, G., & Verplanken, B. (2019). *The psychology of attitudes and attitude change.* Thousand Oaks, London, New Delhi: Sage.

Maj, K. (2002). Zachowanie uprzejme jako czynnik warunkujacy skutecznocc techniki wplywu spolecznego 'niska pilka' [Polite behavior as a condition determining the effectiveness of low-ball social influence technique]. *Studia Psychologiczne, 40,* 93–109.

Marzoli D. & Tommasi L. (2009). Side biases in humans (Homo sapiens); three ecological studies on hemispheric asymmetries. *Naturwissenschaften, 96,* 1099–1106.

Meineri, S., Dupre, M., Vallee, B., & Gueguen, N. (2015). When a service request precedes the target request: Another compliance without pressure techniques? *Social Influence, 10,* 278–285.

Meineri, S. and Gueguen, N. (2011). "I hope I'm not disturbing you, am I?" Another operationalization of the foot-in-the-mouth paradigm. *Journal of Applied Social Psychology, 41,* 965–975.

Meyerowitz, B.E., & Chaiken, S. (1987). The effect of message framing on breast self-examination attitudes, intentions, and behavior. *Journal of Personality and Social Psychology, 52,* 500–510.

Milgram, S., & Sabini, J. (1978). On maintaining social norms: A field experiment in the subway. In: A. Baum, J.E. Singer, & S. Valins (Eds.). *Advances in Environmental Psychology, 1, The Urban Environment* (pp. 31–40). Hillsdale: Erlbaum.

Miller, R.L., Seligman, C., Clark, N.T., & Bush, M. (1976). Perceptual contrast versus reciprocal concession as mediators of induce compliance. *Canadian Journal of Behavioral Science, 8,* 401–409.

Mortensen, C.R., Neel, R., Cialdini, R.B., Jaeger, C.M., Jacobson, R.P., & Ringel, M.M. (2019). Trending Norms: A lever for encouraging behaviors performed by the minority. Social Psychological and Personality *Science,* 10, 201–210.

Mujcic, R., & Leibbrandt, A. (2017). Indirect reciprocity and prosocial behavior: Evidence from a natural field experiment. *The Economic Journal, 128,* 1683–1699.

Nisbett, R. (2015). *Mindware. Tools for smart thinking.* New York: Farrar, Straus and Giroux.

Nyer, P.U., & Dellande, S. (2009). Public commitment as a motivator for weight loss. *Psychology and Marketing, 27,* 1–12.

O'Carroll, R.E., Dryden, J., Hamilton-Barclay, T., & Ferguson, E. (2011). Anticipated regret and organ donor registration – a pilot study. *Health Psychology, 30,* 661–664.

O'Keefe, D. (2015). *Persuasion. Theory and Research.* Thousand Oaks, London, New Delhi: Sage.

O'Keefe, D.J., & Figge, M. (1997). A guilt-based explanation of the door-in-the-face influence strategy. *Human Communication Research, 24,* 64–81.

O'Quin, K., & Aronoff, J. (1981). Humor as a technique of social influence. *Social Psychology Quarterly, 44,* 349–357.

Patch, M.E., Hoang, V.R., & Stahelski, A.J. (1997). The use of metacommunication in compliance: Door-in-the-face and single-request strategies. *Journal of Social Psychology, 137,* 88–94.

Pratkanis, A.R. (2007a). Social influence analysis: An index of tactics. In: A.R. Pratkanis (Ed.). *The science of social influence. Advances and future progress.* (pp. 17–82). New York & Hove: Psychology Press.

Pratkanis, A.R. (Ed.) (2007b). *The science of social influence. Advances and future progress;* New York & Hove: Psychology Press.

Pratkanis, A.R. & Aronson, E. (2001). *Age of propaganda. The everyday use and abuse persuasion.* New York (NY): Freeman.

Pratkanis, A.R., & Uriel, Y. (2011). The expert snare as an influence tactic: Surf, turf, and ballroom demonstrations of some compliance consequences of being altercast as an expert. *Current Psychology, 30,* 335–344.

Reingen, P.H. (1978). On inducing compliance with requests. *Journal of Consumer Research, 5,* 96–102.

Rind, B. (1977). Effects of interest arousal on compliance with a request for help. *Basic and Applied Social Psychology, 19,* 49–59.

Rind, B., & Benjamin, D. (1994). Effects of public image concerns and self-image on compliance. *Journal of Social Psychology, 134,* 19–25.

Santos, M.D., Leve, C., & Pratkanis, A.R. (1994). Hey buddy, can you spare seventeen cents? Mindful persuasion and the pique technique. *Journal of Applied Social Psychology, 24,* 755–764.

Skilbeck, C., Tulips, J., & Ley, Ph. (1977). The effects of fear arousal, fear position, fear exposure, and sidedness on compliance with dietary instructions. *European Journal of Social Psychology, 7,* 221–239.

Smith, D.E., Gier, J.A., & Willis, F.N. (1982). Interpersonal touch and compliance with a marketing request. *Basic and Applied Social Psychology, 3,* 35–38.

Strenta, A., & DeJong, W. (1981). The effect of a prosocial label on helping behavior. *Social Psychology Quarterly, 44,* 124–147.

Strohmetz, D.B., Rind, B., Fisher, R., & Lynn, M. (2002). Sweetening the till: The use of candy to increase restaurant tipping. *Journal of Applied Social Psychology, 32,* 300–309.

Vallacher, R.R., & Wegner, D.M. (1985). *A theory of action identification.* Hillsdale, NJ: Erlbaum.

Van Doorn, E.A., Van Kleef, E., & Van der Pligt, J. (2015) How emotional expressions shape prosocial behavior: Interpersonal effects of anger and disappointment on compliance with request. *Motivation and Emotion, 39,* 128–141.

Vogel, T., Bohner, G., & Wanke, M. (2015). *Attitudes and attitude change.* New York & London: Routledge.

Wallace, J., & Sadalla, E. (1966). Behavioral consequences of transgression: I. The effects of social recognition. *Journal of Experimental Research in Personality, 1,* 187–194.

Werner, C.H., Byerli, S., White, P.H., & Kieffer, M. (2004). Validation, persuasion, and recycling: Capitalizing on the social ecology of newspaper use. *Basic and Applied Social Psychology, 26,* 183–198.

Wilson, T.D.C., & Nisbett, R.E. (1978). The accuracy of verbal reports about the effects of stimuli on evaluations and behavior. *Social Psychology, 41,* 118–131.

Wiltermuth, S. (2012). Synchrony and destructive obedience. *Social Influence, 7,* 78–89.

INDEX

Printed in the United States
by Baker & Taylor Publisher Services